THE
BENEVOLENT
DICTATORS

Interviews with Advertising Greats

THE
BENEVOLENT
DICTATORS

Interviews with Advertising Greats

Bart Cummings

CRAIN
BOOKS

740 RUSH STREET   CHICAGO, IL 60611

Dedication

This book is dedicated to two men who had great influence on my life and befriended me in many ways.

EARL M. CUMMINGS,
my father
born: *November 7, 1885*
died: *October 20, 1952*

ROBERT M. HOLBROOK,
my mentor
born: *June 7, 1899*
died: *October 22, 1981*

Both played important parts in my life at different times which accelerated my career in advertising. Both were great advertising men, but in different ways. Both were truly gentlemen. Both taught me many things.
Bless them!

Contents

Foreword   ix

Acknowledgments   xi

Introduction   xiii

INTERVIEWS

Emerson Foote, agency founder who made a remarkable comeback   1

Charles H. Brower, looms large in the annals of BBDO   21

William Bernbach, one of the world's great creative men   37

Marion Harper, the inventor of the Interpublic concept   49

Jack Tinker, headed the Tinker Think Tank   67

Edward M. Thiele, made a career at the Burnett agency   83

David Ogilvy, doyen of creative admen world-wide   99

Robert E. Healy, saved a floundering empire   115

Edward L. Bond, Jr., 25 years to Young & Rubicam chief   131

Paul Foley, 110 offices in 50 countries under his direction   149

Arthur C. Fatt, turned "soft goods" shop into a winner   165

Arthur W. Schultz, FCB head and Chicago civic leader   179

Neal Gilliatt, shared in McCann, Interpublic hierarchy   189

William A. Marsteller, founder of Marsteller agency   209

Raymond O. Mithun, headed the largest agency west of Chicago   233

Alfred J. Seaman, presided over SSC&B/Lintas hookup   257

Neal W. O'Connor, revitalized Ayer, oldest U.S. agency   285

Brown Bolté, an innovator in many areas   307

BART CUMMINGS

As one of the most distinguished "benevolent dictators" of the advertising businesss himself, Bart Cummings is peculiarly suited for the exercise (having begun his advertising career in New York in 1936), which resulted in this volume recording his conversations with more than 50 leading figures in the advertising agency business in the United States. During 15 years as CEO of Compton Advertising, Inc., during which the agency grew to international stature, Mr. Cummings also was extremely active in innumerable industry-wide activities, serving among numerous posts as chairman of the American Association of Advertising Agencies (1969-70), the American Advertising Federation (1972-73), The Advertising Council (1979-81), and the Advertising Educational Foundation (1972-83). He was elected to the Advertising Hall of Fame in 1978.

Foreword

Why this book?

Since I first began putting this book together, I have asked myself that question hundreds of times. More than once, I decided to give it up. And I suspect many people wish I had. In any case, for better or worse, here it is.

Please don't think it has been all bad. On the contrary. Interviewing the "greats" of advertising has been tremendous. It has given me, and will give you, insights into the lives, the careers, the psyches of many of the most talented communicators and/or marketers in the world.

I have been asked whether there is any common denominator that made these people so successful in the advertising agency business. Yes, and no. There are several characteristics that fit all of them, to a degree. All have had confidence in themselves. A few, perhaps, have had more confidence than they needed. Most of them, however, are quite humble about their achievements. Many did not seek the role of being the "dictator." It was thrust upon them. Only a few fought for their leadership role.

All of them believe in advertising. They knew from experience that interesting, persuasive advertising sells goods and services. Most of them were skillful in leading people, in commanding respect from their lieutenants, in building team spirit, in getting people to stretch their minds and exert themselves beyond the call of duty. And all of them believed in discipline, which to me is the most important attribute required to be a leader.

That brings me to the title of this book: THE BENEVOLENT DICTATORS. How did I happen to come up with that?

In my own experiences as CEO of Compton for 15 years, and in my interview discussions with more than 50 individuals who also have been in command, it became very clear to me that those who have been successful as leaders, are dictators. Sure, they use the brains of those around them; they delegate responsibility. But when the chips are down, when the big decisions have to be made, the dictators make them. Their word is law. And it should be.

But what about this "benevolent" business? That's where the great skill of good management comes into the picture. The *benevolent* dictator must be fair in evaluations and decisions; must be alert to reward success; kind and understanding regarding failures; helpful to those who need it; a father (or mother) confessor when one is required; work longer hours than anyone else. She/he must remember faces and names, birthdays and anniversaries, births and deaths. (A dictator should never be a "buddy" of any employee or play favorites among the staff. Her/his whole life must be dedicated to the success of the agency, its people, its clients. And, believe me, if it's done right, it ain't easy!)

Being a *benevolent* dictator is a great sacrifice. No one should ever accept the role of CEO of an advertising agency if she or he is not willing to pay the price. (Five o'clock departures are not a part of leadership in the agency business.)

Being a *benevolent dictator* is no bed of roses. But it is better than not being one at all.

Acknowledgments

As with most things we do in this world, we are not alone. Most endeavors by anyone are influenced and assisted by many others. And so it has been with me and this book.

Some encouraged me, some gave me technical help in the taping, transcribing and duplicating of interviews. Some suggested ideas which I utilized in the preparation of the book. And Sid Bernstein and Bob Goldsborough of Crain did an outstanding job of editing the book.

I hope Sid and Bob, and those listed below, will believe me when I say, "Thank you for your tremendous help!"

Compton People	*Crain People*	*Others*
Tom Coco	Sheila Churchman	A. Richard Cohen
Margaret Cummings	Gertrude Crain	Woodrow Wirsig
Maria Olshen	Rance Crain	
	Jarlath Graham	
	Ruth Guest	

Introduction

The interviews in this book are transcripts of tapes of exactly what was said to me in an exchange of questions and answers. (Some editing has been done, however.) I made every effort to ask few questions and let the interviewee (if that's a word) talk.

The first two interviews were with Bill Bernbach and Tom Dillon. I did not tape them. I took notes. This was not satisfactory. So I interviewed each of them again with a tape recorder.

In a few instances, I interviewed people more than once. The reason was that I thought of additional questions I wanted to ask them. I tried to improve their interviews.

I interviewed two people over the phone—Charlie Brower and Marion Harper. I had trouble picking up everything Charlie said, because he talked so softly. Marion's interview, however, came through loud and clear.

You may know that *ADVERTISING AGE* selected a few of the interviews and ran them *in part* (excerpts) prior to the publishing of this book. Curiously enough, I received several letters and a few phone calls, usually from intermediaries—but not always—asking me if I would interview so-and-so. Actually, I found this to be very flattering. Also, surprising.

This volume contains the interviews of 18 leaders in the advertising business. In all, more than 50 interviews have been conducted and these may comprise subsequent volumes.

Many of the interviews are extremely instructive. In fact, if you really look hard, you'll find a lot of things you can do to improve your agency's performance—in training programs, new business techniques, fiscal improvements, and so on.

Altogether, I hope you will enjoy these interviews as much as I have. But let me suggest that you not read this book as you would read a novel. Skip around. Read an interview or two, then put the book down. Come back to it another day. By doing this, you will enjoy them much more, and get more out of them as well.

Well, enough of this. Get into the book—and good reading!

EMERSON FOOTE

Emerson Foote was born Dec. 13, 1906 in Alabama. He spent his youth on the West Coast, and began his advertising career with the Leon Livingston Advertising Agency in San Francisco in 1931. He organized his own agency, Yeomans & Foote, in 1935, and wrote an ad for a Chrysler distributor which came to the attention of J. Stirling Getchell, celebrated adman who had the Plymouth account, and led to his moving to New York with Getchell in 1936.

In 1938 Mr. Foote joined Lord & Thomas as account executive on a portion of the American Tobacco account and in 1939 was made the principal account executive on the account. He was appointed a Lord & Thomas Vice-President in 1940 and Executive Vice-President in charge of the New York office in 1942.

At the end of that year, Albert Lasker, owner of the agency, literally "gave" the agency to the managers of his offices in New York, Chicago and Los Angeles, and Lord & Thomas became Foote, Cone & Belding.

In 1948, Emerson Foote resigned the American Tobacco account—the largest voluntary resignation of an account up to that time—and in April, 1950, he sold his one-third interest in the agency to his partners, primarily because of an attack of manic depression.

He joined McCann-Erickson as a Vice-President and general executive in October, 1951, and served as Executive Vice-President, President of McCann-Erickson U.S.A., and ultimately as Chairman of the Board. He resigned from McCann in 1964 largely because of disagreement over the question of whether the agency should handle a cigaret account. He subsequently bought into a small agency, but sold out when that agency was absorbed by Bozell & Jacobs, and he left the advertising business altogether in 1972.

He was a director or trustee of 15 different non-profit organizations, but now has reduced his participation to a much smaller number.

EMERSON FOOTE

Interview

I happen to have come from Alabama. I was born in the little town of Sheffield on December 13, 1906. My father, a cotton and grain broker, in 1912 moved the whole family to California.

I grew up in California. We lived mainly in a place called Mount Washington (near Los Angeles) and I went to Mount Washington Grammar School—a rural school that had only two rooms, grades 1 to 4 and 5 to 8. So they put me through in short order and I found myself entering Los Angeles High School at the age of 11. After a year or so of working, I went to the University of California for one semester.

Where did you go from there?

I was 21 and had held a variety of jobs when I went to San Francisco to work for the Northern California Chrysler-Plymouth distributor. Interestingly, while working there I made my first contact in any way with the advertising business. The agency for Chrysler at that time was MacManus Inc., headed by Theodore MacManus, one of the all-time advertising greats. [The agency subsequently became MacManus, John & Adams, and is now known as D'Arcy—MacManus & Masius.]

MacManus had a man traveling on the West Coast named George Haig, who told me something about the advertising business, and I got a kind of feeling that it wouldn't be a bad business to be in.

The feeling grew when I met the gal that I married. Her name was Sabina Fromhold. She was in advertising, as a copywriter with H. & S. Polk Company in Cincinnati, and visiting San Francisco. I met her on May 2, 1929. And three days later I proposed.

She accepted, and then she went back to Cincinnati; and I

3

didn't go back there again for almost a year. Then I went back, and we became formally engaged, with a ring and all.

Now, during the first night that I met her, I was interested in her work about advertising, because of what Haig had said, and my general feeling about it. So I asked her about it, and we talked, and at some point—she was a copywriter—she said, "You know, I think you ought to get into advertising yourself. I think you would make a good account executive." And I said, "What's an account executive?" So she told me what it was.

So I just kind of filed this away, and I didn't do anything about it. (Incidentally, we didn't get married for nine years, because of the Depression and everything back then, but that's another story.)

Anyway, two years after we'd met and become engaged, in May, 1931, I got fired from my job and decided that this was the time to get into advertising. I got in to see the heads of three of the four eastern agencies in San Francisco—Carl Eastman of N W Ayer; Lynn Baker of J. Walter Thompson; Harry Bucknell of Lord & Thomas—but I did not get a job.

Then I hit the local ranks, and I got in to see Leon Livingston, head of Leon Livingston Advertising Agency. I didn't get a job, but he gave me an assignment. He said he was trying to get the California Olive Industry account, but he was shy of research on the subject. "If you can do a run-down on the olive industry"—this was Friday!—"by Monday, I'll pay you for it." He didn't say how much. So, what the hell kind of research can you do on the olive industry between Friday and Monday? But I went to the public library and looked up olives—and I think that was my only source.

So I came in Monday with a five- or six-page memorandum typed on yellow paper, about the olive industry. Things have changed, Mr. Cummings! So he said, "This is pretty good, I like this, I could use it. Now, how much do you want for this?" I said, "Well, would $25 be a fair price?" He said, "Twenty-five dollars! I can't pay you that for a short-time job!" But then he said, "I'll tell you what I'll do. I'll give you a job at $125 a month."

Exactly what you wanted.

What I wanted. So I got this job at Livingston, not knowing anything about advertising, believe me.

4

I did research work, and finally he put me to doing some copy, and after a number of failures, he was able to use some of it. And then he put me on some account work, and then in automobile industry situations.

Did you get the olive business?

No.

And then Bob Janson, who was general manager of the McAllister Co., the Northern California distributor for Chrysler for whom I had worked, turned over their account to the Livingston agency. Their account meant about $500 a month in fees and commission; that was a lot in those days.

And Leon put me on it, and I began to fulfill Sabina's dream of being an account executive. And it's a strange thing, Bart; if you asked me what, if anything, I've ever done in the advertising business that was unusual, or unusually good, I would say it was my work in handling accounts. Certainly it wasn't as a copywriter, it wasn't as a research man. But I did seem to have some kind of a knack of handling difficult clients, like George Washington Hill [of American Tobacco Co].

The Livingston thing rocked along very well, and I got raised to $250 a month right before I began handling the automobile company, which I had been at before. Then there was an upset. . . .

Late in '34, Livingston hired a kind of efficiency expert fellow, a man named Day. And I came down sick with a case of what they then called "acute inflammatory catarrhal jaundice." I guess they now say it's hepatitis. But I was real sick for about a month, in the Mount Zion Hospital there. And when I came back, I found that Mr. Day had said to Mr. Livingston that he thought I was being paid too much anyway, and I should be cut to $150 a month; whereupon I promptly quit.

Mr. Livingston agreed with that?

He agreed with it, yes.

Then when Bob Janson heard about this, he said, "Nuts to that! You take over our account and handle it yourself." And I said, "I don't think that would be quite right, since it was their account." Well, this dragged along for about a week; I was working for Livingston on about 10 days' notice, something like that. And finally Bob called up one day and said, "Look, if you don't take our account, the McAllister account, I'm going to give it to Harry

Elliott," who was a local, city man. So on that basis, I said, "I will take it." After about a week, the company announced that the Emerson Foote Agency would handle their advertising.

Did you get some other business?

We got some, but if you want to know what the situation really was, I might as well tell you; we launched this agency in space in the McAllister Building, with their guarantee of credit, and they advanced us cash any time we needed it, and we paid it back on the due dates, without interest. The actual capital of the company was $300. (Laughter) $150 belonging to me, and $150 belonging to a man named Louis Yeomans.

He was my partner; he had to be silent, because he was then working for Chrysler as a Northern California field man, as Haig had done previously. But after about seven or eight months of slithering along with the Emerson Foote Agency, Lou left the Chrysler people and came in all the way with me. We tossed a silver dollar to see whose name would come first, and he won, so it was Yeomans & Foote. And we had a nothing business, but we paid our expenses, and we had fun. And our main account was very secure, the McAllister Company.

So, this was, I'd say about September 1935.

And all this time, you were still carrying on this romance in Cincinnati?

Through the mail, yes. I had been since 1930.—No, no, I'm sorry, in 1932, she broke the engagement and sent the ring back, on the grounds that I could not be a very serious suitor, or I would have come back and done something about it. I had a little different view than she had. She thought that we should get married and live in whatever kind of hole we had to live in. I desired making it big first. One day, a number of years ago, I found a statement from the Wells Fargo Bank in San Francisco, showing the balance of the account of the Emerson Foote Agency at the end of the first month of business. 33¢!

As I said, things were going all right, and we hoped to get to be fairly big some day. But along came fate. In late April or May of 1936, the government paid a bonus to the veterans of World War I, and there were a whole slew of ads appealing to the vets to spend their bonus money for this or that, and the automobile people were going after it too.

So I wrote an ad for the McAllister people—a half-page in the *Chronicle* and *Examiner*, with the headline, "Why doesn't someone suggest that the veterans *keep* their bonus money?" A pious story about "We want to do business with them, they have earned this money, and they shouldn't spend it lightly for this and that gadget, even a car." Well, I'll be damned if the ad didn't bring in more business than any other that had run for a long time.

So, this thing caught on. Somehow, the copy came to the attention of Stirling Getchell in New York City. Getchell then had the Plymouth account and DeSoto; he didn't have Chrysler. Getchell had it read over the Major Bowes Amateur Hour, the whole damn ad.

Then he sent for me; he wanted to talk to me. I went to New York, but Getchell said he didn't think they had a job for me at that time, so I came back to San Francisco.

Well, in about three weeks, I got a telegram from Bill Blees, who was Getchell's general manager. Bill had been head of the Buick-Olds-Pontiac Division of General Motors. And it just said, "Report for work on such-and-such a date; salary $4,800 a year. William A. Blees of J. Stirling Getchell." So I had a job.

So I left my little agency. And it was rather hard at first; I had a little dinky office in the Chrysler Building, on the eighth floor. I was put on research work—I had built up this unearned reputation of knowing something about research. And a little bit of work on account work—not much on accounts, some on new business, on preparing new business presentations.

The Getchell thing went along all right, except a curious, a funny thing happened—after about three months, I began to kind of fall apart; I think I was actually homesick for San Francisco. But I couldn't get enough sleep, you know, and I just felt bad. I hadn't had any experience with psychiatrists up to that point, but I got to feeling so poorly that I asked to take a little time off, even though I'd only been there three months. And Mr. Getchell gave it to me. And so I got on a boat, took a cruise back to home, back to San Francisco.

When I got back there, my friends Janson and Yeomans said, "Well, we told you you were nuts to go back there! Stay out of that place; send them a wire you're not coming back." However, I went back; and it was still difficult, but I tried it again, and it was a little bit better, and I tried again to get adjusted to things. And I got sent on my first account assignment, which was the Chrysler Air-Temp, in Dayton, OH.

My time with the Getchell Agency, which lasted from June 1936 to December 1938, worked out very pleasantly. I didn't make a lot of money at that time; I went from $4,800 a year starting salary to something like $7,500. But nevertheless, it was working your way into New York advertising, Eastern advertising, and Stirling Getchell was very nice to me.

Why did you leave Getchell?

In December, 1938, I was offered a chance to go over to Lord & Thomas, Albert D. Lasker's agency, to work on the American Tobacco account. And I well remember Stirling Getchell saying to me, "Emerson, you mustn't do that! This man Hill [George Washington Hill, president of American Tobacco Co.] is a pretty rough customer. You'll be going to work for a fellow who notoriously devours his account executives." Those were his words. But I was young and foolish, going on 32, so I went ahead. I was hired, at $11,000 a year, and I became the account executive in charge of print advertising for Lucky Strike, and worked directly, as all American Tobacco account men did, with George Washington Hill.

And again, it was probably luck; I don't know—it's hard to figure out personal chemistry—but he was the king, and I was the guy at the bottom of the barrel, but we worked together very well. I experienced no outburst of tyrannical behavior that I can recall.

Is it true he always wore his hat in the office?

About 99% of the time. I don't know why, but he did. In 1939, the man who was the over-all account executive on the American Tobacco account, James H. Wright, kind of cracked under pressure. He was removed by Lord & Thomas, and I was subsequently put in as account executive. That was in the late summer of 1939. Then in 1940, Mr. Lasker—and again, I was lucky, because he wasn't always the easiest person to get along with, but for some reason we got along very well, and he proved to be a very good friend—Mr. Lasker made me a vp of Lord & Thomas, and then in July of 1942, I was made executive vp in charge of New York operations for Lord & Thomas. At that time I was 35; Sheldon Coons had gotten $115,000 a year for this job: I was previously paid $37,500, and I didn't get a raise. Based on this, one of the classic conversations between Albert Lasker and me took place. He said one day, "Mr Foote, you've never asked me about money for yourself. I want to ask a very direct question; is that because you don't care about money, or because you think it's a smarter way to handle me?" And I said, "The latter, Mr. Lasker." Whereupon he laughed heartily. But I still didn't get a raise!

However, later that year, we got the agency; he turned the whole thing over to Don Belding and Fax Cone and me.

Why did he do that?

I'll tell you the story as I know it happened, though this may not be the official version. But the time has come to tell it like it was. What actually happened was this. As executive vp in charge of the New York office, one of my main jobs was putting together the annual budget. And while Mr. Lasker was quite generous most of the time with money, he wasn't very easy on operating budgets; he believed in a high profit margin. So, despite my best efforts, I fit the operation of the office into the budget ceiling he had given me for 1943. Late one December afternoon, I went in to see him and said, "Mr. Lasker, I can't make this budget fit operationally. I can't run the office with it. I think that the problem is this: I believe you are tired of the agency business, which is one reason you came up with these low budgets, and I suggest you liquidate Lord & Thomas and close it up." After a long pause, he said, "By God, I think I will!"

Then he called his wife, Mary, and said, "Mr. Foote's made an unusual suggestion; I want to come home with him and talk to you about it." So I went to his house, and this idea was at first not popular with Mary, because she understandably felt the agency was a source of revenue.

But I sat with Mr. Lasker much of the time for about two days, while he was wrestling with his decision. He called in various experts, accountants, lawyers, etc., and then he sent for Cone and Belding, and he closed Lord & Thomas.

Cone and Belding each ran an office?

Yeah, we each ran an office. We were regionalized; Fax was in Chicago, he was in charge of Chicago operations, and Don Belding was in charge of West Coast operations. In Mr. Lasker's plans for a succession agency I was left out for a while. Mr. Lasker decided that nobody could handle Mr. Hill but himself, that he'd close the New York office and let the agency operate with his successors in Chicago, on the coast and overseas. Well, I was kind of numbed by that time. I expected to be out looking for a job, anyway, when I made the sugestion to him about closing. So Mr. Lasker went down to tell Mr. Hill of his decision to close the New York office and what he was going to do and so forth.

Hill said to Mr. Lasker, "I think you're wrong; I think Emerson can handle the accounts well here, I think that he should be in the firm, I think his name should be first, and he should be president."

So that's how it became Foote, Cone & Belding. It was going to be Belding, Cone & Foote—alphabetically. Well, I wasn't going to be there at all in one phase of the planning as I told you. So that's what happened.

How'd the other two guys like that?

They didn't really care. They were kind of shellshocked and knew they were falling into a bed of clover. I mean, who could object? Because the agency, as hard up as it was supposed to be, was still making over a million dollars a year before taxes.

That was very good money then!

And we wound up with 97% of the stock. It was supposed to be one-third interest each, we gave 3% to the treasurer, who had nothing to do with the running of the agency—his name was Bill Sachse—so we each had 32-1/3%.

Were you good friends at that point?

We were friendly; we got along. We were not particularly close friends—like in politics, the senator from one state and the senator from another state 2,000 miles away, they may know each other.

They know each other, but they're not close.

Yeah. And we never did become close friends.

How did you guys pay Lasker?

We didn't pay him anything. Lord & Thomas had about $9 million in net worth, mostly liquid assets, at the time of this liquidation. Mr. Lasker withdrew this, but not at once. We kept the whole thing going with $100,000 we scraped up between the three of us, plus Mr Lasker's generosity in leaving some of his money in the firm for a while and guaranteeing one loan for us.

I borrowed most of the money for my share of $32,333, and Mr.

Lasker arranged a $100,000 loan from A. G. Becker in Chicago, a prominent investment banking firm. We also had, in the first 75 days of the year, Lord & Thomas' previous year's tax reserves—income tax money—to use. We had until April 15—3½ months. We got credit from the Bankers Trust Co. for a very small amount over the prime rate on a million-dollar loan; I worked mostly with them on that, just because I happened to be here. And as A. D. [Lasker] said to me several years later: 'You know, Emerson, isn't it true that you fellows have had no more cash problem than J. P. Morgan Co.?" I said, "Yes." Because we had all the cash we needed from our first day. It was like a rolling ball.

What did Lasker get out of it?

He didn't get a nickel for good will. I think that Mr. Lasker must have been thinking about closing up, at least subconsciously.

He was a very rich man, wasn't he?

Well, he was, yes. Not in a Rockefeller sense. He was worth, I guess, $50 million.

And then you guys built the business.

It grew, yes. We'll skip most of the grimy detail of Lord & Thomas and Foote, Cone & Belding and so forth; and let me tell you how it broke up, and how I got into McCann-Erickson. This is something that, for reasons of policy, I've never told before. I just suddenly realized, a little while ago, that I am entirely out of the business. I'm never going back at my age; I couldn't if I wanted to, and I don't want to, so I don't have to have any inhibitions about this.

I could not possibly relate my life story in advertising without telling you that part of it, substantial parts, were marred by what must be called mental illness. I have abandoned the euphemistic and somewhat confusing term "nervous breakdown," which doesn't mean anything.

It's not that you're babbling or raving, or running around in circles, but you're not well. Well, I was a manic depressive. Most of my trouble came from the manic phase.

I struggled on with psychiatrists for a long time, and had a couple of hospital experiences. This series of illnesses is what cost me my position, my stockholding in Foote, Cone & Belding. It did not cause me any trouble at McCann-Erickson, and they knew *everything* about it because when I got to talking to Marion [Harper], I went out of my way to be sure that he and Mr. McCann knew all that there was to be known.

But it went like this: I think—in 1948, we [Foote, Cone & Belding] resigned the American Tobacco account. This has caused confusion to many people, because it had nothing to do with the health issue. In fact, I thought at that time that cigarettes were good for you. I had been a George Washington Hill man; I admired him greatly. And his successor was a fine man too, Mr. Riggio. But I—we—didn't have the same feeling for him; and I felt—I'd been on the account for about 10 years, 1938 to 1948— we shouldn't get boxed in by the account. So I talked everybody into the idea that we should resign—Fax, Don and Albert Lasker, who fully agreed with it.

You still went to Lasker for advice?

From time to time, yes. On a thing as big as that, I wouldn't think of going it alone. He was completely in favor of it. I guess he wanted us to tell them to go to hell, too. But in retrospect, I recognize that this was the wrongest decision I ever made, because I learned something abruptly afterwards that I didn't know before. I should have known. In an advertising agency, what matters is not control of stock, but control of *billing.* I had been the big man on the American Tobacco account, and the ink was hardly dry on the American Tobacco resignation when I found that I had lost control of my own company.

That's the way it happened. I got kind of upset after this American Tobacco thing, and in about six weeks, I was definitely in a manic phase of mental illness. In my case, it was the classic symptom of being hyperactive, doing too much, scaring people by being so tense. I don't believe I was ever accused of any serious errors of judgment, except resigning the account itself, and that was much later. Also, I believe that Fax Cone believed it was the right thing to do, but Belding, I don't think he was quite so sure.

Anyway, I was hospitalized for about four days with a very strenuous treatment, including electroshock therapy; and then I was put right back to work, which was obviously much too soon. And I had a very fine psychiatrist, and we became good friends. He was Dr. Ralph Kaufman, who was chief of psychiatry at Mount Sinai. He put me right back to work and I did fairly well, but I was badly shaken. I think that some of these techniques are no longer broadly used. Then lithium came along, and lithium has had the same specificity on certain types of mental illness that penicillin has on infectious diseases; they just don't have them any more. They clear up in a matter of days. I think electroshock therapy is fairly sparsely used now, and it's a rough thing.

I had no recurrence of the illness, and I hadn't yet begun to think I had made a mistake resigning the American Tobacco account; it took me about 10 years to realize that. Incidentally, if I had not resigned the account I have no doubt that I would have been able to retain my stock in the agency.

When did these guys make their move on you?

Okay, we got through 1948, and I was still very active; we managed to rebuild the New York office pretty well, and we never lost money there. We resigned the American Tobacco account, and did not lose money in either 1948 or 1949 in New York.

How much billing was that, Emerson?

A total of $11,521,000—which perhaps doesn't seem like much now.

In those days, that was a lot.

That was the biggest account that was resigned voluntarily. I was able to tell the press, who badgered me about it, that we had resigned without the threat or expectation of losing it, which was true. All the more reason we shouldn't have done it. Anyhow, I was quite busy working, and they also made me president of Foote, Cone & Belding International for some reason. But in the fall of 1949, things began to come apart. I began to come apart. I'd been to Switzerland, and completed some arrangements for our Swiss watch account. But I stopped in London, saw a bunch of people and began to get wound up again. And when I got off the plane in New York, my wife, Sabina, thought she saw signs of the manic phase. Again, I say, you haven't got to be babbling or anything, you know what's going on; but you're just not yourself, you're highly keyed and overreacting.

Anyway, when I got off the plane, Sabina sent for Dr. Kaufman, and he said, "You shouldn't go back to the office until you get unwound and calmed down a bit."

And he was still believing in this electroshock therapy thing. So I argued all afternoon to stay away from that, because I didn't like it.

However, Kaufman won, and got in touch with some guy with

a portable machine who came in. I was treated over the weekend, and then went back to the office in a few days.

Now it's December, 1949. I wasn't much good at the office after that. I felt rather discombobulated. I think the worst thing that I did as far as the people at FCB were concerned was to scare people, because of being too tense sometimes.

Were you nasty?

No, not in the usual sense. But once in a while I would lose my temper, which would scare them a bit. It was a little different than just picking on somebody, and it was, again, a matter of not having controls on things.

Early in 1950, Fax and Don, working through the company's attorney, Siegfried Hartman, proposed I take a year off. I was into a manic phase, and I didn't want to do anything that was that reasonable, so I declined. Finally, about February of 1950, they sent me a telegram that ordered me to stay out of the office and go on an indefinite leave with pay. I observed the mandate but I was very worried. I began to figure they wanted to get me out of the company for keeps. And every time I would mention that to anybody in our family, or a doctor, they'd say, "Well, that just shows you that you're not well."

Finally, I found there was too much friction staying at home, because Sabina was watching me all the time, you know—out of her love. I took up quarters at the Hotel Pierre, and a very lonesome life it was. Somehow, I got called onto a jury, and I was serving rather a long time, involving a criminal case. This helped to pass the time. One day I had just gotten back to the hotel from the jury, and a knock came at the door. There was my brother, Stanley, who lived in California, a psychiatrist named Tom Lovell and two attorneys I hadn't met.

Your brother arranged this?

Yes. Sabina couldn't stand it all so she had him come. I argued, saying "Look, if you're going to put me in the Westchester Hospital for maybe three or six months, I'll be all washed up, because our contract with the firm has a special clause." I had designed this contract, and had the lawyers draw it up at the time the firm was founded. The contract provided that if any of those founders died, left the company voluntarily or was declared legally incompetent, the corporation could purchase his stock at book value. But, if any of the three founders should leave the company *involuntarily*, he could keep the stock now belonging to him, with no restrictions whatsoever, just like he bought the stock on the New York Exchange. So it was quite obvious that if I were to be put someplace where I could be declared legally incompetent, they could take my stock at book value. Which they tried to do later. So I remember saying to my brother and Dr. Lovell and the two attorneys, "Look, you're just playing into their hands. They're trying to get me out of the company, to take my stock on a much-less-than-it's-worth basis." But Dr. Lovell said, "That just shows how sick you are." And he added: "I saw Don Belding this morning and he assured me they regarded you as the tent-pole of their business, and they just want you to get well and back on the job." And curiously enough, I think that Belding may have been sincere. I think that somebody *else* was saying something different. Finally, I said to the group at the Pierre, "the jig is up if you put me in the hospital. Let me go out on a farm someplace in Kansas." No, they said that it wouldn't be adequate.

So I was taken out to Westchester Hospital. I didn't sign any paper, I was an involuntary patient—I was there six months. I never had any medication whatever; it was just the rest, and being away from things, and I think I gradually got better.

The next thing that happened, I didn't know this until later, but they had Sabina down to a meeting at the office one day—and she doesn't remember who it was that said this, but it was some responsible official, *not* Cone or Belding—and they wanted her to sign a paper to facilitate my being declared incompetent, not telling her that this was a way they could get my stock. But she wouldn't do it.

Later, one member of the firm, not Cone or Belding, and if you don't mind, I'd rather not give the name out, went to the hospital and talked to the medical director to explore ways of having me declared incompetent. And the director reported this to me later, so I wouldn't be upset by it at that time. The FCB man was told by the medical director; "Mr. Foote is seriously ill, but his condition would in no way warrant his being declared incompetent." So that was that.

Finally, after about three months these attempts to do it the easy way failed. (I was still being paid $5,000 a month, because I was on indefinite leave with pay, but I didn't expect this to last long.) One day, the medical director told me that he had received word from FCB that I was not to come back to the company, and they wanted me to get together with a lawyer to work out the separation details. He came out, and got the picture very quickly. After a first meeting, Fax had said to him, "We think it's best if Emerson leaves his money in the company." He never said flat out, "You won't get any salary." But that was the implication. So I think I did the only thing I could do, I didn't hold on to the stock, for two reasons: One, I was kind of cash poor at that time, relatively speaking, and I didn't have significant investments anywhere else. And I didn't like to leave almost all I had in the custody of these guys anyhow. I asked the lawyer if he could get the book value out, plus something, and he got me two years' salary after that, plus book value.

That was not a good deal.

No. But, after all, I was worried about the cash situation. I got $592,000 for my stock, and I had turned over stock earlier to Sabina for which she got $161,000—$753,000 for 21% of the company, my share at that time. Now, if you think what that ought to have been—and FCB stock went public for three times book value, and book value increased greatly—I would probably have had to give up some stock. But that's beside the point. I knew it was a great deal less than it was worth, but I thought it was the best thing at the time. The whole thing was on a very unfriendly basis. It didn't take place at the office, but at the New York Bar Assn., which I thought was a pretty cold thing. Albert Lasker got into the thing this way: He had said he thought I was just not gaited for this kind of a business, that it was too rough and tumble, and now I had a fair amount of money, and I should never go back into it. But I was determined to get back into it. Anyway, I would say that I don't think this was a villainous plot to steal my stock. I think it was rather just ordinary people operating with ordinary selfishness. I think Don was going along for the ride, with whatever Cone and Bob Carney [the company attorney] told him. I don't think that Fax—and again, I'm speculating freely—cared too much about the money, even though he must have realized this could quicken their wealth quite a bit.

But in summary I was quite angry, although I kept it under

wraps, as far as the general public was concerned. I felt this way; one never knows what one would do under a given circumstance. But my feeling is, searching my soul as hard as I could for the last 32 years, I don't think I would have done to them what they did to me under the same circumstances. I felt that, putting it in military terms, they had left me for dead on the field of battle. They thought I was all washed up in the advertising business.

This is now mid-1951, after I had made it very plain that I was going back in the ad business in one way or another. Belding showed up one day and he said, "Well, if you're going to go back anyway, I think we should put the firm back together again." And I said, "Well, I don't think Fax would do it." He said, "I don't know." So he proposed to Fax that we put Humpty Dumpty back together again, and I understood from Don that Fax was so upset he went to bed for two days with a rash. And that was the end of that.

What happened to Carney?
He became chairman of the board.

I started on the road back, but I didn't try anything early in '51, I just took more time off. Everybody knew I'd had a crackup, and it was described, probably, in more lurid terms than it was. I began to stir around and say, "How do I get back?" And I'll tell you, it wasn't easy. I went to see Stanley Resor of J. Walter Thompson and Sigurd Larmon of Young & Rubicam. Mr. Larmon took me to lunch. They were pleasant and gracious, but they wanted no part of E. Foote. And then I had lunch with Fred Gamble [President of the 4A's] and he said, "I think since you're determined to go back, you'd better just make up your mind to settle for some small agency, and not try to be back in the big time, with your history."

The year dragged on, but I was busy. Fate dealt with me in strange ways. For example, late in 1950, when I was getting out of the hospital, I accepted the job of vice-chairman of the board of the American Cancer Society. The chairman of the board was Gen. William J. Donovan, who knew all about my illness.

Then, one day it finally happened, in 1951, about September. Most of the advertising world treated me like a dirty shirt. I don't blame them really; if a guy's locked up in a booby hatch, well! But two groups didn't avoid me; CBS and Cowles Magazines. They invited me, long after I had left FCB, to their meetings—just as when I was still a big wheel.

And I was invited to a luncheon by *Look* magazine; and I happened by pure chance to sit next to Marion Harper, who was head of McCann-Erickson. During lunch, he said he'd like to talk to me about going back into the advertising business. So we met in a day or two, and within three weeks I was employed again. I suggested that they have their doctors talk to the doctors at Westchester Hospital, and to Dr. Kaufman. And they did.

I got a good report. You see, in all of this, though I was pretty sick at times, I never received discouraging prognostic points of views.

What did Marion have you doing? What was your title?

I went in at McCann as vice-president and general executive, at $50,000 a year, which wasn't bad in those days. And in a very short time, I think like a month or so, I was put on the board of directors, and then in 1952, was made executive vice-president and I served with them for 13 years.

I had a charmed life with Marion, and he was always thoughtful and considerate. I was nine years older than he was, and he seemed to think I filled some role that he needed in there. He put me on a lot of difficult accounts.

What would he have you do? I know you've always had a great touch with people.

I was the troubleshooter. The first account he put me on to save was Junket Brand Foods in Little Falls, N.Y., and they'd just about lost it. It was a matter of pride. Marion didn't lose accounts very gracefully. So I went up there, and we got it straightened out. And then it went from one thing to the other; I kept going to Congoleum-Nairn, which was in a lot of trouble. Finally, one account that was giving us much concern was Esso, which he put me on; I don't think we were in danger of losing it, but we had a lot of trouble with it.

Another account was the Coca-Cola Bottling Co. of Chicago. This company was headed by Harry Kipke, a former famous football coach.

Oh yes, I played for Illinois against Michigan when Harry coached there.

I did some new business, but I wouldn't say I was a spectacular new business man. I was thinking, before this meeting with you, what the hell have I done in advertising that's unusual? And I think, trying to take an objective view, it really was a matter of dealing with clients, going all the way back to Mr. Hill. I certainly cannot say I was a great copywriter; I did write some few good pieces of copy over the years, but I wasn't a regular copywriter. I can't say that I was a great organization man, although I don't think I was a disorganized guy. I seemed to have this curious knack with clients.

If you don't mind, I'll give you a quote from Harrison Atwood, who was chairman of the executive committee at McCann-Erickson. He once said, "Emerson certainly has a way with clients. We have a meeting with a client, he comes into the room and in a short while the client seems to be happy."

And it was a strange thing, because it's mixed up; those few people who try to follow my career have a hard time. I left over the cigarette issue, but this is a different cup of tea entirely than in 1948, and I've never had occasion to regret what I did in 1964. I had been so involved with the health forces that I didn't feel cigarettes were good for people.

We, at Compton, had some tobacco business, but I always admired your stand.

Did you?

Yes, here you were the man who really handled the American Tobacco account; you resigned the account, and ultimately became one of the heads of the American Cancer Society.

One very interesting thing that came up about that: I was grilled a few times in Washington, and when I went to testify, I learned those guys can be rough. One congressman said to me, "Mr. Foote, you used to make your living selling cigarettes, and now you're out crusading against cigarettes. Would you say, or do you feel, that your conversion is the most spectacular since, say, Paul was struck down on the road to Damascus?"

I said, "Well, not quite, because what happened to St. Paul on the road to Damascus happened instantaneously. There were 17 years between my giving up the American Tobacco account and my saying one word against cigarettes."

Why did you leave McCann? Because of this tobacco thing?

Yes. And I expected to stay out of the business completely. My trying to go back was a very serious mistake.

I got mixed up with a little agency. I mistakenly bought in there, and it was a $225,000 loss. It didn't work well, and I had my next-to-last bout with this mental thing.

Because of the mistake?

Well, no, I think it was a mistake all the way through. Then the agency was bought out by Bozell & Jacobs, and I got part of my money back, which reduced the loss to $175,000. And I received a small retainer for five years, and did a little for them.

Now, I think I should tell you one more thing: You can't tell things halfway, when you're in the kind of discussion that I'm in today. My time at McCann-Erickson, my 13 years, was interrupted by another one of these attacks. And a very strange thing—now this shows you the difference between a friendly and an unfriendly environment—I got all wound up and in a manic phase, and resigned from the agency, against Marion's advice, in 1957. Again I spent six months at this place up in Westchester. This time, I wasn't able to avoid medication; I was on Thorazine, and I wouldn't recommend it to a dog. I broke out in a rash with it.

Anyway, I got out of there, took a little job for a while. It didn't work out very well; I invested some money, but I got it back. Marion advised me to come back to the company, at the same salary I was making when I left: $100,000 a year.

I only took one step down. I quit as executive vice-president; I came back as a senior vice-president, with the same salary.

How long were you away that one time?

I was away 13 months. I don't know how widely Marion told everybody in McCann about what I had been doing, but I think that most of the key people knew where I was. I know damn well that he and Mr. McCann knew where I had been!

This was in 1958, and in December, 1959, Marion made me president of McCann-Erickson USA. The next year, it was changed to just McCann-Erickson Inc. And then after Mr. McCann died in 1962, Marion made me chairman of the board, so for a year or so I was both president and chairman of the board of McCann-Erickson, in spite of all these things. So anybody who reads this should take heart no matter what happens to them!

December 29, 1981

CHARLES H. BROWER

Charles H. (Henrickson) Brower was born in Asbury Park, N.J. on November 13, 1901. He spent his childhood in California before returning East to attend Rutgers University. He was graduated in 1925 with a Bachelor of Science degree in English.

After college Mr. Brower taught for a year at Bound Brook High School in New Jersey, where he was also the school's basketball coach. Although he never played the game, his team won the county championship that year.

An advertising course at Columbia College persuaded him to abandon teaching in favor of advertising.

He first applied at the George Batten Company in the fall of 1926, after spending time as assistant advertising manager of Pacific Mills. For a time he was also an automobile insurance adjuster. He was finally hired in 1928 as a copywriter at the George Batten Company by William Benton, later a co-founder of Benton & Bowles, who became a U.S. senator. Four months later the George Batten Company merged with Barton, Durstine & Osborn to form Batten, Barton, Durstine & Osborn (BBD&O).

In 1940 Mr. Brower was elected a vice-president and a member of the board of directors. In 1946 he was named executive vice-president in charge of all creative services, and in 1951 he became a member of the executive committee. Mr. Brower was elected general manager in April, 1957; president and chairman of the executive committee in December, 1957; and board chairman and chief executive officer in 1964. He retired at the end of 1970.

He was a life trustee and was chairman of the board of governors of Rutgers, the State University of New Jersey. He also served as a member of the Westfield, N.J., Board of Education from 1945 to 1958. He was a member of the University Club and the Manasquan River Golf Club.

He was also known as an inspirational public speaker and writer of magazine articles, notably in the *Reader's Digest*. His speeches have been widely publicized and reprinted.

Elected to the Advertising Hall of Fame in 1981, Mr. Brower died July 23, 1984, at the age of 82.

CHARLES H. BROWER

Interview

I was born in Asbury Park, N. J. My father was a butcher. He was a man who never took a drink, as far as I know, but he had a worse habit: he was a dreamer. You can cure a drunkard, but you can't cure a dreamer. And he always wanted a ranch in the West, and he didn't know anything more about ranching than a cow.

Anyway, he traded his butcher business, sight unseen, for a ranch in Siskiyou County, California—up near Mt. Shasta—and he didn't know what was there. So we all went out there when I was three years old. When we got up there, there was snow; we couldn't even get out to what was called our ranch. When finally some of the snow melted, we found out what we'd really bought was nothing but a former farm. A *former* farm.

A former farm? Not a ranch?

It had been bought by a lumber company, because there was woodland, and they had cut it into stumps; and there was a little shack that had one stove, and an iron pipe through the top for a chimney; and that kind of place of course was absolutely impossible for us. We stayed there for a couple of years.

It must have been 1907 when we decided to go back south to Pasadena, because we went through the ruins of the San Francisco earthquake of 1906.

What about your father? What did he do to support the family?

Papa got a job with Metropolitan Life selling "industrial insurance." For this he was paid $16 a week and commissions.

But anyhow, finally we inherited a fortune. An uncle of my mother's died and left us $2,500. That was enough to get us all back East. My mother said she'd been homesick for some reason.

23

God knows why, because we had been in California for 16 years.

I didn't have any money, and I wanted to go to college, so I took a year off and I worked as a farmhand. So I studied for a competitive exam, because if I didn't get in on free tuition, I didn't even have a chance. But anyhow everything worked out, and I applied for a scholarship at Rutgers and got it; and I had $200 I had saved, so I was off to the races.

But I didn't get very high marks at Rutgers, because I had to work all the time. I did a lot of dishwashing; in fact I worked for one restaurant and washed dishes for two hours for my dinner, and then they fired me because I ate too much.

Did you do any writing at all in those days?

Yes, I was on the weekly paper, which is now a daily paper, down there, and I wrote a funny column. It was a column that was just funny, that's all, and I ran that for three years. I was also on the track team—I was a discus hurler. And I managed to graduate just below the middle, I think.

What were you taking, liberal arts, Charlie?

Yeah. I scrambled to get in that because in order to get this scholarship, I had to take an agricultural course in college. And I had, by the way, made my farewell graduation address from high school on the subject of "Why I Would Never Leave the Farm."

So after I'd spent a year on the farm, I knew I'd never want any part of it after that. I thought, "There must be something for you in the world in which you can earn a living without killing yourself; and get paid." So I didn't start thinking when I graduated; I just took the first thing that came along, which was a job teaching high school in Bound Brook, N. J. And I had two classes there, in which I had all of the boys—there must have been about 200—in physical training; and I coached the basketball team, although I had never played basketball, and hadn't even been going to watch the games in college. So all during football season I stood in the gym shooting baskets so I could say I could shoot a basket. And I got $1,700 a year. At the end of the year I got a raise to $1,750. So I left town.

I decided that I would have to do something that paid a little more money. So I, for the first time, did what I think everybody should do who is in a position to look for work: take a real inventory of yourself and see if there's anything you have at all that you can sell. If you have a voice, maybe you can be a singer. And the only thing that I had was this little experience of writing, and I liked to write, so I said, "I think I'm a writer." I didn't know how to become a writer, really. I couldn't write the Great American Novel—I knew I didn't have enough sense for that. And I didn't want to go into newspapers, because just at that time there was a play out called *Front Page*, which "proved" that every newspaper-man was a drunken alcoholic practically, and I didn't want to do that.

I didn't know anything about advertising agencies, but some-body told me about them, and they also told me that there was a professor—Bill Orchard—at the Columbia summer school who taught copy. And so I said, "I'll just pay my 30¢ and go up there."

And I thought things are going to be easy now, because all I have to do is to be the best guy in the class, and then the professor will get me a job. I knew that he worked for an agency, the old George Batten Company. So I did that, and worked and worked and fought and fought, only he didn't say anything much about this nice job he was going to get me! So finally I asked him if there wasn't any job at his agency. He said, "I wouldn't know, because I'm just a proofreader." Ultimately, through answering ads in the *New York Times*, I got a job as a trainee for the Liberty Mutual Company in Boston. And I went to Boston in February and I think I got $35 a week.

And right in the middle of all this, my jaw swelled up, and the doctor said it was an infected salivary gland and would go right down. But it wasn't—it was mumps, and it got downstairs! And it was interesting.

I couldn't do anything much about it except lie in bed there. And when the hospital gave me the bill, I said, "Well, I don't have any money." And they said that I had to pay before I left. And I said, "Well, all right, then, let's be friends, and tell me where I stay, because I'm going to be here all the rest of my life." So they let me out, and Liberty Mutual took one look at me and fired me. One look in the mirror, and I couldn't blame them. I was a skeleton dressed in skin that did not fit. So my old friend, Bill Orchard, the Columbia advertising teacher and Batten proofreader, picked that moment to telephone me that he had found me an advertising job. It was with a company named Pacific Mills, as assistant advertising manager. I explained my health problem to Bill and told him I would take the job if he could get them to wait two weeks. They agreed. I worked there for a year, I guess, but I kept looking around for a job with an agency. I had never been to any agency but Batten; it was the only one I knew about.

And finally, every time something opened up, this guy Bill Orchard would find out about it, because he was wired into the grapevine, and he would call me and say, "Go up and call so-and-so, he has an opening."

Finally Bill Benton, then head of the trade and industrial part of the Batten copy department, hired me. And they'd had a custom, in the old Batten Company, of having Monday morning meetings of the copy department. Bill, who had worked for Lord & Thomas, and thought it was quite an agency, thought that the Batten Company was just junky, in spite of the fact that it had enormous talent at the time. They had Ted Bates [later founder of Ted Bates & Co.] and Chet Bowles, co-founder with Benton of Benton & Bowles, and Bill Benton of course was raising hell. They had a lot of good writers, but they didn't have good jobs. William H. Johns, Batten's president, was pretty old; and he didn't recognize these guys in their late twenties. So things were rather mixed up.

Anyway, Bill *got fired* on a Saturday for having made a "disloyal" speech the previous Monday. (We used to work on Saturdays till 1:00 in the afternoon.) And I came to work the next Monday, and there wasn't a trace of any evidence that I had been hired by Bill—not even a note. Nobody believed he'd hired me. So I said to myself, "He *did* hire me, and by God, I'm going to stay here!" So I found an empty office, and I sat in it for three weeks, and wrote things, and came in on time every morning, and did crossword puzzles. And finally, a fellow by the name of Moe Collette came around and said, "What did Bill hire you for? How much did he offer you?" And that was when I got my first raise. I got raised from $65 to $75 all by myself, by lying. I was so mad I felt I deserved it.

So almost immediately, I went to work on the Wonder Bread account. Ted Bates was assistant account executive. We got Wonder Bread for no reason except that Robley Feland (treasurer of the agency), lived next door to the sales manager. Ted was on Wonder Bread as assistant account executive, and I was writing on it; and I wrote on Wonder Bread for *eight years!* People often asked for some sample of my advertising, and it was all Wonder Bread, except I did some work on Armstrong.

Anyway, the old Batten Company and Barton, Durstine and Osborn merged in May, and I came over in October.

When was that, Charlie?

1928. May 15th, 1928. The companies were quite different. Since the Batten Company had been founded in 1891 and was almost 40 years old when they merged, and Barton, Durstine & Osborn was formed in 1918, they had quite different philosophies, and everybody was quite different. As a matter of fact, everybody in BD&O called everybody by their first names. I called Bruce Barton "Bruce" right away myself; there was something about him that made you feel comfortable. Whereas, everybody in the old Batten Company was called "Mr.," unless he was a kid.

Well, I got to be what they called a Copy Group Head, with Roy Durstine. When the merger came, he said, "I don't give a damn what office you give me, or what you call me, as long as everybody understands that I'm going to run the goddamn place." So he was vp and general manager—that was his title, and he never understood Mr. Johns, the president, who was just sitting there. And Bruce Barton only came there with the understanding that he would never have to be President, never have to hire or fire anybody, or have anything to do with management. He was just the creative man, and that was all he was going to do.

And he wasn't worried about it at all, because he'd discovered that he could support his family nicely on what he could write on Saturday and Sunday. So he didn't care how much he got paid; he didn't care about anything, as long as they'd leave him alone and let him write.

Durstine thought an advertising man who was a real advertising man should be able to do anything in advertising. He should be able to write, he should be able to draw, he should be able to contact, he should be able to figure schedules, he should be able to do anything. So he divided the company into three divisions. One of them was under Lex Chiquoin, one of them was under Stacy Page, and the third was under George Gouge. It was like having three competitive agencies in the same office. It didn't work. When we merged in 1928, the combined billing of the two agencies was $32 million, and of course, this was just about the day before the Depression started. And in the next ten years, it gradually went down to about, oh, $18 million, I guess. And they had no real copy supervision of any kind.

And Durstine appointed what he called a Creative Board, and it was five of the copy and art guys, including me. We were supposed to pass on the copy, improve the copy, and get the standards up. And we traveled around to the branch offices and told them it'd be best to do some supervising at home. Then, of course, everybody hated this, and no matter what they said they were going to do, they didn't do it. And nothing very much changed. We then were known as the Sneering Committee, and they didn't like the way things were handled, or at least they didn't like being kicked around. It made them feel rather bad.

At any rate, Durstine took up various kinds of sinning, including getting drunk and getting in a spat with his wife and divorcing her. Financing an estate on Long Island, he was broke for about a million bucks.

Durstine was ruined. And he obviously had to go. We needed to go right down and help. So nobody on the Executive Committee, of which I was not a member at the time, had enough guts to fire him. But he had married the singer on the GE program, and he had got himself a new Cadillac on hock, and took his wife and went out for rides to see our clients. And we had a lawyer named Gene McQuade, who made him pay until there was no more, as far as we were concerned. So he was out. And we put back the Copy Department, put back the Art Department, as it should have been all the time. And the head of it was Les Pearl, who was an Englishman.

An excellent copy chief and a helluva guy.

I'll tell you an interesting side story. Les was away, and by that time I had sort of become an unofficial second-in-command. And an English lad named David Ogilvy came in to see me, and he was looking for a job. And I said, "Well, we already have an Englishman. We don't need two Englishmen." I liked him, nevertheless, and I told him he could use an office and use the phone, and call other agencies. And he did, but he didn't get anything at all, until finally he joined Gallup down in Princeton and started from there and did very well. I should have kept him and found him a job, but there were many problems. *

In any case, when the war came on Les Pearl resigned and took a commission in the Army, even though he was over 40. And management made no effort to replace him. They wouldn't even let anyone move into his office. They kept it sacred for him.

So there was Robley Feland—he was one of the members of the Executive Committee—and I said to him—I was always very testy with these people, and I expected to be fired, and sort of hoping I would be, because I was disgusted with most of it—I said to Feland, "If you guys on the Executive Committee haven't got enough guts to appoint a Copy Chief, why don't you call the department together and let them *elect* a Copy Chief, so somebody will be in charge?" He said, "Well, what good would that do? They'd just elect you!" Which I thought was rather flattering. So I couldn't take that! And I went back and psyched myself up to quit, and before long, they asked me to come and see Alex Osborn, and Mr. Osborn told me I was Copy Chief. So that was how I got there. All my whole life there has been fighting in some way, you know. I guess everybody's life is.

If there is any hero in the story, it is Alex Osborn. You will remember that he refused to join the original Batten, Durstine & Osborn agency because he was in love with Buffalo, where he lived. In order to get him, they had to open a BBDO office in Buffalo, where he spent most of his time.

With Roy Durstine out, who was going to "run the shop?" Not Bruce Barton. Although he allowed us to make him president, he insisted on sticking to making ads. Mr. Johns was "promoted" to

*Mr. Ogilvy comments that Mr. Brower's memory is imperfect. "I wasn't looking for a job," he says. "Mather & Crowther, the London agency, had sent me to New York to study American advertising. I went to see Roy Durstine and asked him if I could spend some time at BBDO as a observer—unpaid. Roy sent me to Les Pearl, who was then Copy Chief, and Les very kindly gave me a desk outside his office.

"I stayed for several weeks and learned a lot from Les Pearl—and John Caples. I met Charlie Brower several times, but he never refused to give me a job because I never asked him for one. However, about 25 years later he asked me if I would join BBDO as his successor."

chairman but he was too old to do much but shake hands with some of his employees, thinking they were clients. He also fired the office bootlegger (this was during Prohibition) thinking he was an employee who came to work at 10:00 A.M. Ben Duffy was there as head of media and would be president some years later, but he was not thought of as a presidential candidate at that time. So Alex reluctantly took on the job of "running the shop." For seven years, he "commuted" from Buffalo, where he spent his weekends, and lived in the Roosevelt Hotel during the week. During this time, Ben Duffy took on more contact responsibility and was made a member of the Executive Committee. Ben had a couple of things going for him. He was very smart and he just loved people. He could make a client feel that he was personally just as deeply involved in the client's problem as the client was. And this was not faked. He *was* deeply involved. He had two things against him. He had never been able to get entirely rid of his East Side accent. And he had more ways of getting himself into hospitals than anyone I ever knew.

In 1946, what was left of the Executive Committee met for lunch at the University Club and invited Dave Danforth and me. Dave was told that he would be recommended to the board as Executive Vice-President in charge of Contact—a really non-existent job. If a client is unhappy with the agency, he wants to talk with the agency's president, not with a trouble shooter who has been given a resounding title. I also was named an Executive Vice-President and my job was extended to all offices.

Walking back to the office, I said to Robley Feland, "Now that I am an Executive Vice-President, I presume I am on the Executive Committee."

"You presume wrong," said Robley. "The Executive Committee is elected by the Board!"

"Suppose I get someone on the Board to nominate me. You know just as well as I do that I'll be elected."

"Do you know what we will do if that happens? We'll set up a new committee called the Finance Committee appointed by the President, and the Executive Committee will never meet."

Actually this man Feland was a real friend and had saved my skin a dozen times, but apparently he couldn't stand the idea of me being equal to him. Ben Duffy had already been elected President.

Duffy soon proved that he was a real President by getting the American Tobacco account. He was in Florida when someone phoned him to get himself North—the American Tobacco account at Foote, Cone & Belding was said to be "shaky."* FC&B had everything but radio. "Your Lucky Strike Hit Parade" was handled by N W Ayer. According to Ben, he jotted down the questions he thought Vincent Riggio (who had succeeded George Washington Hill as president of American Tobacco) might ask him. Riggio asked the very questions Duffy had guessed in advance, and Ben walked out with the account. Some of the shop cynics recalled that two kids who used to steal ice from the backs of ice wagons, along with a third kid named Ben Duffy, had now grown somewhat in stature. One was president of the Union News Company, who had tobacco stands in most of the nation's railroad stations, and the other was the recognized authority on tobacco at the Stock Exchange. These unbelievers figured that these two old pals, both of whom were very close to Riggio, had given the account to Ben as a birthday present.

As for "Your Hit Parade," we were informed by people in the new client's advertising department that Ayer was looking for a new show because it was impossible to put a purely musical show like "Your Hit Parade" on TV. We said, "Just add dancers and simple plots to the music—add eye appeal to ear appeal." That brought in the rest of the account.

But joy was not unmitigated. One of our favorite accounts was the *Reader's Digest*, which was crusading mightily against smoking. I was informed that we would surely lose the American Tobacco account unless we resigned the *Digest*. Ben was in the hospital, but the decision was not difficult. You may have noticed which one we still have. Neither!

How long was Ben Duffy president?

In 1956, Ben had a stroke in Minneapolis, where he had gone to see General Mills, a client at the time. His right side was paralyzed and his memory gone. Foolishly, we hoped he would recover soon and be as good as ever. Meanwhile, the old question was with us again—"Who's going to run the shop?" Barton wouldn't. Johns was dead. I told myself quite sincerely that I didn't want it. The

---

*Emerson Foote actually resigned the account before this took place.

31

mistake I made was that I also told my wife, who said, "Excuse me, but I think I see your tongue hanging out."

As far as I could figure there was just one other guy who might have a chance. I went to him and said, "It looks to me as though the next president would be either you or me. I'm here to tell you that, if you are elected President, I will work for you hard and faithfully, and if I am elected, I expect you to do the same for me."

He was noncommittal, because he had already been promised the job. Promised it by whom, I am not quite sure, because the president is elected, not appointed. I wasn't very mad, just enough to spend a bit of time alone with each of 25 directors!

The other candidate, sure that he was *in*, went to Hawaii to survey the grass skirts. No one knew where in Hawaii this guy had gone, so Osborn sent a wire to every important hotel in Hawaii, telling him that he was not elected President. Neither was I.

Still hoping that some miracle would return Duffy to us, they elected me Executive VP in Charge. In a few months I was President officially. Immediately it looked like a disaster. One client said he would have resigned before, but he couldn't find anyone to resign to. Revlon ($6 million) jumped out another window.

"How do you expect to replace that?" people asked. "Easy," I replied, trying not to let them see my stiff upper lip. "We'll replace it with six one million dollar accounts." We did somewhat better than that. We replaced it with Pepsi.

But clients were not the major problem. Trying to keep BBDO among the top agencies with a sickly payroll was foolish. It forced our best people out. Our ancient practice: "We grow our own," was ridiculous. You couldn't run even a ball club and just "grow your own."

The government ruled during the war that non-creative people must be paid overtime. We had put in timeclocks, and to keep it "democratic," we made everyone punch in. Everyone, that is, but Barton, who said he would be goddamned if he was going to wind up his life punching a timeclock.

So the important things I did were: (1) added a million dollars to the payroll; (2) started hiring talent from outside; (3) fired many of my best friends, and (4) did away with the timeclocks.

Perhaps the place wasn't what it used to be, but it was a damn sight harder to compete with.

After you got the situation the way you wanted it, Charlie, as President, you had to start thinking about who was going to succeed you.

Well, my thinking was very clear. We needed a new treasurer. And I said, "I've got to fill that job, and I've got to fill it with the guy that's going to take my job." And I had known Tom Dillon for years, when he was Copy Chief in Minneapolis, and when he was Copy Chief in San Francisco, and when he was Account Executive on Rexall in Los Angeles. And he seemed to me to be the brightest guy in the whole company. So I called up Justin Dart, who was the head of Rexall, and said, "I want your man, but I don't want to lose your account." And he said, "Well, OK, I think he's a good man."

So I went out to L.A. to see Dillon, and we had dinner. I said, "You're going to come tomorrow and move back to New York, and be the Treasurer of BBDO. And if you give me any argument I'll kick you out on your ass." So he came back to New York and became the President, and CEO 10 years later, I guess.

What did you do, gradually give Tom more and more responsibility?

That's right. I put him right on the Executive Committee when he was Treasurer. We always had an Executive Committee to act between Board meetings. I guess everybody has that.

Tell me, Charlie, in your career as a creative man, how much did you feel you were helped by research in the development of copy?

I think research is great at counting heads but lousy at looking inside of them. How can a woman tell us what she is going to do, when she doesn't know herself? Claude Robinson—Gallup's partner in the Gallup & Robinson research company—once asked me, "Don't you know, Charlie, that the purpose of advertising research is to dramatize the obvious?" I think the split-run technique that John Caples invented is pretty sound for testing attention and readership. Research can kill good ideas, as well as bad ones. I should like to have seen any research made on that famous Volkswagen ad that Bill Bernbach ran years ago, in which the headline was "Lemon." Research showed that the Reagan-Carter election would be very close. Research elected Hughes and Dewey President. Personally, I would rather have the opinions of a dozen young but experienced copy men than the opinions of 10,000 assorted women. Of course, I have been out of the business for 11 years, so a lot of improvement has probably gone on since.

One of my main activities was giving speeches. I figured that I was not too well known, so I gave almost a speech a week to ad clubs, Rotaries, the N.A.M. and the Economic Club in Detroit. One thing that made me popular was that I was free. The week that John Kennedy was killed I was speaking to a bottlers convention in Dallas. The President was shot on Friday, but I was speaking the Tuesday before. There were about 5,000 people gathered to hear two speakers. One was me. The other was L.B.J., the Vice President. He was to speak first, but he was flying up from Austin through a storm and seemed likely to be late. A member of the committee warned me that I might have to go on first. "OK," I said. "But I worked hard on this speech, and I don't want to be interrupted by this guy or any of his goons." So I went on first, and almost exactly halfway through, I felt a tug at my elbow and heard a whisper in my ear: "The Vice-President has arrived and says he will either talk right now or leave." I sat down. My wife swears I tore at my hair. When he finished proving that per capita wealth of the United States was increasing (this was caused by fewer babies, not by more wealth), he got down, and I got up.

While I was wondering what to do with a broken-back speech, I was surprised by the entire audience standing up and cheering. Either this demonstration or the Devil prompted me to say, "Don't feel sorry for me, folks. The way things are today, the best shows get interrupted by commercials."

One of the things that is happening in the business today is, we have more and more women coming in to responsible jobs. I just wondered if you have any comment about that?

Well, the only comment I have about it is, I have never seen a woman work for a woman. A man will work for a woman, a woman will work for a man, a man will work for a man. But when you get a woman working for a woman, she will not work well. This is what I believe. I have nothing against women. I used to like them.

What do you think today about the size of advertising agencies? It certainly has changed since you left the business, hasn't it?

34

Yes. One thing that happened to me was that in revising the agency, we wanted to go public. And I said, "Oh, my God." And then I quit, and we went public. And I think that they're becoming a holding company, not an agency. It's quite a different thing.

And of course, I know by taking that attitude of not wanting to go public, I gave myself a good screwing, because I got paid off at the rate of about $8 a share.

In mid-1983, BBDO stock was trading in the $40 range. I think the agencies are really turning into monsters of some sort.

Charlie, after being in the ad business for so many years, and now retired from it, are you still pleased you fought so hard to get into it?

Well, I'm very prejudiced about the business, because I just loved it. And I told the boys back there one day that I saw people in the agency my age, who were delivery boys, you know, and they were about 75 years old; and they could hardly walk, just shuffle around like I do now. And I told them that I'd come back and get one of those jobs; I'd do anything to get back in the advertising business. But they wouldn't let me come and shuffle around!

But really, I love the business. It's a thing that I think is really good for a man to be in. You get some awful blows, and some terrific setbacks, but some wonderful rewards. To me, it's the only business I would ever be interested in.

It was Oliver Wendell Holmes who said that "A man should feel the passion and action of his time, lest he be judged never to have lived." And that's what advertising is. You see more of the passion and action of your time in advertising than anywhere else.

What are you doing now to keep busy?

Well, you'd hardly believe it, but I'm writing a book. That's what I'm doing; I'll finish it, maybe, soon. There's nobody alive now that knows as much about the old company as I do, and I have access to a lot of junk around. I can put together a book on the history of BBDO, which would be valuable for BBDO only.

That'd be wonderful!

And I'd give it to them—the young people, and even the older ones, because the people who are there now, most of them have only been there 10 years, and haven't the slightest idea who Mr. Johns was, or Mr. Batten. They probably don't give a goddamn. But I think this would be interesting reading for them. And I won't sell it or even try to sell it, but maybe Bruce Crawford, our President, might have enough money to have a few copies done, and certainly it would be fascinating and interesting to read.

Well, I certainly look forward to seeing a copy of that.

Well, I hope I get it finished so you can. I've had a very happy and very fine life. I was 80 years old on the 13th of November, 1981.

And I have three kids, and the girl is a professor, a medical professor; and then I have another who's a partner in White & Case, a law firm. And I have a boy who's a free-lancer, who's married and has five children. That's the family.

April 23, 1982

WILLIAM BERNBACH

William Bernbach, a New York City native, was born Aug. 13, 1911, and earned a B. A. in English from New York University in 1933. He started his career as an office boy with Schenley Distillers and worked his way up to the advertising department before serving as assistant to Grover Whalen, head of the New York World's Fair in 1939–40.

After two years in the Army in World War II, his advertising career began in earnest in 1945, when he joined Grey Advertising as a copywriter. In 1949 he and Ned Doyle left Grey and teamed up with Maxwell Dane, then owner of a small agency, to form Doyle Dane Bernbach. The agency, which had billings of less than $50,000 during its first year, was the ninth largest in the world in 1982, with billings of $1.235 billion, and income of $175.9 million.

Mr. Bernbach served as President, Chairman-CEO and in 1974 became Chairman of the Executive Committee, but all through the years was recognized as the personification of the agency, which was celebrated for its outstanding creative campaigns for such clients as Ohrbach's, Volkswagen, Avis Rent-A-Car, El Al Airline, Polaroid, and others.

Mr. Bernbach retained a lively interest in philosophy, art, literature and sociology and served on numerous boards and committees. Included among his honors were election to the Advertising Hall of Fame and the Copywriters' Hall of Fame; American Jewish Committee's Human Relations Award; Man of the Year in Advertising in 1963, 1965 and 1966; and the Parsons School of Design Diamond Jubilee Award.

His death on Oct. 2, 1982, at the age of 71 resulted in an unprecedented outpouring of respect and affection from the advertising community and others. He was recognized as one of the foremost creative advertising men of the Twentieth Century.

Mr. Bernbach is survived by his wife and two sons.

WILLIAM BERNBACH

Interview

I'm a New Yorker, a born New Yorker, and I have a tremendous devotion to it. I went to school in New York; I went to public school and high school, and even college. I went to New York University. And when I got out of New York University, it was during the Depression, smack in the middle of it.

When was this?

1933. And I finally landed myself a job at Schenley Industries. Now, prohibition was just being repealed, and I got a job with Mr. Rosenstiel [president of Schenley]—not with him, with his company. I got the munificent salary of $16 a week, with a college degree in my pocket and all. And I was very grateful for it, and I went to work.

That $16 bought something, too, didn't it?

Listen, I was very pleased to have it, and I went to work. I worked in the mail room at Schenley, and it wasn't long before I got to be the head of the mail room—big deal, you know—and just sitting there in between deliveries and working in the mail room, I got ideas and concepts, and I got an idea for Schenley advertising; and I submitted it to Lord & Thomas. Nothing was said, nothing was done.

This was their agency at that time?

Yes. And lo and behold, one day, I open up a newspaper, and there's a double truck with the campaign I proposed. So I had gotten to know Rosenstiel's secretary, and I mentioned it to her very, very modestly; and she took me under her wing, which was a very, very powerful wing. And I said, "As a matter of fact, I have all of the evidence in a letter I sent to Lord & Thomas. I have no copy, but I wrote it out in longhand." I had no secretary, I was just the mail boy. She said, "Well, why don't you try to get that letter back?"

Well, I took myself up to Lord & Thomas, and I was reading a book of poetry at that time—you may know it, you may not—Kahlil Gibran, who was a romantic Indian poet that I, at that moment, was in love with. And I went to call on this girl, who was also in charge of the files up at Lord & Thomas, and she said, "What are you reading?" And I showed it to her, and lo and behold, she was a devotee of Kahlil Gibran.

Ah, what a lucky break!

Yeah. So she went to the files, and sure enough, there was the letter. And I came back, and Mr. Greenlee—who was the head of marketing and advertising at Schenley—was told to put me in his department. Now, he didn't like that, and he said to me: "Don't think, because you went to college, that you're going to be a big shot around here." I said, "I don't think anything about my going to college; I just don't want it to be held against me, that's all."

Well, it went on that way, and soon Grover Whalen came to Schenley as chairman of the board. And he took a great liking to me, and he soon left for the World's Fair [as its president].

I remember that one. The '39 New York Fair.

And he insisted that I go with him [to work for the Fair]. That's how I left Schenley. (I later got the Schenley account.)

When you were in school, did you do a lot of writing?

I always did a lot of writing.

I mean, was there a school paper, or anything like that, or did you write short stories?

Well, in my English classes, I was pretty much always on top of those, and that was a natural bent. I liked it. I enjoyed it very much, and did well.

I did it with heart, too. My brother was an artist, and that's why, later on, when I went to the World's Fair, I worked with Professor Monahan, who was a professor of history at Yale, and I did a book on the history of fairs with him. It was a soft-cover book, but it was very well received, and it was published by the Encyclopaedia Britannica.

It was co-authored. He was the most prominent name in there; he was a professor of history at Yale. But I did a lot of the writing. And so, once, when Monahan was out a few times, our department did all the writing for some speeches for Grover Whalen, and

I got my hand in it, because Monahan wasn't around to do it. He's dead now. Brilliant, brilliant man. The only man I know who got his Ph.D. without writing a thesis. They gave him one on the basis of a book about John Jay; it was so good they considered that a thesis.

Eventually, I wrote all of Whalen's speeches. I became a pretty good speech writer, not only for him, but for various important political people.

Whalen was very important politically, wasn't he? I know he had been New York Police Commissioner.

Yeah. And he was a dear friend; he was grateful for whatever help I gave him; he was just wonderful to Evelyn [Mrs. Bernbach] and me. I was a, you know, a green kid. And he took me on my first plane ride, down to Washington, to be with him, and taught me the ropes. We'd walk into the Carlton Hotel down there, and he'd give me $5 and say, "Now, Bill, what you do is get quarters for these now, because we're going to need quarters for tips and so on." And so I learned the ways. You know, I didn't have that kind of experience.

So we grew very, very close, and until the day he died, I defended him in newspapers. I think I still have an editorial that they made—remember *P.M.*, the newspaper?

They knocked Grover Whalen after he was out of the Fair—with no need for it—and I wrote a letter which they loved, and they saved it for Sunday and made it the lead letter in there, and that further made him feel close to us. He never had a party or an affair without Evelyn or me, and we were just kids compared to them.

That's why I was so loyal to him; he never forgot that I played a part in his affairs, a useful one. Then when the Fair was over I was looking for a job; I was one of the last to leave the Fair, because they began to go earlier, when the Fair was losing money. And I don't know if you remember the old Weintraub agency—I knew Bill Weintraub.

Yes, I certainly do.

That was my first advertising job.

From the Fair, I went to Weintraub, and Weintraub talked with me, was taken with me; and he said, "Look, I have three guys applying for this job." It was a copy job. I said, "Well, I have no experience." He said, "Then why don't you just write me a letter, telling me why you should have this job?" I said, "I don't know why I should have the job; I don't even know if I'm equipped." He said, "Why don't you write the letter anyway?" Well, I wrote the letter, and I remember one guy was from Pedlar & Ryan, and the other guy was from another big agency at that time. And Weintraub called me in, after he had gotten my letter, and said, "You've got the job!"

And I went to work—I was a copywriter then, and did some very interesting things with Paul Rand, who worked for Weintraub at that time. Paul and I became the closest of friends. When I eloped to get married, Paul was with me; he was on the outside. Oh, yes. Every lunch hour for years, we were together, and we were visiting museums together. And there I got that great integration between copy and art, which I innovated, because I would work with Paul, just the two of us.

I helped Paul with some books he was writing, and we integrated our copy and art like it wasn't done before. You know how it used to be done before: A copywriter would write a piece of copy; somebody would take it to the art director, and he would make a layout. We didn't do that. We worked on the *idea* together. Now, when you work on an idea like that together, with copy and art, you're twice as powerful, because you're working on it with two instruments instead of one. And what the copy says, the art doesn't have to say, and so on and so forth. And after a while, the copywriter gets good art suggestions, and the art director gets good copy suggestions, and you get a tremendous integration, which was the hallmark of our work.

And so I began to develop this, and then the war came, and I went off to the war.

Where were you during the war, Bill?

I was down in Virginia, at Fort Eustis, which was a training center, a supply center for men going right across. And I remember, they found out about me in Washington, and the guy who ran public relations, General Somebody in Washington, found out I was at Fort Eustis, and he sent for me. But I had gotten out a day before he sent for me, because I had some kind of bad heartbeat or something, and I was too old, to be honest.

I came back to New York and Grey Advertising sent for me. I got that job, on the same basis, after the first meeting. I know it's immodest, but they needed me, because they were a Seventh Avenue new agency at that time.

Well, we finally pitched some accounts, some big ones like Mennen; and Lew Bonham was the head guy there at that time. Arthur Fatt [then president of Grey] and I made all the new business pitches. I worked very closely with Phillips Jones Shirts, and I got some ideas. After a while, Cy Phillips, who was Arthur's friend (and that was the basis of Arthur's having the account), Cy Phillips said, for the first time—Arthur told me this—he said that he didn't feel he had to attend a meeting, that Phillips was perfectly happy if I would take care of it.

And so we began to develop out of Grey. I played a big part in that; and that's why, when I left I was offered almost a third of the company if I would stay, but I couldn't stay. You know, to have Larry Valenstein [Grey chairman] over me (he was a bookkeeper), discussing communications and advertising, didn't make sense to me. So I finally went out on my own, and I didn't take any pay for a long, long time. About the second week I was in business, a man came to me, one of the famed headhunters, and offered me a job at about $100,000 a year. Now, at that time—

Boy, that was a lot of money.

I never knew so much money existed. But I didn't hesitate for one second—here I wasn't earning anything—because I had this wonderful opportunity to do what I felt was right, to initiate things, to innovate. That was in 1949. And we had a walk-up place on Madison Avenue.

Did you have those two partners with you at that time?

Sure, we opened up.

Ned Doyle was with me at Grey. Mac Dane had a little agency, and he knew Ned. And because Mac already had an agency, all the credit lines were open; he had all those things that you need in this business. And Mac was a good inside man, and a very decent individual. Mac is a wonderful man.

My investment in the company was $1,200, and it was really Mr. Orbach who insisted that I do this. He was really the guy who made it happen.

Was Ohrbach's [a women's wear store in New York City] a client of Grey at the time?

Yes.

I see. He wanted to get you out of there and get you on your own.

I worked with him; I wrote his ads for about 20 years running. But anyway he said, "Bill, you've got to open your own agency." I said, "I don't want to take an account away from Grey; it's their account." But a few months later, he said to me, "Look, I'm telling you now, if you don't leave, I'm going to take the account away anyway." And then I went, and Mr. Orbach—this was not like him, he was very careful with his money—but he paid his bills ahead of time, so that we would have enough money to run our business. And we became like a father and son back then. We had no new business department; we did everything wrong. But every time an Ohrbach ad ran, the bell rang. We won Best Retail Advertising awards—I would say for fifteen years in a row.

It sure did them a lot of good, too, didn't it, Bill?

Oh, boy. Orbach sometimes got so mad, he said, "Here I've built this wonderful store, and all people remember me for is my advertising."

So, in any event, that sketchily is what got us going. Then the others come in—Levy's Bread, Volkswagen . . .

Famous advertising!

I think I also had the advantage of not knowing too much about advertising, and therefore I could be fresher and more original about it. As soon as you become a slave to the rules, you're doing what everybody else does; when you do what everybody else does, you don't stand out. And if you don't stand out, you don't do advertising that gets attention.

You're so right. You changed the business remarkably, you really did. I think you showed the agency business that good creative work will bring business in.

It's good selling. You know, one of the great gratifications I've gotten out of this business is that I rarely make a speech, Bart, where at the end of the talk, the head of some other agency doesn't come up—either the head of it, or the head creative man —doesn't come up and say, "I want to thank you personally for

44

freeing us into good writing and into good art." And I'm very, very proud of that.

If you can sell with good taste as well as bad taste, why not make it good taste? More fun!

You've done something else too, Bill, that I've always thought was remarkable. No matter how interesting or clever the advertising, it centered on the product.

Always. That's a rule around here. Now, the trouble with a lot of our emulators is, they just put the cleverness down. I want the cleverness to stem out of the product. I want to dig into the advantage of the product. The advertising page is not an exhibit place for your cleverness. The purpose of an ad is to sell. And if wit and good writing and good art are going to help make that advantage indelible and memorable, my God, it's the best advertising you can do!

Now, we have to be careful not to think that we're right all the time, because we're not.

Nobody is.

No. You know, I tell my people, I used to carry around a sentence I wrote for myself. It's important for people like us, who are creative, to remember this; and my sentence simply said, "Maybe *he's* right." It's a tendency of some creative people to use their creativity as a crutch. Even if you're wrong, you tend to think, well, you know better than they do. Well, you can't be that sure.

Okay, Bill. I want to ask you a couple of questions. The first concerns how you feel about advertising education, marketing education, in the schools, as a training ground to come into our business, or to go with advertisers, but to come in the advertising business. And then I want to get your thinking on how we in the agency business, basically, but in the advertising business generally handle the press. That's two subjects. I'd like to start off with just what you think of advertising education; whether it's important to us, whether you think we ought to do more to help, or what.

Well, I'll tell you: We have, in our training program, a lot of M.B.A.'s. And I worry about it, and yet I think we should have them. You know, on balance, when I think about it, we should have them, because they've learned the *arithmetic* of advertising. And you can be right as rain; you can say, "One and one make two," and you're right, but it doesn't impress anybody, because persuasion has nothing to do with logic. Nothing!

Now, the problem with an M.B.A. coming in, and I'll tell that to my own M.B.A.'s—and Harvard is wrong for not being aware of this, because when I spoke up at Harvard, and I speak there once in a while, I convert a lot of the students; for the first time, they want to come into the agencies. The problem is, again, let me repeat, that they learn the *arithmetic* of advertising.

Now, that very fact that they learn the knowledge of advertising, and the arithmetic of advertising, will work against them as a judge of an ad. I have found that by and large—I know this is heresy, but I have found out that, by and large, the better the marketing man, the poorer the judge of an ad. Because he wants to be sure of everything, and you can't be sure of everything. As a matter of fact, if you're sure of everything, then all our competition has found out the same thing in their research, and then they will all repeat that goddamn thing the same way in the same ads. And once again, we come back to what I said before; you're right, all your facts are right, but you're dull, because you're saying everything that everybody else is saying.

If you do that, you're hackneyed. And if you're hackneyed, it means that you're no longer vivid, you're no longer fresh, and people are not drawn to you. See? Because you're the *same*. You must be different. An M.B.A. will want research, and if a consumer, in that research, says a certain thing, he'll say, "Boy, that's what the consumer wants; let's use that!" But your competition will use it, too! And it's no longer fresh.

You have to add imagination to it. You have to add freshness to it. You have to add originality to it. Because you will be effective in proportion to the originality of what you say; not to *what* you say, but to the orginality of the *way you say it*. Because if it isn't, if it's the same as the way everybody else says it, where are you? No place.

So, that's one of the problems.

Why isn't there one course at Harvard on creative?

Oh no. Harvard doesn't have that at all. But they do at a lot of other schools, Bill.

I lectured for a year at NYU; I was what they call a Distinguished Professor or something. And these kids have no idea of what creative is. But none!

I said, "I have one purpose in this course; if I can make you leave this course with a respect and a reverence for the importance of an idea, and its memorable execution—if I leave you with nothing but that, I have done you a giant service. Because it's the quality of an idea, and its execution, that will make you successful." I said, "I don't care if you ever draw a line or paint a picture or write a sentence. If you can't do it, that's not the important thing. The important thing is for you to feel how important it is, and look for it. If you can't do it, get somebody who can do it, and get somebody who can do it better than anybody else can do it."

Shakespeare took all his plots from the penny history books of his day! There was no new material in that; but by God, it's what he did with it! And that's artistry; that's what creative is. And that's what makes people look, respond; that's what makes you touch people and move them.

Well, now, this is the kind of thing I'm talking about in advertising education. I'm not talking about ...

They're not given an advertising education.

Well, it is given in some places; there aren't any Bill Bernbachs around giving it. Of course, they teach them research, they teach them account management, they teach them the financial side of the business, and so forth; and all of this, I think, is a good thing—

Fine! I have nothing against that. I want it. I don't want my creative to come out of something that's not sound. On the other hand, what a pity it is to have all those facts and figures, and then have them drop dead because they're cold and dead and never brought to life.

Well, the only other thing I wanted to ask you about is this whole business about how we use the press. Now, you get a good press, personally, because you're so much admired.

Well, yeah, but that's different.

But what do you think about the trade press, Bill? Do you have any comment on it?

It's no different from the regular press, and I have a thing against the press. First of all, I think that communications is what the world's going to turn on. The world turns on public opinion, and that's formed by communications. And yet, it's the only element of our society, the press, that has no check on it. And it's prey to their instincts, to their own motives of survival, conscious or unconscious. That shouldn't be. And so, you have to think in those terms when you look at the press. They're looking for a provocative story above everything else.

January 18, 1982

MARION HARPER

Marion Harper, Jr., is a business writer and an adviser to business on marketing policy and practice. He was born in Oklahoma City, Okla., May 14, 1916. He graduated from Phillips Academy at Andover in 1934 and from Yale University in 1938. He holds an honorary doctorate from Salem College.

Prior to his resignation from the Interpublic Group of Companies where he held the position of Chairman of the Board, he had devoted nearly thirty years to creating the company as well as to developing its antecedents from a four hundred-man organization to one employing over seven thousand people in forty countries.

During this period he had an unusual opportunity to see international marketing at work in some of the world's great businesses. In 1960, Mr. Harper received the Parlin Award of the American Marketing Association for contribution to the advancement of marketing.

He has served as Chairman of the American Association of Advertising Agencies and of the Advertising Research Foundation. He has been decorated by the Brazilian government and lived abroad for four years in the 1970's. Out of his second lecture at INSEAD, Fontainebleau, France (May 24, 1974) came the notion for the major subject which he has been researching: "The art of strategic decision-making in the large corporation or public service institution." He is the author of *Getting Results from Advertising* as well as numerous articles and papers.

MARION HARPER

Interview

I was born, and live now, in Oklahoma City. My basic childhood could be summed up very simply. I was a fairly good student; in junior high school, I won the Sons of the American Revolution Medal. My mother (my parents were divorced) expected me to work and I did—newspaper routes, etc.; she also insisted upon my learning how to speak and present myself well, and I was active in debating, winning a letter in junior high school. I was encouraged to have extracurricular interests; I was five times president of the United Daughters of the Confederacy Children's Chapter, and oddly enough, I was president of a WCTU chapter. That has changed a little now. I used to take pledges out and get them signed.

All during that period, I was expected to worship, and I joined a Southern Methodist church my grandfather had built. I joined that church and resigned to the minister when I was about twelve years old. I resigned over a principle: I held that the church had no business taking collections from children who were too young (two to four years of age) to understand what they were doing.

I was always impressed with my father, and he had been in advertising, particularly in retail selling here, and I had always been aware of his career. His father, who lived in Oklahoma City, had kept up the contacts, and beginning in 1928 or so, I used to go East for vacations.

In 1932, I went to New York City for nine months prior to going to Phillips Academy at Andover, Mass. During that period, Dad was at General Foods, and I began to meet people in the advertising agency business.

Your father was in marketing there?

He was a Vice-President; he was President of Hellmann's at one

51

point; he was in charge of Birds Eye introduction, and he was in charge of Maxwell House, which is how I knew and was exposed to the Benton & Bowles people.

In 1932, I went to Andover, stayed there for two years, graduated with honors, won a speaking competition; and I think about that time, or shortly after that time, my father went to the Blackman Company (forerunner of the Compton Advertising Agency.)

I went to Yale in '34, and was there, of course, through '38. I worked at least one summer at Blackman (now Compton)—I'm not sure, it may have been two. I was assigned to Research. I worked another summer later in that period, interviewing on new drug products that a group of people were planning to introduce. I asked a number of executives in the firm what to study, and was told to major in psychology, which I did. I studied under good men, and graduated with honors.

I was very much influenced by the research orientation and the advertising orientation of the people I met. I became interested in copy testing and made that sort of a side interest.

What happened after college?

I worked for four months selling house-to-house, at my father's insistence. When I came back to New York—it was January 1939 —I told my father that I'd made up my mind to go into advertising.

At this point, I went to the Royal Bank of Canada, where I was interviewed for a trainee post. I went to Macy's to be interviewed for an executive trainee post. The thing that discouraged me completely—and changed my father's mind as to my having some other career—was that before going to Macy's, I had to study for three weeks to find out what examinations they gave to applicants. . . . what scores they accepted, etc. For example, if on the intelligence score you were below 120, they didn't take you. On the I.Q., if you were above 130, you were too bright! So you had to position yourself very narrowly. Well, I studied very carefully. I had done enough work in college to understand the problem. And I took the tests. Lo and behold, instead of some bureaucrat telling me that I had the job, I was called in immediately to see the psychologist. He told me that I could have a job as his assistant, because I had "hit" the test so accurately! I said, "To hell with that."

At the Yale Club, I found that there was an office boy's job open at McCann-Erickson for $14 a week, and I just took it. It so happened that this was not an office boy's job, because the company had decided to enter into a young men's training program. During that period, I attended numerous courses, was introduced to all the departments, kept copious notes, and was lectured to ad nauseum.

After a few months, I was asked to analyze the old L. M. Clark and Daniel Starch readership reports, to work on copy testing, and to see whether or not, out of all of the data, someone could make some kind of synthesis that would be useful creatively—that is, that could be presented to the creative people, and that would influence·their work. And I devised a method of predicting readership scores, which was put into a presentation which lasted for seven years as to what the principles were.

Well, the odd thing was, I was then exposed to all the creative people in the various offices, and then was able to meet and to sample, if you like, their kind of thinking. Based on that, they formed a Copy Research section in the Research Department.

In the Copy Research Department, I was then fortunate in the sense that I acquired Dr. Hans Zeisel, and Dr. Herta Herzog. He was a superb statistician, even though a lawyer. Dr. Herzog had been married to Paul Lazarsfeld, and had a particularly unusual reputation in two fields; that is, in daytime serials, in the analysis of what program elements seemed to work, and in devising new psychological approaches to research.

Later, I became Director of Research; my wife (Virginia Epes) became head of Copy Research, and in many respects she did a better job than I did.

All during this period, I worked on new business very extensively, and I suppose I went all over the United States, in essence, making calls. We were a very sleepy, old agency in those days. In 1939 we had reached the end of the road, I think, and—well, in '41, I remember, we had about $19 million worth of billing. I know it sounds absurd, but we had 400 people; and we had a few offices overseas which Mr. McCann had started. Some of those were very good, particularly in Germany and in Brazil and Argentina.

I became a Vice-President at the age of 26; I was assistant to the

President in late '46 and '47. One of the most formidable problems during those days was to develop a professional organization. And we began, in '47, what was called the Continuing Clinic of Agency Operations. What we did, in principle, was we took the very best people that we had, we worked at night and weekends, and we asked questions in writing of all of our people around the world; and then we synthesized all of that into what they considered the best practice, and the best practice in the industry, and then we conducted seminars throughout the world, to upgrade the professional practices of our people.

In 1948 I was named President of the company; McCann became Chairman of the Board. I was 31 years old.

In those days, J. Walter Thompson was first, with about $70 + million in billing; Young & Rubicam was second, N. W. Ayer was third, McCann was fourth or fifth, then Lord & Thomas (later Foote, Cone & Belding). The whole top ten, I suppose, plus another ten or fifteen, did about half a billion dollars in volume.

My job here was to take an agency which had fine character, had a good international facility, had a rather sound reputation, but certainly was not very bright creatively, and find a way to turn it around and make it competitive in the marketplace. And it was in that period, in the '50s, that the concept of the holding company was devised.

What brought you to that, Marion?

Well, basically, the principle that I had was as simple as it can be: 1. that to attract good people, we had to have a larger business; 2. that it became very clear to me that the very best clients made the best agencies; 3. that these clients would have product development concepts and products, new products coming, and those new products should not routinely be given to some other agency, because of some idiosyncracy of the management or because of possible product conflicts. We should be able to provide a facility whereby we could say, even to our opponents in the company, if there were any, "We have an agency that you can have." But by concentrating all of the client money in one holding company, the concept was that we would be able to give them good service anywhere in the world, be able to solve any problem anywhere, be able to make an investment in new products, and be able to continue to do basic research and basic studies in communication.

And out of that, the first agency acquired was Marschalk & Pratt. Now Harry Marschalk made good sense, because we shared the Esso account with him. And it made good sense, because I had a different problem, in the sense that I had to bring the fine men that I was working with, Mr. McCann, Mr. Atwood, Mr. Anderson and others, to a point where they would accept this idea without knowing what the idea was too quickly. After all, they were rather older men, and they were very conservative. And so, Marschalk made good sense, because everybody was saying to himself, even though I was not saying it, "Well, he'll absorb it." I never did, obviously.

And then later, we went on to Erwin Wasey, Pritchard Wood, Jack Tinker & Partners, etc. Financially, all during this period, we had very little resources. I remember at two meetings around 1944–45, I remember there was a meeting in which the primary problem was how to get enough working capital above a half-million dollars to continue to service the growth!

I remember I was put on the Executive Committee in early '47, and the first vote the committee took was to dismantle all of the overseas companies. Mr. McCann, Mr. Atwood and I voted to keep them, and the two other members—we'll leave them nameless—voted to sell them. And I made the difference. During the period that I was building the holding company concept, of course, I accepted the principle of expanding the business internationally. I don't really have any record, but I think that we had opened in 16 countries that we were not in during that period—Italy, Spain, Sweden, Finland, Belgium, Switzerland, Austria, South Africa, Japan, Hong Kong, Australia, India, Canada . . .

A tremendous expansion all at once!

Well, I only point that out to say that we had three expansions running simultaneously, and all of these on what I regard as limited resources for the job. The first expansion I just outlined; all of those took money. The second expansion, of course, was we were acquiring other agencies. And the third expansion was, we were attempting to go into the marketing services business, that is, be a separate research company, a separate sales promotion/merchandising company, etc.

Looking back, I think one of the mistakes that one might have pointed out to me at that point, had I been more sensitive to it, would have been that basically we had three elements of growth running simultaneously, two of which were mandatory in my book, but the third we might have postponed. By taking on all three, we strained the company unusually.

All during this period, incidentally, without exception, we carried a basic research budget and we always programmed monies into experimental work and into so-called basic research, that is, applications.

I entered the computer field through John Felix & Associates. Looking back, it probably would have taken a great deal of money to go after Control Data or IBM. And I suppose in one sense the original Jack Tinker & Partners (one of the units set up by Interpublic) work was experimental.

One of the mistakes I probably made was that I let Jack Tinker & Partners take its first client, which was Miles Laboratories. I probably should not have permitted that, or I should have continued some immediate provision for experimental creative principles. Because what happened was that the client began to eat up the people, and in the long run experimental work was driven out because of day-to-day pressures of making money. I might add that one of the great satisfactions I've always had was that the Miles business in the first four years went up about 65%.

The reason was simple. One of the things that Dr. Herzog did was go over all the research that had been done on Alka-Seltzer since 1923. And in that we found the answer—one answer at least—to the sales problem of Miles and Alka-Seltzer, namely: you could read the research one way, which people did at Miles, which called for one tablet per drink: we read the same research as recommending two tablets. So we simply doubled the dosage in all of our advertising. This made a fundamental difference and of course it was backed by the medical people, it was backed by everybody. It was right there in front of them but they never saw it, and the agency never saw it.

Another curious thing which I learned through the Tinker activities concerned creative work. Mary Wells (now head of Wells, Rich, Green), was in charge of the creative work under Jack, and Mary couldn't tell the difference between a *very good* commercial, meaning a commercial that would last longer than three weeks when aired, and a commercial that was *superb*, that might go three months. And this reminded me of something my father had told me years before, that one of the problems in raising Holstein cattle is that you fall in love with the animals you have. I always felt that our creative people had a tendency to fall in love with their creative product and could not too easily discriminate creatively between the very good and not very good, even though it might be better than most.

During this period we had a practical problem also, which was the problem of our people. We were training our people—were exposing them to each other, were exchanging them, had training programs, etc., and we also decided to go outside and bring in seasoned people who—their tenure might not be forever—but the point was that around them we could build teams of people.

And this was one of the three problems the industry gave us. The first problem was the industry rejected the concept that you could have a holding company. The second thing they rejected was the idea that you could have competitive products in the same house. And the third thing they rejected was that you could bring in top people and suddenly make them part of the team, so to speak.

You brought in some awfully good ones.

Yes, we did. Some of the people that we had with us who have gone out and done very well were, of course, Pete Peterson, who's chairman of Lehmann Brothers, he was a very young man in the research function; Mary Wells, of course, who came from Doyle Dane; Stu Watson, who's gone on and become chairman of the board of Heublein; and one man that never received enough credit, but who was very influential in our company in terms of stimulating us to the kind of organization we developed finally and into many of the personnel policies we developed was a man named George Park. Now George had been on Ralph Cordiner's staff at G. E. when they turned that shop around, that company around. And of course we had Hans Zeisel, who went on to Chicago Law School; Bill Free, who started his own agency, etc., etc.

Well, I would say with Bob Healy and Emerson Foote, you brought in two great people.

Well so much for that. Our people were of constant interest to us, and constantly important to us. During that period several things on the client side happened. Of course we acquired several very important clients, some of which you know very well: Coca-Cola, General Motors, Miles, Carnation, Westinghouse, etc. Now we had several odd incidents during that period, the most amusing of which I suppose, which tested our principles, was the resignation of the Chrysler business. We had the Chrysler account—we billed around $27 million—which was a lot of money in those days. And we came to the conclusion that Chrysler was not going any place.

I remember at one point I, through Jim Cope, who was public relations director, told the senior officers at Chrysler that either they were going to seize the 25 largest markets of the United States with top management attention, taking them away from the field, or that I had to resign the account. So I remember being brought in and Jim Cope said to me, "By God, Harper, you've won! Look at the people we're sending!" So I looked at the list and promptly resigned the account. Because all they had done was shift the old sales force around.

I had once before told Tex Colbert and some other men that they could take the business if they didn't conform a little bit more to better business practices. And we took the General Motors Buick account and the GMC Truck account. We exchanged $27 million for about $14 million. It was not a very popular decision among some people. But as time has borne out, I think it was a brilliant decision, because the agency now has Chevrolet, which is at least $140–$150 million; it has Buick, it has GMC Trucks and occasionally has an institutional assignment.

Another great account during that period was the Coca-Cola account, and this brings me to a kind of interesting problem: that is, when agencies go public, what is it that they can't do? Now we all know what they can do. As a matter of fact it was under my chairmanship of the Four A's that we debated this subject, and finally agreed that we had the right to go public. I remember, incidentally, that the people who opposed me most on going public were three: Fax Cone of Foote, Cone, & Belding; Bill Bernbach of Doyle, Dane, Bernbach; and Norm Strauss of J. Walter Thompson, all of whom subsequently went public.

John Crichton [former editor of *Advertising Age* who became President of the American Assn. of Advertising Agencies] and I used to talk about this problem of the public agency, and this now gets back to the Coca-Cola reference I gave earlier. I think in the first six months we invested a million dollars in the Coca-Cola account; that was a lot of money in 1959–1960. And we made that investment without any income, because I insisted that they give a much longer notice to D'Arcy (the former Coca-Cola agency) than they were thinking of.

Our assignment was very simple; Coca-Cola had been steadily deteriorating in market position in the United States, and the question was what to do about it. And, we turned, once again, to trying to understand the marketing aspects of the business and trying to understand the consumer facts of the business. That's where we began, and then from there, we moved to the creative side. And once again, that investment of a million dollars, which seemed like a lot of money then, has been proved worth while over the years, because the business did turn around, basically by following the principles that were enunciated then.

Now, the question which you always have as a public agency is, could you invest a million dollars today, or let's call that $3 million? Could you even do it, because after all, you have many investors who are not in the agency. Is it fair to them? And so, John Crichton and I always felt, and even though we supported going public, that somewhere in ten or twenty years two problems would emerge, possibly three. But the two problems we had in mind were the fact that the generations that were then running the agency would achieve a very large and substantial reward, but what about the second and third generations, particularly the third?

The second area that we worried about was this: How would a marketer be able to handle new product operations? How would an agency be able to finance either long-term market declines which he had to reverse, or the cost of researching the marketing possibilities of new products? Often in those days, we took the position that we were an entrepreneurial business; we had been private since 1912; we had a right to find out anything we wanted to without asking anybody's permission. And we paid for the research, and we never expected to be remunerated! Because we got that payment back by increased media commissions. So the question always continues, whether in a public agency that can be done. It certainly cannot be done extensively.

I think all the fears that we had have dissipated in that connection, especially with regard to the investors down the road, the second and third generations. I don't think it's been a problem, do you?

Yes, I think it's coming.

You do think it's coming?

One of the problems I worry about in the next ten years—it might be five years or fifteen—is the consequence of two things. One is the adoption of the holding company concept, and the other is the going public, both of which I can safely say I've been very much identified with and greatly supported during the '60s and '70s.

Well, here's what bothers me. I believe that I've always been happy in the agency business; I've spent my life in it, and I have no regrets for having done so. But if one takes a long hard look at the agency business, he must come to several conclusions, tentatively at least.

One is: the rank and file of smaller agencies, whether these are 4,000 or 5,000 or only the 750 or so listed by *Advertising Age*—agencies with one man or no people as employees—there's great room for the so-called local or regional agency. I have very little doubt about that.

My doubt concerns the top 25 in billings and revenue. Maybe it's 20, maybe it's 26, I don't know. Now, here's what bothers me about it. The top 25 are, at the moment, in a very competitive scramble for finances, a very competitive scramble for internationalism, in a very great scramble to grow and to be bigger. In fact, there are several predictions around that by the year 2000 or so, there may only be 10 "great agencies."

I think there's a good chance of that.

I don't think so.

You don't?

No, and I'm going to explain why very carefully to you, because no one else will probably ever listen—I probably will never say it to anybody else, I'm not sure. At any rate, here's what bothers me. This is a nuts-and-bolts view of the agency business. In the first place, you exist solely to help your client. There is no other rationalization for the advertising agency business. In the beginning, our job was to fill space, and for that, we received a commission from the media. By now, the amount of money which is involved in, let's say, a $250,000, 30-second Olympics commercial in 1982 is already, by the time you multiply that, already beyond the ability of most agencies to finance. So that it basically is the guarantee of the client anyway, directly or indirectly. Now, what puzzles me is that, by putting the emphasis on facilities, and by putting the emphasis on finances, we are putting our emphasis where we cannot hope to match our best clients. Our best clients will always have more money, and our best clients will always have extensive facilities, to the extent that they want it. Up to now, they haven't wanted an advertising facility.

Okay. Now, the advertising agency business—my second point —is going to sleep, because it looks back to the '30s and thinks about house agencies; and it says, "Well, house agencies won't amount to anything." They're probably right. But what they are *not* right about is that marketers are going to develop some new solution, in my opinion.

One reason I think it's true is that, if you study, let's say '79 or '80—and take the 100 largest advertisers; the largest, Procter & Gamble, spent well over $600 million; the smallest client of the top 100 is Mazda, with about $18 million. Now, there are only, as I remember the figures, about 70 agencies that are larger than $18 million. Now if I cut that down, and I say, "All right, let's go to $50 million," at this point there are only about 30 agencies larger than that in billing. So what I keep coming back to in my own mind is, with the enormous growth of billing, with the oncoming new product proliferation, with mergers, etc., on the part of manufacturers, it's almost inevitable that they can do anything they want to do. And for the first time, the advertising budget plus the direct marketing budget is large enough for them to want to do something about it. We keep looking at advertising as the thing to focus on; of course, that isn't true. Because, for example, the direct marketing expense other than advertising, well, you use your own figure, it's at least $120 billion, it probably is $200 billion.

So if I add the two together, that means the manufacturers are spending about $250 billion in information management. I'm assuming that a catalog is information, that a sales meeting is information, etc. Now, from the manufacturer's standpoint, he must look at his bottom line, and he must look at the total money he spends in information support; and he cannot look, finally, just at advertising. You know, for most of our lives, advertising has been a relatively small item. But advertising is now getting to the point where in dollar size alone, in the major company, it's a major part of business.

Now, the public company—that is a long answer, I realize, but nevertheless relevant—the public company in the agency business makes its money, fundamentally, not from the ideas it has, but from the multiplication of those ideas in media. All right. Now, the multiplication of those ideas is done by—excuse me—lesser people in the agency business. Now, these people can just as well work for a manufacturer as work for an agency. I remember once, one of the best creative men I ever knew and ever worked with was a man named R. E. Thompson. Thompson came to me one day, and he said, "I think I have an idea for Chrysler. I have an institutional campaign." He reaches into his pocket, pulls out an envelope; on the envelope, he has written a single set of words, "The Forward Look." And "The Forward Look" turned that company around when we ran it.

Now, wait a minute! That has nothing to do with offices in Venezuela or London. It has nothing to do with the ability to multiply. It has nothing to do with nothing! It does not require the same caliber of mind to produce "The Forward Look" that produces the multiplication of "The Forward Look." And of course, the crudest example of that is in the airline business, where all schedule advertising could just as well be done by an airline as an agency.

So the question really comes down to, how do you pay an agency? In the coming years, what I'm afraid the question is going to become is, "How do we pay for the idea that was on the envelope, and *we* will do the multiplication." And note one other thing. When you get to 6,000 people, let's say, or 5,000, 4,000 or whatever, they constitute a kind of permanent bureaucracy. Now, there's no reason to pay for that bureaucracy if you're a manufacturer. You can do it cheaper. One other thing I notice with great alarm is that the agency business no longer pays competitive salaries for top positions.

Therefore, if I give the company a monopoly, so to speak, on resources, which they have; I give them a monopoly on objectives, in other words, strategy; I have passed the research function to them and they have a monopoly of information—I am just a step away from a new problem, which is that they can have any number of creative consultants, pay those people, and multiply the things by in-house work. Maybe I'm just seeing a ghost, but the result of this would be that you would have a marked increase in permanent staff in a manufacturing organization. Because one of the things that happens, and I regret that I have to say this, but it's true—if you take a large advertising agency, and you list its largest accounts, you find that the smaller accounts are subsidized by the profit produced by the larger accounts. For example, in the automotive business, if you don't make 5–7% operating profit, there's something wrong. Okay, the reason you don't *finally* make it is because you pass it on for redistribution through agencies and other outside organizations.

Okay. I just can't believe that in the last analysis, the very smart people who are in the top manufacturing organizations in the United States are not going to look at this and say, "Wait a minute, this isn't right! We're entitled to keep the profit agencies make from our advertising and reinvest it on our own behalf!"

And moreover—this is my last point—I'm increasingly worried about a new problem which I see signs of when I watch television, namely: so many advertisements today, in this recession economy, are using simple product attributes, or they're using competitive claims, naming competition. They are moving away from what we used to think of as image advertising, or advertising of appeals or motivation, or whatever you want to call it—selling-appeal advertising, buying-appeal advertising—they're moving away from that to a more informational form. And in a way, electronic media kind of asks for that, particularly as it reduces the time which you have to use creatively in getting a message for an advertiser across. Therefore, there is less need for the unusual creative skill.

I realize all this sounds impossible, because the agency business is at its peak; we have many great mergers and amalgamations going on, and so I must sound like an idiot. But the fact of the matter is that, what the manufacturer is going to decide, in my opinion, is that the answer to the question: "When do you stop creating?" is the most important question in his life.

In a public agency, in a holding company agency, in a company in which eight or ten percent of the stock is held by officers, and that's what we're coming to, then you're going to have to ask this question: "When do you stop creating?" Because if you create beyond a point, it costs money. If it costs money, it creates expense. If it creates expense, it creates loss. You can't have that in a public company!

And so, I just wonder if, in the last analysis, manufacturers will just sit around without creating some new entity. I'm not arguing, mind you, that they will have a house agency. I'm simply arguing that they will create an entity which incorporates the information resources into some single unit, and which achieves the integration that I, perhaps, tried to achieve and didn't, which perhaps in some respect Y&R is trying today.

Now, the Y&R experiment is a funny experiment, too. Because —and this is really my last point on the damn thing—let's imagine for a minute that Wunderman [Wunderman, Ricotta & Kline, a direct response agency in the Y&R fold], which is a very profitable business—let's say that they do $125 million. Whatever. At any rate, the Young & Rubicam advertising portion of the business is so much bigger in size, and the people there are the people who have the clients. Now the fact of the matter is, the people at Wunderman are not quite the same people that are at the agency. And if you had to make a choice, and you're a Y&R executive, you are obviously always going to have to favor advertising over, let's say, direct-response advertising; because general advertising produces more total bucks. So that, in a way, is another reason I'm not very happy or sanguine about the future of the very large amalgamation.

I'm not saying that for ten years it may not be good; I'm not saying that the public holding company is not practical. All I'm saying is that I wonder if we don't have a conundrum-producing problem here, the conundrum being whether the manufacturer is going to sit still and finance this? Because he's the one who's financing the mergers and the amalgamations, he's the one that has to be content on the resolution of the competitive problem, he's the one who has to put up the money for the new product development, he's the one who has to finance the overseas office, etc., etc. I just don't believe that whenever you get to, let's say, General Foods spending $400 million in advertising, and perhaps a billion dollars in the management of information totally, including research and advertising, I don't believe they're going to sit still!

Maybe ten years from now, one or more of these companies will create entities where the answer to that question is "We'll give the do-it work to our in-house facility, and we will use five or six outside creative consultants." This brings you to another problem; it's an awkward idea, but you know, all of us in advertising promulgate a single thought, namely: that you can only get a good idea from one agency. That's, of course, nonsense.

In all the work I ever did, I came to the conclusion that about 75% of all advertising was relatively ineffective. What was effective was the amount of money being spent. But that's being cancelled out by competitive activity today.

Marion, can I ask you just a little bit about your thinking on advertising education? What kind of people should we be attracting to the advertising business?

Well, I have a funny problem again with regard to the holding company and public agency concept. Anything that increases the distance between key people in the agency and key young people acts to the disadvantage of the agency in the long run, and of the individual, obviously. Now, one of the things that I believe is urgent in education is that you have, for all intents and purposes, immediate access to the top people, if you're a trainee of promise. Top people in the advertising business, both on the manufacturer's side and the agency's side, should involve themselves in eyeball contact with people who are going through any kind of formal education. Otherwise you vitiate the whole process.

I believe that a good deal of what is taught in the common textbook is rather ridiculous. That is, I believe that you can acquire all the basic information in a very small amount of time, in formal training. What you can't acquire are the finesse, the techniques, the experience, the applications. And therefore, it seems to me the one thing that the Four A's or someone like that could do is, by getting funding together, to expose these people to more practical case histories, and have them discussed, not just by a teacher and the class, but by people who have prepared the case history and people who've had the experience, even people who are in dissent. So I suppose I'd like to see more case work.

And the third thing is, I'd like to see some dissenting voices.

Let's say cable. I think there are 16 cable entities accepting advertising today. I think more time should be spent reviewing their
future, the future of AT&T, the future of electronic media generally, than just talking about "How do you make a commercial?"
The problem involved is, if HBO continues to not accept commercials, and Shell, Max, and View do the same, sooner or later
advertising is going to have a new problem, because it's being
barred from a medium that was proved to be effective in reaching
people. And mind you, that people are *paying* to see, in part not to
get advertising.

I guess the last thing that bothers me about education is that not
enough attention is being paid to what is going to be the problem
in the next twenty years. I believe there'll be a very large increase
in criticism of American business. A lot of that criticism is going
to spring from the advertising which these people are running. It
isn't that their self-interest is not critical and important, but
they're going to have to show that their self-interest belongs to the
common interest. In my opinion, the way that advertising is going, it doesn't pay much attention to the common interest. And I
don't believe you can say, "Well, this should be done in some
other form." Not really, because my guess is, most of the criticism
of business is going to come either from a product experience, or
it's going to come from advertising. And maybe those are related.
Because, in principle, the promise you make in advertising often
exceeds the delivery of the product.

They have to respond to what is going on.

I think the advertising agencies are currently responding to
changes that are behind them, and I'm afraid the changes that
they're working on aren't relevant to the future they're going to
face.

That's my worry. That doesn't mean it's right, that doesn't
mean I'm right.

May 11, 1982

JACK TINKER

Jack Tinker, perhaps the mostly widely recognized of Twentieth Century advertising art directors, began his advertising career in 1927, at the age of 21, when he joined the staff of N. W. Ayer & Son, America's oldest advertising agency, then headquartered in Philadelphia.

He developed the facility of merging art direction and copywriting, so that he became one of Ayer's key creative people, involved with many of the agency's principal accounts. He created the ads that introduced the Ford Model "A" to America during his seven-year stint at Ayer.

From Ayer Mr. Tinker moved to J. M. Mathes in New York, where he spent five years before joining McCann-Erickson in 1939, an affiliation which continued until 1960, except for one year at J. Walter Thompson in 1942. He served the agency in a variety of executive posts, culminating as Creative Director and Senior Vice-President. In 1952, he received the Art Director of the Year Award from the National Society of Art Directors.

In 1960, Mr. Tinker was asked by Marion Harper, then head of the McCann-Erickson/Interpublic complex, to set up an organization whose sole function was to be creative exploration and development—a project which emerged as Jack Tinker & Partners and for ten years exercised a major influence on American advertising with off-beat approaches for such advertisers as Braniff Airlines, Alka-Seltzer and Buick Riviera.

Serious illness forced him to withdraw from the active agency front in 1971, but he continued his activities as a book illustrator and painter. He lives at Lake George in upper New York in the summer and Florida in the winter.

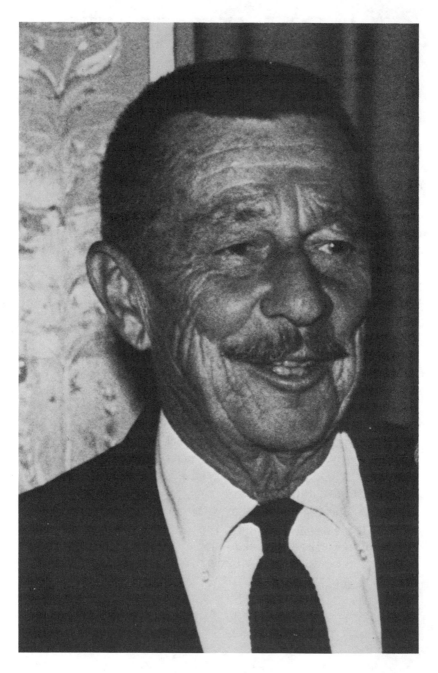

JACK TINKER

Interview

I was born in Pittsburgh, January 17, 1906. I grew up in the old farmhouse which belonged to my grandfather and served as a family residence for all of his daughters, my mother being one of them. All of us grew up there, and so we were a large family in spite of the fact that I was an only child. I went to Peabody High School in Pittsburgh, as did my wife Martha.

Eddie Gott, who became chairman of U.S. Steel, and Frederick Close, who became chairman of the board of the Aluminum Company of America, also went to Peabody. We were famous for people who didn't appear to have a future.

The next school I attended was the Pennsylvania Academy of Fine Arts in Philadelphia. But my father didn't want me to follow the career of an artist, and so I attended Carnegie Tech for about a week and that was enough to prove both to Tech and myself that my future lay elsewhere. So I talked the family into sending me to Pennsylvania Academy, which at that time was a beaux arts school. You came and went as you saw fit. No attendance kept; no records of any kind. And it was in the old Pennsylvania Museum which was on Broad Street and a fine school. Some of our really great painters went there over the years—Thomas Eakins, Robert Henri, Sloane.

As I look back, I actually believe I might have been afraid to go to Carnegie Tech because I knew that I had a talent. I could make thoughts appear on paper with almost no effort. And this skill isn't given to everyone in graphic terms. So I really wanted to pursue that.

I had been encouraged by teachers in high school. The art teacher in a high school carried very little influence, but my art teacher was a woman and she felt that I had a skill that should be pursued, and I began to believe it, and I certainly enjoyed it. I wanted to go someplace where I could improve whatever ability I had, and the best one at the time was this Pennsylvania Academy. So I went.

And I had an apartment with another guy in town and it was a dreadful temptation to do nothing, because right out of high school with ordinary, middle-class background to find yourself in a wacky world of long hair and sandals was very tempting.

My father actually came down at the end of the first year and a half and asked for me at the registrar's office. And they said they had nobody there by the name of Tinker. He said, "Well, I've been paying the bills; he must be here." And they looked it up again and they said yes, but he really hasn't attended the school very often. And he went out to my apartment and discovered that I was enjoying life there and he took me out of school—and back to Pittsburgh.

Your father had a brewery; did he want you to come in there with him?

I don't think so, because at that time we were closing in on what later became Prohibition. I went to work in the stockroom of Club Aluminum Co., for a short period of time. I remember I lost my first pay check on the loading dock playing a game called Red Dog, which I had never heard of before, but all the truck drivers knew—and when all the smoke cleared away I didn't have any money.

Then I worked at a gasoline station for a year. During that time I also decided that I would like to go back to Philadelphia because in my mind it had some association with a world which I wanted to participate in.

I persuaded my Dad I would not spend my time doing nothing. And I went back and I went into the advertising business—but I don't think anybody knew I had entered it. I saw this sign on the side of a brick building which said N. W. Ayer & Son Advertising and I didn't even know what it meant except that I had a vague idea that it had something to do with the art world. And I went in and went through the normal channels of employment. Somebody said, "Well what do you want to do?" And I said, "Well I don't know, I'll do absolutely anything to get into this business."

When somebody said, "Do you do anything?" and I said, "Well, I draw." So they introduced me to Vaughan Flannery.

I believed then and I believe now he was one of the most important contributors to the direction and the graphic and visual ends of advertising. And he hired me.

When was this?

The year was 1927. I was 21. I worked there six years, during which time Martha and I were married. I started for $25 a week. And before I was married I lived on Hershey bars; when we were married I was up to $50 a week.

We lived in Germantown, which was a pleasant part of Philadelphia and over my head as far as income was concerned. But I liked it and I liked the business and I had a feeling that it was exactly right for me. I could use what talent I had and make it pay both for the person who was paying me and for me. I was getting the most out of what I had to give.

Everybody who started at N. W. Ayer in those days started in what was called the Business Department. It didn't make any difference whether you were going to be a writer or an artist or an account executive or in the financial end—you started at the same thing.

And they had a martinet who ran it. I thought he was an elderly man; I realize now that he must have been very young. Every morning he inspected all of us kids, because we really were young people. He looked at our fingernails; we had to have stiff white collars, white shirts and obviously a complete suit that matched, no sports jacket or any of that stuff. And many of the young guys working in that department were working literally for nothing. They were standing in line to come to work. Most of those were university graduates or business school graduates.

What were you doing?

Delivering mail. In essence it was working out of a central mail room and rushing about filling water carafes and delivering the wrong mail to the right person, and generally learning the business. And as you moved along, you learned for a period of up to six months; if you were, for example, going to go into the business end of advertising or marketing, you might be allowed to pick up and read an occasional paper that had something to do with your interests; and if you were going into the creative end, once in a while you were allowed to work in an evening, let's say in the bullpen, where you would paste things up.

Eventually, that's where I went after I'd done my stint in the Business Department; then I moved into the Art Department. The art director-in-chief, Vaughan Flannery, was quite remote in the sense that—physically, as well as emotionally . . . he lived kind of by himself in what I thought was a magnificent office *with* a secretary.

After about a year and a half, I became a supervisor myself. And at the end of the fifth year, Jim Mathes, who was one of the senior members of the firm of N. W. Ayer, moved to New York and started his own agency. The reason for starting was that N. W. Ayer would not handle liquor advertising, and he had an opportunity to pick up the distibutorship of Johnnie Walker in this country, and along with this started an agency . . .

Both the distributor and the agency?

That's right; then he picked up Canada Dry and added that to the stable. Later he got Kellogg's away from Ayer. He had a lot of influence, and he took about half a dozen people from the agency, and I was one of them, and that brought me to New York.

How long were you with Jim?

Another five years. I seem to run in five-year cycles.

I was an Art Director. It was a far less structured outfit than N. W. Ayer, which was a very rigidly structured organization; which, at the time, I think, was good. But at Mathes, I would have called myself, if you asked me then, a supervisor, because I thought I was better than just the ordinary art director, because I could issue some orders to other people. From there I went to McCann . . .

Why did you leave Jim?

Very age-old reason—money! He did not honestly believe in paying large salaries to anybody.

If you remember, the business tends to be very much like professional baseball. The creative persons, particularly—and I can speak for them better than I can for any other departments—they were loyal to their profession, to their peers, and to the accounts they worked on, but not necessarily to the agency. And if somebody walked up and said, "How would you like to come over to X

Agency for so many dollars more?" and it looked like you weren't going to fail in the attempt, you usually did it.

This was pretty much a visual age, anyway, except that radio was beginning to be important.

I'd say the peak, and at the same time, almost the beginning of the downhill side of what one could develop in the graphic end. Print was enormous. Radio was beginning to be a strong selling force. But I think the art directors, in those days, along with the writers, saw the best years they ever saw. And in my case, because I really couldn't make up my mind, frankly, whether I wanted to be an illustrator or an art director, I was sort of doing both— moonlighting. I was illustrating for magazines, I had an agent on the side who was showing my work, getting me commissions . . .

Under an assumed name?

No, under my own. And nobody really objected to it—I did it at night, mind you, and to this day I have depended heavily upon my ability to have a thought or a notion and have it explode in my head and end up on paper in a visual form that other people can understand. A writer does the same thing with either a pencil or typewriter. But I had an advantage, I felt, over other art directors who, while they may have had ideas, were not as facile in projecting them in a way that the lay mind could see what you're talking about. So I had the bulge on the field at that time.

Okay, when you went over to McCann, toward the end of the '30s, it was for money. What were you working on, do you recall?

Yes. The first account I worked on was the Ford Motor Company. The Model A came out while I was still at Ayer, and I worked on it there. Then McCann picked up part of the Ford account, and I worked on it again. I also remember American Gas Company and American Mutual Insurance—

Mr. Friendly? That was your creation, I think?

Yes, the character, and I did the artwork, which was unusual— caused no end of trouble, as you might guess.

Because you got paid?

Then later on, when I ran the department, I would not allow anybody else to do it. I gave up that practice because it really did screw things up. But I did it and I enjoyed doing it.

How long were you at McCann before you ended up running the department?

It was during the first year of the war, the first year of our participation in the war—'41–'42.

It started off with an old friend of mine by the name of Ed Graham, remember? Well, Ed went into the Marine Corps as a correspondent, and he thought he was doing me a favor, so he put my name in too, and I went down to Church Street for the physical. And I sat there two days in my underwear, and eventually somebody examined me and I passed, and then the last question was "Where did you go to college?" and I said, "Well, I didn't go to college. I went to this art school." As soon as I said that, the noncommissioned officer, whoever he was, said "That's all. Put your pants on and get out," he said. And I did, and I tried two or three other people just to see why he stopped dead.

Anyhow, that was when I went from McCann to J. Walter Thompson. As I say, I was the supervisor, and I thought, "Gee, I'd like to be more important than this."

I had a discussion with my immediate superior, who was Leland Stanford Briggs, who was running the creative department at McCann at that time. Well, he was sympathetic; he didn't see how this could be accomplished in an art place. So I left, and Thompson gave me a job, and it was an excellent job, working on Lux. The gal in copy writing (I remember referring to her as the "Red Queen") was the dominant figure on the account and ran the Lux copywriting with an iron hand. But we got along very well, and so those were very happy experiences when I was there.

Walter O'Meara and James Webb Young were alternating—six months on and six months off—as creative heads of the office. And Walter turned out to be, for me, a very good thing. I enjoyed his company, and he saw to it that I worked on quite a few accounts that he was called in to do special things for. I think they were called "institutional advertising," which meant that you had large space, one big picture, an ideal thing for an art director.

I was a year, just exactly a year, at Thompson, and I woke up one morning and went to the office and discovered that there had been two promotions. I was a supervisor—and two other guys, who were supervisors, had been elevated to something called a Vice-President.

And I hadn't, so I went immediately to Stanley Resor (head of the agency) who was a nice old gentleman, and I presented my case and said I understood exactly how (I'd only been there a year) these other people certainly deserved it, but I felt that I couldn't stand this humiliation, and that I was going to have to resign. I don't think he was broken up, but he was sure as hell surprised. And I did; I resigned, and by nightfall I was back at McCann, and that time I did succeed in making Head Art Director.

Okay. Now, here you are, head of the art department at McCann Erickson, and you're a Vice-President?

No, that's another story. A year or two after that, my mother died. She was from Harrisburg, and that's where the funeral took place, in the bosom of all these other cousins and uncles and aunts, and I went there for the funeral. And it was while I was at the funeral, the phone rang, and it was H. K. McCann, who said he wanted me to become a Vice-President and a director.

He had me confused, but I accepted, as you might guess, willingly and with enthusiasm. Anyhow, I did become a vice-president and a director of the company. This must have been, let's see, toward the end of '47. But then, shortly thereafter, Marion Harper began to rise out of the slime of all of the rest of us, and he went up, as you know, like a rocket.

What happened to Harry? Did he retire?

No. H. K. remained in the saddle, and in my view he was a supporter of Harper, but perplexed by this new phenomenon, because Harper is a research man who came up with the technique of determining just how many people actually read an advertisement. And this became, as you may remember, the greatest selling tool of that particular period in the advertising industry. And frankly, all the creative people, and all of the account people, too, were pleased, and at the same time, confused; and the creative people added another note—they were a little unhappy with all this, because it began to add restrictions over which they had no control, really.

But Harper could sell advertising campaigns, not incorrectly—I don't mean to imply that it was a charlatan's move; it wasn't, it worked like a charm—but it helped the average businessman to see in advance what his money might possibly be doing for him when he spent it for advertising. Well, he thought so, and of course,

Harper thought so, too. Well, Harper soon became (with the exception of McCann himself) the head man, the head influence in the company—

I can't remember how young he was, but he was in his thirties. Well, when he finally became President, and McCann stayed on as Chairman, Marion walked into my office one day and said—as a matter of fact, he didn't ask me, he just told me that he thought it would be a good thing if I could serve as the creative head of the business. And it frightened me so badly—for several days I didn't come to the office—I didn't quite know how to do this. Because you know, in those days copywriters, although art directors would never admit it, copywriters were *really* the elite.

They thought they were, certainly.

Right. And I had visions of these people tossing me out of the 47th floor window. Anyhow, it ended up that I took the job, and it worked very well. I stayed that way as head of the creative department until—oh, I would say, the middle Fifties, when I became Chairman of HOAC.

HOAC?

An acronym, I believe, for Home Office Administrative Committee. This was an adventure of Harper's, trying to govern the home office of McCann-Erickson by a committee without having to make up his mind as to who was going to be the President. So I was Chairman. I figured he made that move because I had a lot of friends, I was easy to get along with, and I didn't appear to be any great danger to the marketing or business end of the business; they could put up with that.

Now let me ask you a question. I know that from just being a visualizer, you became a very good copywriter, you became a good concept man. Tell me about that development.

Well, I always wrote! I mean, from the beginning, when I first went to school, I messed around, I wrote and illustrated three children's books when Martha and I were first married, to supplement my income. They were not terribly successful, but I would make anywhere from five to eight thousand dollars on a book. Lippincott published them. I was no Charles Dickens, but I mean, I just put one sentence after another.

So I had always been familiar with the concept of writing, although I always had to do it longhand, which was a terrible time, and at one point (and this was after I was working at McCann), I'd started work for several years on what I fondly hoped was going to be the Great American Novel, and I think my hand just gave out at about 50,000 words, and so did my patience, and I sent the manuscript off to Anderson, who read it, and the publisher sent it back with another terse note saying it was difficult to write a historical novel with nothing but imagination. I was allowed to figure out just how bad I was.

But I did write, and so the copy department accepted me on the basis that "You are writing just concepts" because I seldom wrote anything more than an idea, and then hoped that somebody would put some meat on it.

Well, the concept is, to me, the guts of the business, and then you let the spear-carriers fill it in—the wordsmiths.

That's right.

Not that they're not important, but it's the idea that's important, and that's the concept. Now things are going along pretty well, and then all of a sudden Jack Tinker & Partners is formed.

Well, that's right. You see, when I was being the creative director, and then actually becoming the administrator of the home office of McCann-Erickson, I also took on the creative directorship. And that meant I did a lot of traveling those days, and—

Domestic and foreign offices?

Uh-huh. and I remember spending a lot of time in London, some in Paris; ostensibly I was trying to help straighten something out that was not straight. I did a lot of that and I didn't care much for it, and I didn't see where my role in the business could go anywhere except further and further into administrative work and further away from the ground where I felt safe. I knew what the hell I was doing in the other; in this one, I never could count over ten without taking my shoes off, and I really got very frightened when confronted with marketing problems and that sort of thing. I had no training other than instinct for that. So I had already worked out a deal with McCann where I was taking two months off every year.

And at that time I was very important in the Coca-Cola scene, and in those days we had the beginning of the Buick account and Standard Oil. They were big ones, and I did a lot of contact work as a creative liaison, that sort of thing. But that, too, made me nervous, and finally I said "I think I'll retire." And I talked myself into it, I talked Marion Harper into it, and he said, "Well, instead of giving up altogether, why don't you take your pick of people and start some kind of an organization where you could do what you want, come and go as you see fit, and work on problems that are bothering all of us from a creative standpoint?"

And I said "Fine," and figured this thing out, and wrote a paper on it, what it amounted to, and what it could accomplish. I have to admit he thought of it before I did. As a result, we formed Jack Tinker & Partners. The name was chosen carefully so that no one would believe that any one person was the head man. We had four, a representative of the creative department (other than myself), and a marketer and a research person. Four of us, all of whom had problems.

Don Calhoun was the writer, and he had the most fertile mind that I ever ran into in the advertising business. It certainly was not the most different one, but he had this immense ability to be given a picture of a product, and he could come up with a way of communicating to the buying public that which they should know. He really was uncanny with that.

Myron McDonald was the marketing director. And he, too, was a brilliant guy, and had been the account man on most of our big accounts and had been replaced on every occasion because of some appeal from his clients. They never doubted how bright he was, but they'd get so they couldn't stand him around. And Herta Herzog, who was a Viennese and had been trained as a concert violinist, and had polio when she was in her twenties, and then went back to the university and came out of it as a psychologist and research person. She was the fourth partner.

We opened our doors on the 47th floor of the Waldorf Towers without the Waldorf Towers knowing that we were a business. We were there one year. During that time the first piece of business that we had was the Bulova Watch Company Accutron Watch, although when we got it it was a piece of machinery that had been spun off from the Space Program. They knew they could turn it into a watch, or turn it into a power source for a watch.

And that was a fascinating time for us. We dealt with the top engineers and the top marketing men at Bulova, names I cannot remember, but Omar Bradley was, at the time, the Chairman of the Board. That was also interesting. And that was a big experience. We did the whole damn thing from start to finish. We designed the watch and the marketing concept, which at the outset was introduced by outfits like Abercrombie & Fitch.

Did you go to jewelers later?

That's right. Anyhow, that was the first thing, and just as that was going we introduced the Riviera, which was a Buick Division model which had been created by General Motors and put up for grabs really, to see which division would manufacture it. Pontiac wanted it very badly and Oldsmobile wanted it very badly, and on behalf of Buick we presented a campaign and a marketing plan. It was accepted; Buick Division got the car and we felt very proud of it. It had one flaw, as I look back on it, and it didn't take long to find it out. As a result of our advertising, it looked and sounded too expensive, and they had a problem. We classed it by its appearance and by the way the thing was handled, so that it stopped a lot of people in their tracks because they were afraid to ask, "How much is that car?" That had to be changed.

But then we were bounced out of the Waldorf Towers by the City of New York, who discovered, because we were bringing telephone cables from one room to another, what we were doing, and they said, "No way!" Then we moved to the Dorset Hotel. We started this whole thing in 1960, and in 1967 we had eight floors at the Dorset, and as most people remember, we had, among other accounts, Miles Laboratories, whose best-known product was Alka-Seltzer. We'd done some things for them which made them happy, and made us relatively famous. And we started what later became known as Ivory Tower boutiques, and it became a very successful thing, and we made a lot of money.

And we made one serious error—"we" meaning the four people. Mary Wells had come to work for us. I contacted Mary, who had worked at McCann in the copy department as a youngster, when I was the head of the creative department. I barely knew her at the time, but then she was at Doyle Dane and, as you know, did very well there. Ned Doyle took a real interest in her and invested money for her in Polaroid, I remember. She was doing very well.

We needed somebody, and I was having trouble with Don Calhoun, who couldn't stand any competition—personally, it upset him. Mary was coming to work for us, and she became, in a very short time, one of the principals—that made five of us, and finally Don quit, he got so teed off at Mary. And in 1967 Mary asked me if I had ever thought of quitting and starting our own agency. And she kept that up; she'd been talking about this for some time. We then got the Braniff account; we met Harding Lawrence on a visit to California for Continental, which was a McCann-Erickson client, and Mary and I went out there because the Los Angeles office was having a bit of trouble with Continental.

We went out and we met Harding, who at that time was the right-hand man of Robert Six, head of Continental. But when we got back, we discovered that Harding had taken a job with Braniff as the head man, and he called up, asked me if we would be interested. We went down to Dallas. He had taken the job, incidentally, because it was small enough that he felt he could make a big dent in the operating of this kind of airline, as against, for example, Pan Am which, incidentally, also offered him a leading role.

So we said, "Sure, we'll throw in." And we took the business, and you know the rest of it. We did all this stuff, and today there must be four or five people around town who'll say, "I said, let's paint every plane differently." I'm one of them, I said, "Let's do it," and Mary, I'm sure, will tell you she said it, and both Rich and Greene will, and the truth of the matter probably is, we all did it sitting around at night, as we did those days, together.

They were with you at that point?
They were with us at that time.

You had Wells, Rich and Greene right there with you?
Together, yes. And from the standpoint of the client, that was an enormous success. I don't think we ever made a great deal of money, but we sure made a lot of gold marks for ourselves.

At that time we never placed any ads.

That's why Mary wanted to start on her own, right? That does make the money.
We got to this point where, after Mary had talked about withdrawing, finally she got serious about it. "Why the hell are we turning over all this dough to Interpublic? Let's strike up a deal."

We got a lawyer, and we tried to work out a scheme whereby Interpublic would skim off a little more for us, and they considered it. At least Mary told me this. I never really knew whether it went before the board or whether Healy—at this time, Healy was pretty hard-nosed, and I think he would have said "No" right off the bat. But anyhow, they did say "No," and I went to Florida for a two- or three-weeks' vacation, and Mary called me and said she was quitting. She told me what she was going to do; she was going to take Harding's account and maybe even Miles Laboratories. Harper called me, and I came back, and we went through a series of meetings in which we would offer Mary everything that you could legitimately offer her, and then we'd plead and then we'd offer more, and finally she quit. And then I had a heart attack, and that took me out of the picture. Now, I remember when I awakened— let's say two weeks later, when my wheels were working—I said, "That's it." I'd always wondered how the hell I'd get out of this business. I really didn't know how to get out of the business.

The heart attack told you.

That's right, and I thought, "Man, what an excuse."

I did go back, actually, for a couple of months—because by that time, Jack Tinker & Partners began to collapse. I'm sure it wasn't just because I collapsed; maybe it was the combination of Mary and myself. We had some very able guys, but they, I'm sure, didn't have any feeling of security with the two leaders out.

They were shook up. And Mary took fifteen people, and all of them were good ones. So I went back and tried to help them through an interim period, and that's when Myron McDonald was made head of Jack Tinker & Partners. Then he overshot the field and tried to become president or chairman of the board of Interpublic or some other move, and Healy, I guess, grabbed him by the coat collar and threw him out, and he left. And that's when Healy came to power there.

Well, let me ask you: young people are always saying, "I have certain talents; I'm a writer, I'm an artist, I'm a researcher"—you know. In your judgment, does advertising education help you get into the business or doesn't it? What develops a writer? Can they be developed in college?

Based only on my personal experience, I would say that the greatest number of proficient advertising writers were the result of

journalism courses or some kindred studies such as English literature or creative writing. Now, that doesn't mean there weren't,
and still aren't, great advertising creative writers who had no formal background in that sort of thing.

Come right off the street. Like Rich and Greene.

You remember, I ran a full page ad—it may have been in *Advertising Age*—in which we offered a salary of $20,000 for an art direc-
tor and for a writer, *no experience necessary*. All they had to do was
come in, show up and talk to me. So we hired two people, and
Hugh Greene was one of them. And he had a kind of natural
instinct for it, really.

The other one was Lois Quarry. And she's still in the business
someplace and doing very well, so I've heard. But in answer to
your question, I think that the majority of writers had training in
the mechanics of their trade.

August 8, 1981

EDWARD M. THIELE

Edward M. Thiele was born in Roswell, N.M., in 1914. He grew up in Chicago and attended public schools there. He graduated from Denison University, Granville, Ohio, in 1935. He became one of Denison's trustees, and in 1962 received the Denison Alumni Citation as an outstanding alumnus.

He worked for the Shell Oil Company as a Marketing Supervisor, for Derby Foods as Advertising Director, where he contributed to the growth of Peter Pan Peanut Butter, and for Swift & Company, where he was responsible for the advertising for a number of products. He entered the agency business with H. W. Kastor and Sons agency as an Account Executive.

Mr. Thiele joined the Leo Burnett Co. as an Account Executive in 1951. He was made a Vice-President and Account Supervisor in 1954 and a Director of the agency in 1958. During these years, he supervised a number of major accounts, including Campbell Soups, Procter & Gamble and Philip Morris.

Mr. Thiele served as President of Leo Burnett Co., Chicago, from 1961 through 1970, moving up from Executive Vice-President in charge of client service, a post he had occupied since 1958. He retired as Vice-Chairman of the Board of Burnett in 1974.

He served one year as President of the National Advertising Review Council (the advisory committee to the National Advertising Review Board). He was a member of the National Business Council for Consumer Affairs, a Presidental group of prominent businessmen; and a member of the Sub-Council on Warrantees and Guarantees. He was Chairman of the American Association of Advertising Agencies in 1971–72. He was Vice-President and director of the Chicago Association of Commerce and Industry; a member of the Information Advisory Committee of the Department of Commerce; a Director of National Outdoor Advertising Bureau, the Consumer Research Institute, the American Red Cross, and Lake Forest Hospital.

Edward M. Thiele died November 17, 1982, at the age of 68.

EDWARD M. THIELE

Interview

My father was a rancher, and we lived in Roswell, N.M., for two or three years, and then we moved to Chicago where I lived most of my life. I went to Morgan Park High School, and to Denison University in Granville, O.

I played football in high school and in college. I played with Woody Hayes, as a matter of fact. He was at Denison while I was. I never was a star. I also was interested in dramatics in college and high school; and I studied art part of the time, and I've since kept up with the art, and now I take lessons, and enjoy it very much.

I just got through with a portrait of Petty, my wife, and one also of my daughter, Pleasant, who's the oldest daughter; and I painted them from photographs, and I find it very, very difficult to get the eyes, particularly. But they liked them, and they do look pretty much like them.

I majored in English and dramatics, with a minor in art, but that was very minor; but I enjoyed dramatics very much.

OK, you were pursuing English and dramatics, and what was the hope? To go into the theater?

No, not really, although I had an opportunity to go to Hollywood when I graduated. In the senior play, which I had a leading part in, I had an offer from a talent scout who happened to be in the audience from Universal Pictures. And I was tempted to go, but my Dad, who was there for my commencement, said, "Not on your life, son!"

So I came back to Chicago, and got a job—that was kind of tough in 1937, with the Depression on. I got a job with the *Chicago Evening American* in the merchandising department, and that consisted primarily of putting signs up in grocery and drug stores and other retail outlets.

How much did they pay?

$14 a week.

Aha, a college graduate, at $14 a week?

Right. And that lasted for about a year and half, and then I went to work for H. W. Kastor & Sons, an advertising agency in Chicago, now defunct, but a pretty good agency in those days. They had Welch's grape juice, Zenith radio and Tums ("Tums for the tummy") and some Procter & Gamble business. We had introduced Drene shampoo and Teel dentifrice, and had American Family soap, which was a very well-entrenched brand in Chicago.

I started in the research department, and soon became an assistant account executive; our supervisor at that time was Bill Karnes, who later became president of Bates. Kastor was a good place to start, because it was small; with very, very bright people.

There were originally seven Kastor brothers. They started in St. Louis, and they were a great copy agency, primarily in mail order.

Were you married by then?

I got married in 1940, to Pleasant Williams (her nickname is Petty), who also worked at Kastor; she was secretary to head of the radio department. We got married in June of 1940, and I was broke. I had been fired from Kastor the week after our wedding announcements went out.

What a nice present.

Yes. But Kastor lost Tums and Welch's grape juice all in the same week. They had to reduce their staff, and I was one of the ones to go.

I cast around for a job for a while, and Pete Peterson, who was Petty's boss at Kastor, had gone to work for the Republican National Committee—that's when Willkie was running for President. Pete hired me to work for the Republican Committee for National Recovery. That was really a blind for a way to spend money for the Republicans. The Hatch Act had come in. They would only allow a certain amount—$6 million—to be spent on the Presidential election, and this was a way to pour more money in.

It was a semi-church organization, and the plan was to put out this propaganda in churches, YMCAs, anything that had any kind of a religious connection. My territory happened to be the State of Michigan. I bought myself a car for $120, went over to Michigan and started to tour the state. I filled the rumble seat and the rear trunk with literature, and started out.

Petty and I would go from town to town and stay in tourist homes; they didn't have motels much in those days, so we'd get a tourist room for $1 a night. But we had a good time; it was a good break from office work.

I really wondered whether I was doing any good in this job, so I went to see Mr. Reinhold, a Lutheran preacher who headed up this committee. I said, "I just wonder if I'm taking your money under false pretenses? I can't feel anything happening out there." He opened his desk drawer and said, "Don't worry, young man; here's an indication of whether you're doing any good." He pulled out a check for $2,000 from Harry Olds, the head of Oldsmobile, and said, "This came in last week after you'd been to Lansing." So I took a new interest in the job, and realized something was happening.

That lasted until the election, and I like to say that Senator Vandenberg and I carried Michigan for Willkie. One of the few he won. But it was quite an experience, and worthwhile. Fortunately, I made enough money at it to get us back on our feet, and we bought a little furniture. Then I started to hunt for a job, again, and I really scoured Chicago.

This is now the late fall of '40?

Yes. And I finally took a job that I really didn't want very much, with Shell Oil. Even though the war was in the offing then, gasoline had not yet been rationed, and Shell was still an aggressive company. I was what they called an area service supervisor, a glorified term for a salesman. I called on gas stations, had to show them how to operate and made sure they carried a full line of Shell products. I got fired from the job, because I lost my temper with my boss and threw a telephone book at him.

Why did you do that?

My previous boss allowed me a $25-a-month pad on my expense account because things were tough, and I just couldn't make ends meet; we had a baby by that time. I think I was making $160 a month, and I just couldn't make it. So they said, "Well, put $25 on your expense account." And this new guy came in. He was a new broom, and he was sweeping clean. He said, "What's this $25 on your expense account, Ed? That's $25 more than anybody else turns in." And I told him that Mr. Peterson had allowed me to put that on. He said, "Well, from now on, it's off." I happened to have a telephone book in my hand, and I threw it at him.

Then I went to work for Continental Can in the stockyard plants, which primarily provided cans for Armour & Co. And it was a terrible neighborhood, with the stockyard smell all around, and no air conditioning, and hotter than Hades in the office. It was a miserable place, so I left after about six months and went to Derby Foods, a division of Swift, which made Peter Pan peanut butter. Well, we were very successful at Derby, because we had Needham, Harper & Steers—Needham, Louis & Brorby then— and they recommended we go on daytime radio five days a week. It proved a real bonanza for Derby. They developed a kids' show by the name of "Sky King," which later turned out to be one of the big ones like Jack Armstrong and some of the other ones. We were very big on premiums; we once sold 900,000 treasure rings, and rings were the hottest thing you could put on the air. These rings were very ingenious—they glowed in the dark, had secret compartments and signaling mirrors. A boxtop and 10 cents was the going rate. And in a year, we had increased sales nationally by 50%. It really was a bonanza for Derby Foods.

A boxtop with peanut butter? You must have had an "outsert" sticker to tear off.

Exactly right. I outgrew that job, though. I needed more challenge, so I went to Swift and handled ice cream, ham, bacon, cold meats and hard dog food. I worked with J. Walter Thompson and McCann-Erickson and had good experiences with them. I guess I did all right, because I ended up with raises every year.

I spent about four years with Derby and Swift. But by now I had three kids, and I still wasn't making enough money to satisfy Petty or me. And I started to moonlight a little bit: I invented—it was hardly an invention—a cake decorating kit. I went to a food chemist and got him to prepare a cake decorating outfit, which consisted of a tube with sugar frosting in it, so you could write "Happy Birthday," or whatever, on a birthday cake without getting a pastry tube all messed up.

I didn't have the money to get a patent. But we put together a kit, consisting of paper doilies and a small package of powdered sugar. The idea was that you'd get a plain cake, without any sugar frosting on it, and you'd put the paper doilies on it, and then you'd sprinkle the sugar on it, and carefully lift the doily, and you'd leave the pattern on the cake with sugar. And a tube of the name-writing frosting went into a box and sold for a dollar.

Well, it never materialized, because I contacted *American Weekly*, and I was going to buy a small piece of space on their food page. Their rep called me and said, "Ed, you know that cake decorating idea you had? There's a guy named David Noyes who would like to talk to you. He's a very brilliant man, formerly executive vp of Lord & Thomas." David Noyes was a consultant to a little outfit called Reddi-Wip. [Reddi-Wip was whipped cream in a can.]

I went down to St. Louis, and Noyes introduced me to Mark Lipsky, who was chairman of the board of Reddi-Wip. I talked to Mark, but David Noyes had already greased the skids, and I really had the job as general manager when I walked in, I learned later.

Mark finally said, "What would it take for you to go to work for me?" I said, "Well, I ought to get $25,000." He said, "Well, that sounds fair enough; you ought to be worth $25,000 to us. I'll tell you, though, we'd like to give you a little incentive. I'll put a little bonus in there that will give you 5% of the profits before taxes." Little did he know that the company would make $6 million or $7 million that first year. And they owed me, according to that contract, some $300,000. That's a good deal more than I'd bargained for; I had no business making that kind of money. So they sent their lawyers up to Chicago, where my office was, and we settled—I was building a house at that time—and I think I settled for a $75,000 bonus, which was still pretty good.

Just built you a house—not bad!

Ruthrauff & Ryan, Chicago, was the Reddi-Wip agency. They had the business when I came there, and I didn't want to change. They did a good job. We put Arthur Godfrey on radio, and we advertised in *Life* magazine, and had a budget of, oh, $800,000 or $900,000.

That job lasted a long time, four or five years, and it was a marvelous experience. The Reddi-Wip Co. was a vital, stimulating place. Mark Lipsky was a salesman *ne plus ultra*, the best salesman I ever saw in my life. I was there for about four years, and decided I should leave: I wanted to go into the agency business. So I called Fairfax Cone, whom I knew slightly; Maurice Needham, whom I knew quite well and Leo Burnett—theirs were the agencies I had

decided I wanted to work at. And I got a date with Fairfax Cone—
he put it off for a week; and Maurice Needham agreed to see me.
I talked to Maurice and got a lot of good advice but no job offer.

Then I had a date with Leo Burnett; I called him cold, and said,
"Mr. Burnett, my name is Ed Thiele; you don't know me, but I'm
with the Reddi-Wip Co., and I think I've got something maybe
you could use." He said, "Come on up."

I went at noon the next day and he was not back from lunch
yet. I waited for about 20 minutes and he came in and fell all over
himself apologizing for being late. We went in his office and I gave
him my background and finally he said, "I think we can use you."
Sure enough I got a job, and I was thrilled. It wasn't quite as much
money as Reddi-Wip—in fact, it was considerably less. But I didn't
have some of the problems I had at Reddi-Wip. And I was hired
just before the Kellogg account came into Burnett.

That was in 1951. I think I was hired primarily to work on
Kellogg. But as it happened, the Kellogg account was delayed for a
month or two, and here I was, just sitting around when we got the
Charles Pfizer business, a pharmaceutical company in Brooklyn.
We got the agricultural end of that business. I didn't know anything about agriculture or animal husbandry or anything else,
much less pharmaceuticals. But Leo came in one day and said,
"Big boy, do you know anything about pigs?" I said, "Not a damn
thing, Leo." He had a textbook—"The Care and Raising and
Feeding of Swine"—that he threw on my desk, and he said, "Start
learning. You're going to go to work for Charles Pfizer." So I read
the book and was fascinated because that really is quite an industry. You know all about that, Bart. You were raised in Rockford.

I worked for Swift on the killing floor.

Pfizer had some terramycin residue, from the big vats they
cooked pork in, just sitting in the rain out in their yard, outside
the cooking area. This was going to waste, and they found that it
still had quite a little medicinal activity in it, but you couldn't use
it for human medicine. So, they conceived the idea of feeding it to
cattle and hogs. It was almost magic in the way it made hogs gain
weight, and one of their scientists knew that a sow came into heat
every six months. And if you could wean the baby pig sooner she
would come into heat sooner, and you could perhaps get three
batches of pigs a year instead of two; that would be a 50% increase

90

in the pork business. So they experimented and finally invented a product by the name of Terralac, which was terramycin and powdered milk, with some vitamins. This was to be given to baby pigs one day after birth. John McKeen, the chairman of Pfizer, got so worked up that he got a corner on powdered milk—he literally cornered the powdered milk market in the U.S.

We introduced Terralac in Illinois, Iowa and southern Wisconsin, the major hog areas, and it took off like gangbusters. But what they didn't figure was that the average farmer knows little or nothing about sanitation.

Baby pigs were put in chicken coops and manure bins and died as a result, having no mother to keep them warm.

It occurred to me we should tell Pfizer immediately—the sooner they stopped it the better. I called Leo and I said this isn't going to work, and he was bitterly disappointed because he was as excited as John McKeen was. He said, "Well, I guess you better call John McKeen, Ed." So I called McKeen, and he said, "I hate to hear that. What shall we do?"

I said, "If I were you, I would discontinue marketing; hopefully we'll figure out a way to instruct the farmer better."

He agreed, and he stopped it right then and there. Then, he called Leo and said, "You know, this guy Thiele has got a lot of guts and nerve. I congratulate you for having that man on our account." And you know, Leo never forgot that.

After I'd been on the Pfizer account for about a year I got put on the Tea Council account as well. The Tea Council consisted of the countries that raised the tea as well as the countries that packaged the tea and we met at 500 Fifth Avenue in New York in a big conference room, once a month. These people would come from all over the world—India, China, Japan, Indonesia—and it was quite a United Nations meeting when we all got together and it was a very interesting and instructive account.

That's Leo Burnett's first taste of television. You may remember "Take Tea and See."

Well, we tested that out in Buffalo, with really blanket television. We bought spots until they came out of our ears in Buffalo: "Take Tea and See." We wanted to see what the ceiling on tea was because coffee was by all odds a big seller and tea was limping along rather badly.

Well, this test market was fantastic. I had gone down there with a guy by the name of Don Tennant who was a television writer [now the head of his own Chicago agency] and we called on grocery stores and you didn't have to be a genius or a research expert to feel the impact of that advertising. Tea sales went up something like 100% in a month and it was very successful and we expanded that nationally and it was a success nationally although we didn't use it in the weight that we had in Buffalo.

One of my next accounts was Campbell Soup. We were chosen to introduce frozen soups for Campbell. They were an immense success at the outset, but eventually turned out to be too expensive. They couldn't compete with Campbell's regular canned soup.

I'd been on Campbell for a little while, and at about that time we got some Philip Morris business—Marlboro cigarets which we tested in Texas. And that famous ad with that cowboy and the tattoo.

Featuring Andy Armstrong [a famed Burnett creative director].

Yeah—right. The ad was published in Dallas, as a full-page newspaper ad. And that was another raring, tearing success—that brand really took off. Marlboro had been a very feminine cigaret. It had pearl tips, as I remember, and came in a tin can and cost about three times as much as regular cigarets. We redesigned the package and made the ads, and Philip Morris really was astounded at the way that brand took off.

I don't think the cigaret industry ever experienced anything like it before.

Suddenly we found ourselves with a successful brand on our hands from a major company, and that took a good deal of my time. And then I was in New York about three days a week; then we got the Nestlé business. That gave us Nestlé, Tea Council, Charles Pfizer, Philip Morris and Campbell Soup on the Eastern seaboard, which is more business than we ever had. So, I was made the Vice-President in charge of the Eastern operations, or some such title.

I spent two or three days every week in New York. About that time, '55 or '56, I started to work on Procter & Gamble. It was a real challenge, although I had worked on it earlier at Kastor; but things had changed a good deal since the '40s. At Burnett we had

Camay soap and a shampoo product, which was only an experimental thing, and a hair curler, a permanent wave. So then I became vp in charge of Procter.

Did you still have all that stuff in the East, too?

Yes.

Gradually taking over the agency!

I had a good part of it. It was about $55 million in the East, and Procter & Gamble, of course, was important billing. And P&G was really an experience for me. I will never, never cease to be amazed at how wonderful that company is. And to me the biggest lesson I learned from Procter is their practice down there in Cincinnati of heading every letter or memorandum or opening every meeting with "The purpose of this letter, memorandum, meeting is . . ."

You knew why you were there and they never forgot that. It was a wonderful lesson and it's surprising how easy it is to write a letter when you decide in advance what you want to say, what the purpose of the letter is; the letter writes itself.

Well, we had a lot of fun with those meetings with Procter and the budget meetings were particularly exciting. Once a year you got together with all the brass, as you well know.

I went through them for 30 years, Ed.

I'm sure. The brand men are all keyed up, they rehearse the agency and make sure that everybody has the same answer to the same question in a hotel room two or three days before the meeting and when the brass starts to stick pins in you you really are prepared. And that was a good lesson too.

Well, along about that time I was made a Vice-President of the agency. And in about '56 I was made Executive Vice-President and . . .

Were you in charge of client service or just a lot of brands?

I was in charge of client service for about half the brands.

And about that time we started to look into Europe; it fell to my lot to go over and talk to agencies in Europe in terms of expanding over there and internationally, so that took a good deal of time.

In 1961 I became President. Dick Heath, who had been President for some years, retired and Leo talked about retiring as he did for years. But he didn't retire, God bless him. My one argument in all my life with Leo was that he didn't know when to retire; I think it was too bad because he stayed about five years too long. He slowed down considerably, and he got a little bit doddery. But he was an inspiration still to the creatives, which was his main purpose in being there anyway.

And people revered Leo; he was a wonderful, wonderful man to work for. Generous to a fault, he always insisted that the clerical people receive the utmost consideration in salary and profit sharing.

In fact for many years executives did not share in the profit sharing. The company was allowed to put 15% of their salary in and the executives did not share in that. The highly paid people just did not share to the same degree, I think they shared up to $15,000 and beyond that anything they made went into the profit sharing account and those that weren't making that important money shared in those profits.

You finalized the deal with the London Press Exchange, I believe.

Yeah, we'd looked at several agencies in England, and the London Press Exchange seemed to offer the biggest opportunity because it was one of the larger agencies in London, and they also had quite a little international network. They had 31 offices in 29 countries. As it turned out, most of the offices weren't much good. But we didn't know that then, and we didn't have time to look at all 31 offices. So we made the deal, and it's been good for Burnett. It prospers. We've had trouble in a few places. We had trouble in Paris and in Germany, but through no fault of anything Burnett did, or the London Press Exchange. It was just the exigencies of the agency business.

The important thing is that you got involved in all this and became international. It changed your thinking.

Oh, yeah, we thought that business was going to fall our way the minute we got that network of agencies, but it took a long time to really develop. And now we've got Marlboro in most of the countries and Kellogg in many of the countries and Nestle in many of the countries, so it's finally come into its own.

What about the spirit of Burnett, the kind of people that you wanted to attract and a little about Leo's philosophy?

Leo was the heartbeat of that agency, and he was so highly

respected by everybody there that the morale was absolutely tops all the time. The only animosity that I every felt in that agency was between the creatives and the account people—occasionally the creatives would get mad at the account people. That happens to some extent in every agency.

It's universal.

Yes. But the creatives wanted to present the advertising. They wanted to dictate what was said in the advertising, and they treated the client like he didn't have any business messing around with it. And unfortunately Leo felt the same way. He was a tough, tough guy when it came to selling an ad that he thought was right.

If he and the creatives thought the ad was right, and if he had to go down and sell it himself, he would. It made it tough many times, particularly at Procter—boy! And Procter had, you know, that one-paragraph copy platform—"The purpose of advertising is—" He said, "I can't tell them what the purpose is." Damn it, it's a good ad, that's all they have to know."

The really remarkable thing about the company, I think, is its Chicago location and its lack of branch offices. Leo literally saw every ad that went out of there. Towards the end he got so that he couldn't quite see them all because we got so big. But he saw every major ad that went out, and insisted on it, as a matter of fact. Leo worked until 6 o'clock, took a briefcase load of stuff home, and died at the dinner table.

I remember his funeral in Chicago. Mayor Daley came, and I was a pallbearer, along with other directors. It was a sad day. He was buried in a cemetery on the North Side, and the funeral cortege was immense. It must have been, oh 500 cars, maybe, blocks and blocks, and people came from all over the country—clients.

As I understand it, Ed, he did a lot of sharing and putting together for people, as you said earlier and he made a lot of people rich. Not that you didn't work yourselves, I don't mean that—but he shared, didn't he?

He shared the wealth. The stock was widely held in the agency and the agency has always been profitable. In fact, the last couple of years I was there I deferred a good deal of my salary and lived on my dividend mainly, and that reduced the taxes and helped me in my retirement.

The fact that we didn't have any branch offices was one reason the company was profitable. Most branch offices are just a drain, they're just pure expense and you can't call them profit centers even though the client who may be nearby makes a profit.

Did you every talk about going public?

Yeah, but Leo was always against it. He felt he would lose control of the agency, which I don't think necessarily would be true. He was always negative, but he would not have stopped it if the directors decided to do it. But he decided not to, and it was a good decision.

Do you have any thoughts about advertising education and bringing kids into the business?

I think the best training for the agency business is selling, whatever area you're in. If you are a creative man, you have to sell your copy. If you're an account man, you have to sell your ideas. If you're a new business man, you have to solicit business and be a good salesman.

I also believe in a liberal arts education; that's what I think is the most important thing. Not only does it broaden you and give you a little introduction to history, art, English and the languages, but it makes for a better life, in my opinion. It broadens a person's perspective; I really believe that's the right background for a man in the advertising business.

Do you think MBAs are important?

It's pretty hard to get a job without one, they tell me, I haven't had much experience with that. But certainly Procter & Gamble insists on their MBAs.

It's going the other way now, Ed.

Is it really? Well that's wild . . .

What I'm really concerned about is advertising overwhelming itself. That isn't very clear but there is so much advertising—the television is so busy, the radio, all the media—it's so much with us that I think it is starting to rub off a little bit or just bounce off.

Not being as effective.

Just too much competition. And with the problems that are arising in the network world now you wonder what is going to happen when all these cable deals get going and it just increases the competition.

Well I'll tell you, no matter where you turn you're going to be listening to commercial messages.

Right. I am amazed at the price they are paying for television shows nowadays. It's unbelievable. I've been out of the business now for just about 10 years but the prices they pay are just unfathomable to me.

OK Ed, let's talk about the Creative Review Committee at Burnett.

Well, in the early days Leo was head of the Creative Review Committee and then for many years Draper Daniels was its head. The committee consisted of the top account people and the top creative people and it just wasted so much time. The meetings were too big and just almost unbelievable. Sometimes we'd sit there and look at storyboards and ads for three hours on one account and Leo would never be satisfied—always something more, something more; change this, that man was a real driver, but what a lovely guy. He could get material out of a creative man better than anybody I ever can conceive of. And they'd just break their backs to please him.

Well, the end result seemed to work and that was the basis of making the Burnett agency work. And I think it meant better advertising for the client primarily, and I think it was wonderful for that reason. But, boy it was hard work.

There were a lot of people sitting around that table?

Oh, often 10 or 15 people in the room and a lot of time wasted. I remember when I became a vice-president, Dick Heath was sitting in the meeting and I had hit him the week before for a raise. Dick always cleared everything with Leo, so he wrote him a little note during a lull in the meeting, and he evidently said to Leo we're considering making Ed Thiele a Vice-President and a substantial raise in salary, and what do you think?

Leo wrote back a note, I've still got it, I'll show it to you sometime. He said, "Ed Thiele is one of the most creative account people we've ever had in this place and I'm all for it, he deserves the vp," signed Leo. Well, that's one of my prized possessions.

April 6, 1982

DAVID OGILVY

David Ogilvy is the founder, a Director and formerly Creative Head of Ogilvy & Mather International, the fourth largest advertising agency in the world.

He was educated on scholarships in his native Scotland and at Oxford University, where he majored in modern history. Leaving Oxford at the bottom of the depression, he became a chef at the Hotel Majestic in Paris.

In 1948, he founded Ogilvy & Mather in New York. Today, Ogilvy & Mather has billings of over 2 billion and serves more than 1500 clients in 33 countries.

Time Magazine has called him "the most sought after wizard in the advertising business" and *Newsweek* referred to him as "one of the innovative giants of U.S. advertising."

Ogilvy's book *Confessions of an Advertising Man* has sold more than 600,000 copies in eleven languages. His book *Blood, Brains & Beer* is autobiographical. *Ogilvy on Advertising*, published in 1983, outlines the fundamentals of advertising and includes numerous examples of their execution.

He has been a Director of the New York Philharmonic Symphony, Chairman of the United Negro College Fund, a Trustee of Colby College and a Governor of the American Association of Advertising Agencies.

He is a Trustee of the World Wildlife Fund, a Commander of the British Empire, and the first foreign member of the Advertising Hall of Fame. Adelphi University awarded him a Doctor of Letters in 1977. He lives now in France and is a consultant to the agency.

DAVID OGILVY

Interview

I was born in 1911. My father was Scottish. My mother was Irish. When I was three, my father lost all his money, and from then on we were a very poor family. My father's total income was less than $1,000 a year, which was difficult with five children to educate.

I got a history scholarship to Oxford, but I got some sort of block, didn't do any work, couldn't pass any exams, and got thrown out, which was very traumatic. I sort of ran away from the cultured, civilized life, and tried to change class and become a workman. I went to Paris and got a job as a chef in the great kitchen at the Hotel Majestic. That was a good antidote, because I *had* to work there—bloody hard work. There were no trade unions; I worked a 63-hour week, standing up, hot as hell.

Then I discovered that the only people who make any money in the world of cooking are the head chefs, and you can't hope to get one of those jobs until you're at least 35. I was 22, and I couldn't face 13 years of that heat and that poverty. So I took a job selling kitchen stoves, back in Scotland. I did that for a few years, and I got good at it—door-to-door selling of expensive kitchen stoves. One day, the company said to me, "You're a very good salesman, you've got the best sales record. Will you write a brochure for our other salesmen on how to sell our stoves?" So I wrote it, and it got me a job in an agency in London, which is now our London office. I did that for a bit.

Was that Benson & Mather?

It was Mather & Crowther. My older brother was there; he was seven years older than me. He helped me get that job.

I was doing very well in that agency, but it began to eat me. Every time I got promoted, I thought people would say, "Ah, yes, but that's his elder brother's influence." I wanted to prove I could

101

do it on my own. I'd become terribly interested in advertising, and I read every book that had been written on the subject until then. I became obsessively interested in advertising, and I have been all my life. It's really my only thing.

So I thought, "Well, the place for advertising is the United States." In those days, American advertising was about 30 years ahead of any other country. It isn't now, but it was in those days. I thought "I want to go where it's done best." So I came to the United States. I had to get a job in a hurry. George Gallup hired me to go to Princeton to do research for the motion picture industry, and that was the best thing that ever happened to me. I learned an awful lot from Gallup. I learned the research business. And at that time, he was Research Director of Young & Rubicam, and he was doing factor analysis, which has been a great interest to me ever since. Gallup has had a huge influence on me. He only paid me forty bucks a week. There was I, going to Hollywood all the time, and dealing with big shots like David Selznick and Sam Goldwyn. I was *dealing* with them; I had meetings with them, alone! I was on the telephone to them all the time. For that, Gallup was paying me 40 bucks a week!

Then the war came, and I went into the British Secret Service —which sounds much more romantic than it was. I don't think I was very good at it.

OSS had just come into existence, and it was difficult for the United States, because they'd had no foreign intelligence service, and they had to get one in a hurry. So we helped them. We'd got a lot of know-how that they didn't have. We helped Donovan and his people learn the trade, which they did amazingly fast. At one point, I was giving OSS about 80 reports a day from my sources.

After the war, I didn't know what the hell to do, like so many people. I bought a farm in Lancaster County, Pennsylvania, among the Amish. I've always been hipped on the Amish. I did that for two or three years. But I was a lousy farmer.

You were married then?

I was married, and had a son. I came to New York, and started an agency.

Now, I'll tell you why I started an agency. In those days, I thought Young & Rubicam was much the best agency. It was the only agency I wanted to work for. I admired Raymond Rubicam very much. But I thought they'd never hire me. I said to myself, "I can't get a job there, so the only thing to do is start my own agency." Years later Raymond Rubicam said to me, "David, I can't understand how we missed you, because we knew you. How did we miss you?"

I started the agency, and from the first day, Rubicam was the great influence on me. He took a fatherly interest in Ogilvy & Mather. I used to see a lot of him. Rubicam always said exactly what was on his mind. One day, he'd be so blazingly rude about some campaign of ours he'd seen, and tell me how lousy it was, and I just wished the earth would open and swallow me up. A month later, he'd talk about some campaign of ours that he liked. It was so wonderful, his praise. He was a great influence on me, his whole attitude to the agency business. Today, Ogilvy & Mather is the third or fourth biggest agency in the world. Out of the four top agencies in the world today, two of them are the lengthened shadow of Raymond Rubicam. Such has his influence been on me. I sometimes think that Ogilvy & Mather is more "Rubicamish" than Young & Rubicam.

Well then, Ogilvy & Mather got started. I was the Research Director. It's the only thing I knew anything about in those days.

You had a partner.

I had a partner, Andy Hewitt.

I didn't have any money—only $6,000, and it wasn't enough to start an agency. So I borrowed the money from two London agencies, $100,000.

And they made a condition: "You are an Englishman, so you can't run an agency in the United States. Nobody would take you seriously. We'll loan you this money on condition that you hire an American to be your boss." I should have said, "Fuck you," but I didn't.

I didn't know many Americans; I didn't have much to offer my boss; I'd got no money, I'd got no billing. How could I go out and hire an American hot-shot? But I did happen to know Andy Hewitt. So I hired Andy to be my boss.

Alas, we got on very badly indeed. We fought the whole time. I was always critical of everything he did, and he knew it. He was always having migraine headaches, because I was so foul to him. It was dreadful. So one day, I resigned. But it was Andy who left the agency. It was touch and go whether we would survive. I didn't know if the whole thing was going to go up in smoke. But we survived. We were what would nowadays be called a "creative boutique." Those words hadn't been invented in those days. We got a reputation for being a hot creative shop.

One day, a party came from Procter to scout us. Four or five men—I forget who they were. They came in my office, and I'd got some of my fancy ads from *The New Yorker* on the bulletin board in my office—you know, things like Hathaway Shirts and Schweppes and that sort of thing. I thought, if the Procter people see this, they'll never hire us. They'll just think we're fancy. So finally, I said, "For Christ's sake, stop looking at those ads!" And one of them said to me, "You've solved those problems well, and we think you'd be able to solve different problems well." But the next week we got Lever Brothers. First come, first served. Lever came first.

Lever Brothers was a terrible account in those days. It's very good now, but it was very bad then, just after they'd fired that architect—Charlie Luckman. We did some good work for two or three of their products.

Anyway, we'd got this creative reputation—

Incidentally, I want to remind you that you did come in to see me at that time, when you had gotten Lever. Do you recall that?

I'm glad that you recall it. I was too shy to remind you of the fact that I offered you a partnership in Ogilvy & Mather. I left your house about 10 one night—I think it was a summer evening —and you said you'd let me know on a Thursday. On Thursday you called up and said, "Uh-uh, I can't do it, because I've told them here at Compton what's going on, and I've been told that I'm to be the next head of Compton."

That's right.

Then, one day, we got the Shell account. That was the decisive thing in the history of our agency. It really put us in the big time. It was $13 million, which was an awful big account in those days, twenty years ago. Some people wondered whether we could administer anything so big and complex. But we did. We had a wonderful period of new business. For seven years we got every account we competed for. We never missed once. But the trick on that was that we never competed for an account unless I knew we could get it. I couldn't stand failing a new business contest, especially when it was released to the papers that you were one of the runners-up. We had a very hot period; we were as fashionable as hell.

What do you think the magic was, David? Was it your creative ability?

Yes, it was. We'd got five or six famous campaigns. I was also a good salesman. I got a reputation in the agency business for being a creative hot-shot. I was a moderately good creative man, and did some good campaigns, but I was a lousy creative director. What I did best was new business. The day that agency opened, I made a list of the six accounts I most wanted to get—it was a silly, childish thing to do but I did it—General Foods, Bristol-Myers, Campbell Soup, Shell, and Lever Brothers, and one other—I got them all, finally. It took a long time. It took eleven years to get Shell.

After that we changed from being a creative boutique, and got to be a proper agency. But all those years of fantastic success, I lived in mortal terror. I was always terrified of losing clients. I ought to have had a ball, but I was miserable with fear all the time.

However, you were very wise, David. In addition to your tremendous creative ability, and your unsurpassed ability to get new business, you built the agency into, also, a marketing organization. Now, I knew you were looking around for someone, and I called you and urged you to see a fellow named Esty Stowell whom I knew very well. I don't know if you remember that.

I do indeed.

And I know you hired him.

Had you known him at Benton & Bowles?

Oh, yes, very well, and admired him tremendously. You see, he came after his Benton & Bowles exit, which was a horrible thing. He should have been made the head of that agency; he wasn't. He came to see me after he'd taken a year or so off, and was looking, but I honestly didn't have the kind of position that he would fit. He should have had my job, and I should have left, really. In any case, I called you and told you that I hoped that you would be willing to see him, and you did.

I had a hell of a time persuading Esty to come out of the woods and go to work again in advertising. He did great things for us. I said to him, the day he arrived to work, I said, "Listen, Esty; we've got a good creative department, and I'll run that, and you take everything else. I don't know anything about marketing at all. I don't know anything about media. And I'm a hopeless manager. I'll do the creative thing; you do everything else." So for a few years he did everything else. He made us respectable. He is a very admirable man—honest, painfully honest. Much more honest than me.

For example, we had Standard Oil-New Jersey. We had a chance to get Shell. Esty almost died when he heard that I was going to try for Shell, when we'd already got an oil company. I said, "The fact that one is $13 million and the other is $2 million does not make any difference to you." One day we had a chance to get Lipton Tea, but we had Tetley. He wouldn't let me touch Lipton. God, Lipton was something like $8 million, and Tetley was $1 million. Esty is the most honest, decent, moral man I know. He made us respectable, and he got some good people in here.

Today the marketing function seems to be disappearing from the agency world. There was a time, which you remember very well, when the marketing people in the agencies were better than their clients. That may not have been true at Procter, but it was at most of our clients. We started hiring business school hot-shots, and our clients, a lot of them, relied on us for marketing service. But today, they're hiring better marketing people than we are, and they do it themselves. The future role of the account executive is, in my mind, rather obscure at this moment. We just bought an agency in Chicago, a direct response agency, called Eicoff. He doesn't have any account executives at all. He just has the people who write the ads, and the time-buyers. The time-buyers are on the telephone to the clients all the time. They run a commercial in Cincinnati or in Cleveland on Friday night, and by Monday morning they know exactly how much they've sold. If that commercial hasn't sold, they cancel the time slot and buy another.

I was a lousy creative head, because I did it all myself. That's not the way to have a good creative department. I also was doing the new business. It was very dangerous; I thought, "Christ, if I get hit by a cab, the whole thing's going to go up in smoke." But gradually it got more stable. We got more good people. My first two years, I couldn't pay anybody more than $10,000 a year, so I was always trying to get bargains, and there aren't many bargains around, you know? But then we got billings, and enough money to get a decent research guy, a decent media guy, and so forth.

I had an appetite for personal publicity, and that helped us in our early days. But it got to the point where I didn't want any more personal stuff about me. I wanted to promote the *agency*. So I dropped out of the limelight, and stopped making speeches and swanking around. That gave my very able partners a chance to blossom, like Jock Elliott.

Eight years ago, I'd organized myself out of a job in New York. I really had delegated myself out of a job, and I would sit in my office in New York trying to think of something to do. The guys in the other offices were working their asses off, and I hadn't got anything to do. So I went to live in France. I got out of the line. But I'm a director of the company, still. I conduct an enormous correspondence with our people all over the world. We went international. Esty thought I was nuts. He said, "You 're British, and you're hypnotized by all that foreign stuff, but this is where it's at, here in the United States. Don't go off into that foreign thing. Just concentrate everything we've got on the United States." Well, I didn't agree. Today, about 50% of our business is outside the United States.

And very strong. The agencies which don't have business outside the United States are having problems.

For the last eight or nine years, I've been living in France. I travel a great deal. I come to New York quite often. I was in Houston two or three times last year, and Chicago.

I know that you're very inspirational to these younger people.

My difficulty is to stay relevant. I don't know how you sell bubble gum. I have a horror of speculative presentations in new business. Ken Roman, who runs our New York office, says to me, "You're just plain wrong! We make speculative presentations nowadays, and that's how we get accounts. There's no better way to get them."

How do you feel about research in relationship to the creation of advertising?

I'm glad you asked that question. A great many advertising campaigns are produced every year, thousands of them, and a lot of them are pre-tested, or post-tested, but nobody ever stops and says, "Hey, let's *analyze* the scores that we've been getting. Let's try and find out what works and what doesn't work." This is what I learned from Gallup. I'm obsessed with it. I think our agency knows more about what works than any other agency. Years ago, I started putting factor-analysis findings onto slides for use in indoctrinating our people. I call them "magic lanterns." We've got 25 of them now, on all sorts of subjects. We've got one on typography; we've got one on television as a medium; we've got one on financial advertising; one on corporate advertising, which your daughter Ann * wrote; one on issues advertising. We've got one on coffee advertising, one on chewing gum. And so on.

What do you really mean by factor analysis? Do you get all the factors and then analyze them? Is that what you mean?

Here's the sort of thing I mean. We find that celebrity commercials are way below average in changing brand preference. We find that the readership of advertisements set in reverse—that's white type on a black background—is almost nonexistent. We've got hundreds of these factors. Our creative people don't like this stuff. It imposes on them a discipline which they resent. We've got a marvelous creative man in San Francisco, called Hal Riney, who makes great commercials. I would never dream of trying to impose my research discipline on Hal. But most of the people who do advertising campaigns are rather run-of-the-mill people. If you impose a dogma on them which is research-based, you save them from wasting so much of the client's money.

Occasionally you get a genius who's also got a head on his shoulders. Okay, leave him alone. But most creative people, I find, if you can indoctrinate them with this stuff, they will produce better advertising. By "better advertising," I mean advertising that produces more results.

There's a fight going on in our agency on this issue. It's not an unpleasant fight, just a philosophical difference of opinion. The

---

*Ann referred to is Ann Cummings Iverson, management supervisor on the Shell account at Ogilvy & Mather's Houston office, and oldest daughter of Barton A. Cummings.

whole idea of any discipline is unpopular in all fields. Look at contempoary painting. Look at contemporary music—there's no harmony in it. Look at contemporary poetry. The whole idea of discipline is unpopular. For years, it was difficult for us to persuade an art director to work at Ogilvy & Mather. They wanted to be free spirits, and didn't think they would be free here. But I'm quite unrepentant about it. I'm determined to build a corpus of knowledge in our agency.

Some years ago, Stanley Resor tried to buy us for Thompson. A marvelous old man. He said to me, "You know, every year, we do all these advertising campaigns, we spend hundreds of millions of dollars for our clients. What do we *know* at the end of it? Nothing, absolutely nothing. Four years ago I put a group of four bright guys to work, to identify some factors which are present in successful advertising." I asked, "How many factors have they got now, Mr. Resor?" He said, "I'm proud to tell you, they're now up to twelve." I was too polite to tell him that I was then up to 96. Gallup and I correspond occasionally on this subject. He's a great man.

We've got a magic lantern called "Procter & Gamble."

Oh, really?

Yes. It's about Procter & Gamble's philosophy of advertising, what they do and why they do it.

While a lot of creative people don't want any discipline, there are a few in this advertising world of ours who like a *dogma*. Why do people join the Catholic Church? They like having some sort of discipline, something firm to hang on to.

Now I'll tell you what I think is important in the agency business. First of all, it's wonderful if you can get your agency a good creative reputation. Secondly, I think new business is terribly important, and it's underestimated nowadays. I think leadership is very important, and it's difficult being a good leader in an agency, with so many neurotic people around. Good financial management is very important. A few years ago, I don't know if you remember this, the big, rich agencies started diversifying. They went into all those strange fields.

Particularly Doyle Dane Bernbach. Remember?

Mary Wells burnt her fingers. J. Walter Thompson made some awful mistakes.

Foote, Cone; even Y&R diversified. There was a move among

my partners for Ogilvy & Mather to do it. But I dug in my heels. I said, "No, no, no, we're not going to do it; we're going to stick to our knitting." I'm proud of that. All the others burnt their fingers, and we didn't. Success is often what you *don't* do.

This is true. Knowing when to keep still and mind your knitting is very important.

We knew something about advertising, and I didn't think we knew anything about those other things.

Doyle Dane put a lot of money into Georg Jensen and lost a bundle.

Nowadays, the fashion is to go around buying other agencies. It gives me the creeps. If this trend continues, in a few years, there are going to be about ten giant agencies and a lot of little local agencies.

The medium-size agencies seem to be out of luck.

Let's talk about people for a minute—and their education. I suspect that every young person would like to know what you think they should take to prepare themselves to come into this business.

I don't think they should study advertising at the undergraduate level in college. That's a hard thing to say, because there are so many people teaching advertising; 70 universities and colleges in the United States offer courses in advertising. Some of them even offer degrees. I think that's a sad waste of time.

I don't think that's a good thing. It was Maurie Needham [founder of Needham, Harper & Steers] who persuaded me of this thirty years ago. I was very fond of Needham. I think it's better if college students get an education in geography, or economics, or physics, or Latin, but not advertising. I want people whose education has not been in advertising. I don't like saying that, because I don't want to start every professor of advertising thinking I am his enemy.

I used to be very hostile to the young people, particularly the young creative people. Then I changed my mind. I was in our Frankfurt office, and saw an exceptionally good campaign. I asked to meet the copywriter who had written it, and she was brought into my office: she was eighteen years old. I took her to one side, and said, "Leave, and go to college. Get an education." She did.

The head of our office in Frankfurt has never forgiven me. Maybe she'll come back to us.

Good for you, David.

I like people with well-furnished minds. One of the difficulties about hiring people in the agency business today is that it's mostly television. I can predict whether someone can write print ads—if they've been editor of their college newspaper, or can write well, or are interested in selling. But how can you predict that someone will be able to write good TV commercials? I don't know. If anybody else knows, I'd like to hear from him.

Well, that's interesting, your point of view on advertising education. I've spent a lot of time working with advertising education, those that are advertising majors. They have to take a lot of liberal arts. And if all they took was advertising education, I would agree with you 100%. But they don't; they have to take a language; they have to take English, they have to be able to write. They have to be able to do a lot of things that I don't think you realize.

I don't believe in people going straight from college, or even business school, into an agency. I advise them, "Get a selling job, preferably selling to consumers, not selling to the trade. Get some sales experience. Then, if you possibly can, get a job in a research outfit." I happen to have done both of those things, and found them very useful. Many's the argument I've had with copywriters. For example, a copywriter will come in with a headline. I'll say, "I know what that word means, but does the housewife know what it means?" "Of course she does." I'll say, "I bet she doesn't. You've been brought up in Manhattan, or Westport, Connecticut. You don't know anything about the people who live in America. Get in a bus, and go to Iowa, and spend a week on a farm there, and come back on a bus; and if you still want to use that word in a headline, go ahead and use it."

It's marvelous if copywriters can start in direct response, where they can taste blood. They can write an ad which can outpull another ad by four to one. They then realize the difference between good advertising and bad advertising. And then they come into the agency business. They're going to spend the rest of their lives trying to sell things, and not to be fancy entertainers. Our business is infested with people who've never sold anything in their lives.

That's right. They don't know people; they don't know how to deal with people, how to talk with people.

We are what we were. Take Bill Bernbach, whom I respect so much. His background is completely different from mine. Sometimes I look at a Doyle Dane ad and say to myself, "I don't know who wrote this, but I'll bet he has never had any experience in direct response, or he couldn't write a headline like that."

The horrifying thing to me is to see the way people in big manufacturing companies fall for "creativity." I can take them a commercial which is sound as a bell, full of consumer benefit and demonstration, and they'll say, "It's not *creative.*" So you go back with a commercial written by one of these entertainers, and they love it.

I've always moonlighted, all of my life. My partners don't mind my doing it, and I'm always encouraging other people to do it. For the last three years, I've been employed by Campbell Soup Company as their consultant on marketing and advertising.

What you typically see is that advertising expenditures have not kept pace with inflation. A $10 million budget today buys only as much advertising as a $5 million budget bought eight years ago.

Let me ask you: we've talked about women a little bit—this girl over in Frankfurt, for example. But women are coming into this business, and becoming more important all the time, and they're making great contributions. Have you any comment about that?

In early years, I was against women in the agency business. I had an unfortunate experience with one, an awful woman. And then I changed my mind. Most of the things we advertise are bought by women and used by women, but most of the advertising is written by men. Idiotic. And it is still true outside the United States. What the hell do men know about it? I wouldn't put a woman on a cigar account; why put a man on a tampon account. Ogilvy & Mather now has more female account executives than males. In France, a woman in our agency gets pregnant. The agency has to pay her for six months, when she's having her baby. Then she comes back, works for a year, and has another baby. She has a whole family at our expense.

That is irritating.

We had a wonderful copywriter here for years, called Reva Korda, and she had two babies. I couldn't grudge her two babies. But a couple of years later, she came into my office wearing a maternity dress. I said, "Oh, Christ, Reva!" She said, "I just put it on to tease you."

Is she retired?

No, she's now got her own consultancy, bless her.

I'm proud of the fact that some of the campaigns I wrote years ago are still around. I wrote the first Dove advertising about 27 years ago, and my campaign's still running.

Well, your Hathaway campaign is still running.

It's almost 30 years old.

Well, you've had a tremendous success, David. Tell me about what you do over at your chateau.

I start the day by going to my desk, and then I look out of the window, and I think I must go and see if such and such a plant has come into flower. I'm apt to garden till lunchtime. But my wife says I work about seventy hours a week. I don't know when I'm working and when I'm not working. Poor buggers like Bill Phillips and Jock Elliott get bombarded with notes from me. When I gave up being chairman, I should have done the decent thing and gone away. But Jock asked me to stay around. I try to raise our creative standards. Now Jock has retired, and Bill Phillips has given me a three-year contract, to my great surprise. I also travel quite a lot for the agency, and I'm very active in the World Wildlife Fund. I've been on its Executive Committee for some years, and that's given me a great interest.

About three years ago, the German head of our Frankfurt office quit, to my horror. I sent Jock a telex saying, "What would you think of my going to Frankfurt?" I worked for a year in our Frankfurt office.

I've traveled an awful lot in the United States, and know the country better than most of the people who work in New York agencies.

I'm sure you do. There's a lot out there, too, David.

There's a lot out there.

April 20, 1982

ROBERT E. HEALY

Robert E. Healy, who has been an honorary chairman of The Interpublic Group of Companies, Inc. since 1973, had been chief executive officer of the company from 1968 to 1971.

Mr. Healy joined McCann-Erickson in 1952 as Vice-President, treasurer and director. He moved up to Executive Vice-President in 1955, and Chairman of the Board of the domestic company in 1960.

In 1962, Mr. Healy became the first President of Interpublic, S.A., headquartered in Geneva, Switzerland, and was in charge of Interpublic's international operations. After almost three years in Geneva, Mr. Healy, in August 1964, carried out a personal plan of partial retirement. In July of 1967 he accepted an invitation to return to Interpublic on a full-time basis with special financial and development responsibilities. In November of that year he was elected President and chief executive officer of The Interpublic Group of Companies, Inc., and chairman in February 1968. He served in this capacity until April 1, 1971 when he relinquished the presidency and chief officership, remaining as Chairman.

Before joining McCann-Erickson, Mr. Healy was associated with Colgate-Palmolive-Peet Company, Inc., where he was Vice-President in charge of advertising. In this post he supervised the company's relationships with its various advertising agencies and managed the sixth largest U.S. advertising budget. Earlier, Mr. Healy had been with the Johns-Manville Corporation, as assistant to the vice-president in charge of sales promotion.

Mr. Healy is a graduate of Pace College and the recipient of an honorary DCS degree. He is also a member of the College's Advisory Council, and over the years has served on the committees of numerous philanthropic and professional organizations.

ROBERT E. HEALY

Interview

I was born in Brooklyn and spent my childhood in Jamaica, Long Island. After local elementary and high schools, I went to Dwight Preparatory School, and I graduated from there. I liked figures and decided I'd be an accountant. So I went to Pace Institute and took business law and accounting.

I had been a little shy—I was known as a very prideful person. So I figured if I was going to get on in the cruel business world, I'd better stick my pride in my pocket; otherwise, I'd have a problem. I decided to sell Hoover vacuum cleaners door-to-door. And that was the greatest experience of my life; I'll never, never forget it.

Was this in the city?

In New York, Long Island, Bronx, all of them! I took subways, buses, everything. And you had to carry the cleaner. I looked strange there.

You got to know human nature very well, because you had to get in that house. Because when you made a demonstration, seven out of ten times you'd make a sale. And I found out about the psychology of the human mind, particularly at home. And that held me in great stead. I did very well.

And I got married. After I got married, I said, "Well, I'd better get something more substantial. Now I'm no longer prideful; I can knock on that door, go in that dirty house, white house, black house, it makes no difference to me." So I went down to the Pace Placement Bureau, and they sent me to the Johns-Manville Corporation, which was looking for a budget clerk in the sales promotion department. So I went up and met a guy by the name of Ken R. Dyke, who hired me. Ken was sales promotion manager. So I graduated from being a budget clerk to assistant to the sales promotion manager, because we did all our own brochures, we had a house organ, we had artists, copywriters, photographers—and

117

when I went there, there were 129 people in the operation, because we also had field sales promotion people all over the country. By 1932, we were down to 29. I was still there.

The old Depression set in. And of course, in a depression, guys who work budgets are very much needed. And that's when I gained more responsibility, because we were so short-handed.

Dyke was offered a job as advertising manager of Colgate-Palmolive-Peet Company in Chicago; and after he was out there about a month, he got lonely and called me. He offered me a position. I said, "What am I going to do?" He said, "I don't know, but we'll figure it out when you get here. You want to come?" I said, "Sure." So the first of January, 1934, I went to the old Palmolive building in Chicago. And there again, I had to set up something they never had, which was an in-house production department, because we did all our own sales promotion material, window display, dealer broadsides, salesmen's brochures, coupons, 24-sheet posters, one-sheet posters. And I got to know some of the finest artists, and also some of the finest ad men in the business.

Who was your agency at that point?

At that time, it was Lord & Thomas and Y&R. That's when I first met Tony Geoghegan, whom I consider one of the greatest media people of all time. Then along came Bill Benton and Chester Bowles, and Lyman Chalkley, whom I was very fond of. Then, when the Colgate family had regained control of the business from the Johnson family, who were in Milwaukee, we moved back to Jersey City, where the main Colgate plant was.

Ken left Colgate in 1936—he got caught in a political squabble —and went to NBC. When he left, he said, "Bob, I'll tell you something: *"That's* the coming thing, television." I said, "I agree with you."

Mr. Little was then President of Colgate, and he asked me to stay after Ken left. I became a brand manager, working on many of the various brands at Colgate. And in 1942, they made me advertising manager. Now I began working with Bob Lusk, Ted Bates, Bill Esty, Phil Lennen [all agency founders or principals].

I met you in 1936. I was an office boy at Benton &
Bowles. I used to deliver packages of ads and artwork to you.

Then Roy Peet took over the Colgate management, and then Hugh McKay followed him. That's when I got in a bind, and decided I was going to leave, because Hugh McKay was an over-bearing personality, and I've found out in my life that unless you're happy at your job, there's no sense continuing. And it so happened that Chester Bowles had offered me a job, going to work for Benton & Bowles. When Little found out he called me in and said, "You can't do it. Bob, you have too much at stake here, and I want you to stay here." So he fired McKay and made me advertising manager.

In 1946, Mr. Little made me vice-president in charge of advertising.

Do you recall the date when the Ted Bates agency was set up?

We set Bates up as an agency in 1940. He started with Colgate and Continental Baking. And he took our old friend, Rosser Reeves, away with him, and a guy named Clint Ferris—a very quiet, low-profile guy, but a great copywriter, in my estimation.

So, Colgate's business grew, and the advertising budgets grew, and I got to know Stuart Sherman very well, and Art Marquette (of the old Sherman & Marquette agency in Chicago). I was making a lot of money. But Colgate, in those days, had no provision for deferred compensation, or any stock option plans. So I figured that Mr. Little was going to stay there till they kicked him out, like Countway at Lever Brothers. And I thought too much of him, and I wasn't going to be around when they carried him out. But I knew what a great salesman the man was. So I talked to my (then) wife and my dad, and I said, "I'm going to quit, and I'm going to spend a year with that decision, because I know if I go to Mr. Little, he'll change my mind, he's such a super salesman."

He could sell you out of anything.

So I made a decision that young men shouldn't make—I was 49 years old at that time—so I stayed with him for a year, and I went to Mr. Little and said, "Mr. Little, you've been very kind to me; you've taught me the business—not only advertising but sales promotion, salesmanship; but I've decided that I have a duty to my family, and I have to be going. You pay me too much money, and I can't keep a nickel of it, the government gets it all; and it isn't often in a family that somebody comes along who's capable of making a lot of money."

I said, "I think I'm capable of it, and I'm going to give it a shot." And he didn't believe me, of course, because he thought I had another job, and I said, "I can leave at any time." Well, he said, "Let me think it over." Next day he called and said, "No, you've got to stay and help me, because we've come into some new contracts for television; the Colgate Comedy Hour is on"—and I'd negotiated that for him.

And all the planning for the following year, '52; I did it all. Nobody knew in the business; nobody knew except Mr. Little and my wife, and I thought about it myself. So when it came to January, I was still on the string. I hadn't gone looking for a job, I didn't have a job. So I said, "Mr. Little, I've got to get moving; time's running out." And he said, "Look, Mrs. Little and I are going down to Clearwater for a vacation, and I want you to come down and see me." When I arrived, he handed me two books, and said, "I want you to study these tonight and tomorrow morning, and we'll have lunch tomorrow and we'll discuss it." And one was a program for a deferred bonus plan, patterned after the General Motors plan, and the other was a program for stock options— everything that should have been in place. And I read them, and I complimented him the next day at lunch. I told him, "The plans are absolutely great; too bad I can't do anything with them, but I can't change my decision. It's irrevocable." So we parted the best of friends; and I took an apartment in the old John Murray house on Madison Avenue, and that was my office. Agencies offered me space, but I said, "No; I'm going to be a free man." And then the news got out, and the "feels" started coming; and there were a lot of "feels" and a lot of lookers.

Now, I'd known Marion Harper a little bit, and he got hold of me, and we talked and we talked, and about three months later, after surveying the field, I said to Marion, on the first of April, 1952, "Okay, I'll join the ship." So with my background in business law and accounting, I came in as treasurer and director of McCann-Erickson. That was the only way he could bring me in . . . without upsetting the so-called "people business." So I took up my duties and became an agency man.

John Anderson, who had been the treasurer, retired, so I got that shaped up, and I said I wouldn't work on anything competitive to Colgate—in my mind—for one year, because I knew too much. Then Mr. Little sent over the lawyer, Walter Reynolds, to see me, to see if I'd done anything against the company, which I hadn't; so he called me up and said, "Well, meet me in the Ambassador"—the old Ambassador—for a drink that night, and I did, and he handed me a bonus check.

How nice.

He said, "You didn't qualify," but he said, "You helped me so much, and did all the planning, and Walter tells me you're not working on anything competitive to the old business." He said, "Here, take this." I said, "I don't want it." He said, "No, you can have it." And he said, "Don't forget, the number's 1111, any time you want to come back." And I thanked him very much.

So we went on, and after a year I began to become very active in account work, and we were on a brand new business strike then, with Emerson Foote and Bill Berchtold, and Marion, so I became a member of the business team. I started working on a few accounts, and then came our greatest period of growth.

I became manager of the New York office of McCann, and chairman of the board of McCann International, and chairman of the board and chief operating officer of McCann-Erickson. Then Marion started the Interpublic concept, so he asked me to go to Europe to set up worldwide operations, because I'd worked international for years.

I said, "I will, if my family will agree." In the meantime, I had divorced, and married Wayne and had two young sons. So she said, "That will be a great experience, for the children as well as myself; I'd love to go." So we went to Geneva. And I set up shop, and we had an old French villa, right on Lake Geneva.

We stayed there for three years. But when I began to get a little feel of business and ability, I decided that when I reached age 60, if I could afford it, I was going to sort of semi-retire. I could never fully retire; I was too active. So on the 15th of August, 1964, I became 60 years old. On that day I left Geneva, and went right down to Plantation Key, Florida, where we had a lovely place right on the ocean, which had been rebuilt. I had 13 acres right on the ocean, and a deep-water tarpon pool at my front door.

So I worked—Marion had wanted me to stay on, still, and travel the world for him. So I did special assignments, and then I came to New York for board meetings, exec committee meetings, and I spent the time at the Key. Everything was going along fine, and then when Interpublic got in a little trouble, Marion asked me to come back and take over as head of the operations committee, and see what could be done to get the financial problems settled.

So I came back, and started to work actively, and evolved a plan I thought would take care of the financial problems at that moment. We were just short of cash. And at a meeting in November, the Board decided that things weren't happening fast enough, and no decisions were forthcoming, so they asked me if I would be president and chief executive officer.

Marion stayed on as chairman of the board, and he was going to work on new business; I was going to take over the client side and the administrative side. But Marion was too active a personality, and he just couldn't stand another man heading it up, and in February he resigned, and then I ended up chairman of the board. And with the help of all my associates and good clients, we were able to turn the ship around.

Who were your associates at that point, Bob?

Paul Foley, Neal Gilliatt, Bill Taggart, Don McNamara, Frank Sherer, Elliott Plowe, Armando Sarmento, Carl Spielvogel, Bryan Houston. But all we did was cast aside a lot of the non-agency-related corporations.

Were you public at that time?

No, no. We couldn't go public; we needed cash. I found a friend at Chase Manhattan; $13½ million.

Didn't Bryan Houston help?

Bryan was a great help to me because he knew Tony Cole of Chase. And that's when I learned the philosophy, "Never be negative. Always be positive." Anytime anybody made a negative statement, I shut the meeting right off. I said, "No more," because negative people don't go on like I have.

And we got what we needed. We had three great clients—the Carnation Company; the Coca-Cola Company; and the Heublein Co. They advanced us $5 million in advance billings, which gave us more time to feel the marketplace; because everybody we talked to in the investment banking field wanted a piece of the action. And I decided I'd brought too many people into the business; I didn't have to give part of the business away, it was enough! As I said, we found Bryan Houston and Tony Cole, Jack Cooper, and we were negotiating along, with some very creative work, which is too complicated to go into here.

Yeah, but it was wonderful, wasn't it?

Absolutely fabulous. And, as later events proved, the company turned around; and Marion always wanted to take Interpublic public, and even had the Four A's change their by-laws so public companies could be members of the Four A's.

So I decided that that was a good idea, because we were growing very fast and had great requirements for capital, and this was a way to get money. And Bill Hogan was the chief financial man. Bill had retired from American Airlines a year before we asked him to join us.

We worked it out with John Morgan of Smith Barney. We were going to take the company public two years earlier, but the market went dead. So we withdrew, and in 1971 we took the company public. And a strange thing about life, as I said, is the small circle. I was sitting in Jersey City, where the closing took place, and I looked right across the street, and there was my old office. I want to tell you, it was real nostalgia.

I guess the highlight of my coming back really wasn't turning the company around; it was having the confidence of my associates, who bought, cold cash, $3,600,000 worth of debentures— with no promise of anything, except they had first call. This even amazed Wall Street, amazed the investment bankers and Chase Manhattan. They never figured this was possible. But we did it. And I said that was the most fulfilling moment of my life, because I went around the company and solicited pledges for the debentures. They all got paid very well. They all made a lot of money; but at that time there was no sign of anything except confidence. And they had it. That I consider the greatest thing that ever happened to me in life.

Now just to get down to philosophies, I have a few that I follow along with positive thinking. One is, "Sit loose and stay fluid; don't make any commitments; don't close your mind. Don't have a vertical mind; have a horizontal mind." Be a good listener; most people are not. I believe in that. After we had a meeting, I'd go around the room and say, "Write down on a piece of paper what the problems were and what the decisions were." And then I'd read them, and I was shocked! So I said, "Boy, I'm going to change this."

Another philosophy — "No gratuitous statements." Don't put your head on a chopping block asking for somebody to cut it off. Because the world is full of people with gratuitous statements who lived to regret them. And, "Be a good communicator." It's a two-way street; it takes two to talk. Don't make promises to clients without going back and talking to your own people and knowing you can make the date. That's what I call a gratuitous statement. And don't mix your social life with your business life. Sure, go out and have a good time; go to dinner; stop. The two are entirely separate, in my book. I've seen too many sad stories where the social life got in the way of the business life, and many happy relationships were ended. My daddy used to say, "Don't sleep in the gutter with anybody, because the next morning, you'll regret it."

So I decided I wanted to go back bone fishing, once I got the business turned around; I was going to do it. I'd built my succession. And I asked Paul Foley to come over and become the chief executive officer.

Why did you select him?

Paul, in my opinion, is one of the great copywriters of the business, and I've known a lot of them—particularly in our business—Jack Tinker, Bill Esty, Phil Lennen, Ted Bates, Rosser Reeves—and Paul is a likeable personality. And I figured it was time to promote a creative guy and give him a shot, and it'd be great for the organization. And I had great faith in Paul. I told him I'd be a great help, but I would never interfere; and I didn't want to call him president/chief operating officer, I wanted to call him president/chief executive officer, so he'd know he'd have no interference. I said, "No problem with that. What the hell, you want to go call on clients the same way? You want to write some copy? You can't compete with the agency, but you can write some copy if you want to." I said, "I think when you come over here and get used to it, you'll thoroughly enjoy it." Events proved he did.

Does "over here" mean over to Interpublic?

Right. Over from McCann-Erickson. He was the Chairman of the Board and chief executive officer for Interpublic.

And had you made him the head of McCann?

Yes.

How many years ahead of that? Not long, I think.

Well, the first thing I did when I came back in the business in
'67 was ask Armando Sarmento to come back and join Interpublic,
and run the international operations. I considered Armando then,
and I still do, as the finest advertising internationalist in the
world. So Armando came over, and Paul took over McCann. And
under that leadership, you know what happened to McCann, what
happened to Interpublic—it grew, grew, grew—still growing, more
acquisitions. As you know, we just finalized the Lintas idea. The
31st of March. So we now own 100% of Lintas. And that's a
tremendous operation, and gives us three worldwide systems. And
that's where the business is. Even our old friends at Esty and Ted
Bates have found that out.

So that's the way the business is going. I've got to tell you, for
excitement, the agency business has got it all over the client side.
You get involved in many more situations. You have just as many
personality problems; you still have a sales department, and a research department; you've got a creative department, an account
executive department; business is that way. You can't run away
from it. And another thing I've found in my life; you have to
discipline yourself. If you don't discipline yourself, you get in a lot
of trouble, because you get nervous. And nervous people never
make a success. Concerned people, yes; but nervous people, in my
opinion, don't do the job. You see, a nervous mind is not a good
mind to make a decision.

Do you still go back for board meetings?

Oh, yeah, once a month.

You know, I have so many friends there, and the people I
brought into the business, they call for advice and counseling, and
I say, "Well, you know, I'll be really glad to give it to you; but
remember one thing—it's free. I don't have to suffer."

Well, you've had an amazing career, Bob, I'll tell you.

Well, I've had three careers. I got as far as I could go at Colgate,
in my opinion—maybe I could have done better if I had stayed—
but I was perfectly happy with that. Then I got as far as I wanted
to go with McCann and Interpublic; and I came back, and had a
third experience.

I was going to say, you started out learning how to sell.

Right. I went out in the field on any account I handled, and I rode trucks, Coke trucks, bakery trucks, drove automobiles, went into garages, showrooms, supermarkets, Mom and Pop stores, all over the world, because I wanted to know what was going on in the marketplace. There's only one place you can find out; go there yourself and see it.

Then I was very fortunate in my upbringing, because my Dad was an internationalist; he was a lumber expert, and sold lumber all over the world. And when I was a young lad, he took me outside of our own continent, when I was still young, still going to high school; and I could see the cultures, how different they were from ours. And it's held me in good stead, because when I became an internationalist with McCann, I'd *been* there. When I went to live in Europe, the main thing there was looking back at your own country. Then you can understand the criticisms by other people of you own country much, much better. When anybody comes to me for advice about living abroad, I say, "Well, if your family can go, go; it'll be the greatest thing in the world, not only for you, but for your family. You'll *never* regret it."

And I know how important you think creative is, because of what you did with Foley. I know it's hard to pick out any one person, because you went through so many great creative people there.

Right. Well, Jack Tinker, of course, was out of the picture entirely because of his health; but I would have never considered Jack—he was too nervous to become the head.

I know you've always been interested in young people and their education, and those that came into our business—what kind of an education should they get, to come into the advertising business—on either side, client or agency?

I think for a young lad starting out, who is not highly creative—in other words, very artistic or very word-minded—it is better to start on the client side of the business. I think it's a tenderer side; they are more lenient in bringing you along, much better disciplined than on the agency side, and as I said earlier, I believe discipline is very important in a young man's life. Plus it exposes them to the corporate way of life at a young age. And you can understand the inner workings of a client mind, which I assure you, Bart, is entirely different from an agency mind, because their options are entirely different, and the greenhouse they live in is an entirely different kind of a greenhouse. They have to do all kinds of things; they can't specialize. When they come in young, they've got to roam the field and find out where they want to fit in. I think it's easier.

Then if a guy really applies himself, really communicates, keeps his hand in, keeps reading all the books he can get his hands on, he'll see what he wants to do, whether it's writing copy, being a research man, or a media director, a production man. Account executives, of course, they're a strange breed, they just happen.

What do you think about education for all this?

I think you have to have a formal education if you want to be successful, in today's market. I think the day of the idea that you had to be an M.B.A. to get anywhere is going by the boards. It had its time. But that doesn't mean to suggest that if you want to be an M.B.A., I don't mean you shouldn't. You know, get a formal education. Nobody ever went wrong, in my opinion. I didn't. You're taking business law, accounting, as your major—plus journalism, which when I went to school, many years ago, was not offered as a course. But I learned it myself, through the school of hard knocks.

Of course, today they teach a lot of advertising in college.

Excellent schools. Also, have confidence in yourself. Don't be a nailbiter. Without confidence, nobody's going to go anywhere. And the greatest sign of that is Ron Reagan right now. One thing Ron's got is confidence. A lot of problems, but he gets out there and he just exudes confidence. Always confident.

Another thing for young people: Always be wanted. When you're not wanted, look out. If somebody wants to talk to you, talk to them. It doesn't cost anything. But if you really are going to talk at a serious level, be man enough to go tell the people you're working for that somebody has asked you to talk to them, and you feel a fairness to yourself to have that conversation. Don't let them find out the hard way, because that's going to be bad on you. Nobody is penalized for being an honest man.

Now, one thing we've been talking about: you were talking about the male animal all the time. But you know, we have a lot of women in our business today—in fact, I think more women than

127

men. And in very responsible positions. How do you feel about that?

Some of my best friends are women. Margot Sherman, I think, is one of the really great people, even though she's an ardent feminist every time. And Mary Wells—we've had a lot of women work for us, and we still do. Jo Foxworth, she was there. And we have a great gal now at McCann-Erickson called Penny Hawkey.

I believe that over the last decade, gender has not been a consideration that enters our minds when we are staffing at any level or in any spot. I think this is a startling change for men of my age, but my point is that in our business the change *has taken place.* The reason I think it has happened is that real talent and dedication is and always has been so difficult to find that we cannot possibly cut ourselves off from such a rich source on the basis of gender. This brings me to another point that I think I am at the time of life to make: very few people are really any good at our business. I have never been able to figure out why, because, God knows, we can use all the help we can get, and the life we offer is rewarding in every sense of the word. Also, we all have legions of superbly gifted people flowing through our offices, and legions more begging to come. But the number of genuinely effective professionals seems always to remain small.

What do you know about Phil Geier?

Well, Phil started with us as a trainee in our Cleveland office, worked for Marschalk Company, the old Marschalk Company. And we brought him to New York, to McCann-Erickson. We brought Jack Powers out of London, back to the States, and made him president of McCann, so we needed a replacement. And we decided Phil Geier should get a shot at it. And Phil exceeded our fondest expectations. He built McCann at that time into the No. 1 agency while he was there. Good advertising man, good client man, excellent salesman, and knows no hours. He has one of these damn tape recorders. Never gives up; he's the greatest memo writer in the world. I said to him once, "You're going to make all the paper companies rich." He said, "Why is that?" I said, "You write too goddamn many memos." So, he's doing fine.

A workaholic.

He did the SSC&B deal that everybody thought couldn't be done. And Paul Foley did the Tom Adams/Campbell-Ewald deal, and nobody had that idea before. Paul had it because fundamentally he had ties there; he came out of Detroit, he'd been a motor guy all his life until he came to McCann. So, when Paul had a question to ask them, he got a receptive answer, and he put together that deal.

It was a good one.

Actually, for both Tom and his people as well as ourselves. Because it gave his people access to our worldwide operation, as well as broadening Tom in that respect. Tom didn't know a goddamn thing about overseas, Europeans; he found out doing stuff for us.

Oh, Joe Culligan used to call me "Mr. Clear," because I believe in clarity. Another great friend, Professor Paul Frischauer says, "You know, you're like butter; you get a clean cut." I believe in not wasting anybody's time. If I have something to say, I say it, and I've said it as succinctly as I know how to say it, and as clearly as I know how to say it.

April 3, 1982

EDWARD L. BOND, Jr.

Edward L. Bond, Jr., retired Chairman of the Board of Young & Rubicam, Inc., joined the agency in 1946 as an account executive, shortly after his discharge from the service following World War II.

During his 25 years with Young & Rubicam, his career took him from Account Executive to Vice-President and account supervisor, to director of the Account Management Department, to Executive Vice-President and general manager and, in January, 1963, to the post of President.

In March, 1965, he became Chief Executive Officer of Young & Rubicam, and in January, 1968, Chairman of the Board. He retired in 1972.

Born in Clarksboro, N.J., in 1913, Mr. Bond attended Washington & Lee University and later New York University. He entered the Army as a private in 1941 and was separated from the service as a major in 1946.

Mr. Bond had served on the Commerce Information Advisory Committee of the United States Department of Commerce; as a trustee of the United States Council of the International Chamber of Commerce; on the Board of Directors of the Council of Better Business Bureaus, Inc., and as a member of the Board of Advisors of the Council for Financial Aid to Education, Inc.

He also served as a member of the Board of the International Executive Service Corps; a member of the Advisory Council of RIAL (Religion in American Life); on the Advisory Board for Young Americans for Responsible Action; Director of the National Multiple Sclerosis Society and of the New York Chapter of the American Red Cross; and in advisory roles with Columbia University's Graduate School of Business, Thunderbird Graduate School of Management in Arizona, and Hampshire College in Massachusetts.

He has held many posts with the American Association of Advertising Agencies and in 1968–69 served as its Chairman.

EDWARD L. BOND, JR.

132

Interview

I was born in a little village in southern New Jersey—a town called Clarksboro—and it was a doggone good life, as I look back on it. There were four boys in the family, and my father raised tomatoes and peppers and corn and alfalfa and pigs and sheep and cows and horses and goats and chickens.

And the only memorable thing that Eisenhower ever said, as far as I'm concerned, was "We were poor, but didn't know it." I don't think my father ever had, at any one time, more than maybe $5,000. He bought the farm for $7,000; it took him most of his life to pay that off. Four boys, all pretty close together in terms of age; and we fought a lot, but we had a hell of a lot of fun.

We worked the farm all summer, and went to school, more or less, the rest of the time. And Dad was a semi-educated guy; he had been through grammar school and through part of prep school when he got very sick and had to leave. He went to George School, which is a Quaker prep school in Pennsylvania. And the doctors finally told him he had to go out West for his health and live in a better climate for a while, for a couple of years, so he did. He got into a surveying party and laid out the town of Provo, Utah. And I went there on a motorcycle a couple of years ago and looked at it. It was very exciting.

But anyhow, they were great parents. My mother was nigh unto a saint, and she'd have to be to have four snotty boys screaming and hollering and breaking arms and legs and tearing each other up. And it seemed to me there was a catastrophe every other day.

None of us got very well-educated, for two reasons. First, we didn't have the money, and second, we didn't have the brains! It was just about that bloody simple. Anyhow, I went through grammar school literally in a one-room school house.

133

I had a rich uncle, an international lawyer, and a pretty good one. He got enamored of automobiles, and he took me to school one day in a red, brass-radiatored Mercer. That was very exciting, one of my early great memories; and I've loved automobiles and motorcycles and airplanes and stuff like that ever since.

I went two years to Swedesboro, N.J., High School, and then two years to George School. And I enjoyed it; it was a good thing. But I really was not a good student. But I had one teacher that would have made the difference. His name was Walter Mohr, he's dead now—he was the only teacher I ever had that made me want to learn. Every other teacher . . . .

How did he do that?

Well, maybe it was partly the subject he was teaching—history. And he made history, just by force of his knowledge and character, he made it interesting, and come alive, and made you want to know more. And he was far and away the best teacher I ever had.

When I finished high school there, my parents expected me to go to Swarthmore, where I had been entered at birth because other members of my family had gone to Swarthmore, a Quaker college, and so it seemed to my parents that that's where I should go. Well, I decided, being a recalcitrant type, that I wasn't going to go to Swarthmore, the hell with it.

I couldn't have gotten in anyhow, even in those days. But my father, having come from Virginia, I'd spent a lot of time as a kid down there. I started looking at colleges in Virginia. And eventually I decided, if we could scrounge up the money, I would go to Washington & Lee, a small, nice college.

It doesn't rate very high, I guess, academically, but it's got a beautiful campus. I went by there last year, and you know, they've spent $67,000,000 and screwed it up completely. It's now a big university, thousands of students, and you know, it's got as much character as a concrete block. I liked it the way it was. I was a bit of a Civil War buff, and "Marse" Lee is buried there, and VMI is next door, and we were kicking the hell out of them and vice versa.

I was there for a couple of years, and then ran out of money and quit. I quit and went to work in a factory in Camden; the McAndrews & Forbes Company, a licorice factory. And I was a night shift worker; they worked around the clock, you know. 7 to 3, 3 to

11, 11 to 7. The most god-awful existence a man can live, you know. Your stomach never settles down, you never get any sleep, you feel like crap all the time.

And here you were, about 20 years old, I guess. Nineteen, twenty?

Yes, something like that. And finally, I got to know some of the people, the head of the chemistry laboratory. The main product was licorice extract. I'd have to tell you more than you want to know about licorice.

I really don't care about it at all.

Anyhow, I worked there for a while. But I was not cut out to be a chemist. I really wasn't interested; I was just trying to keep my soul and stomach together. But this uncle—the international lawyer I alluded to earlier—who lived across the road from us on the farm, said, "Why don't you come up to New York and work in my office, and I will help you go to school, and I'll pay you. I'll pay you a little money, and help you go to school if you want to do that." That seemed like a pretty good thing. So I came to New York, and he had an office at 501 Fifth Avenue, right across from the library; and he paid me $15 a week, on which I lived. That was *everything;* that was food, board, booze, women, you name it, transportation, everything.

And then, I picked the nearest college to his office, which was Washington Square College of New York University; and I took my classes in such a way that I'd go to the office at 8 a.m. and work until a quarter of eleven, get on the subway, go to Washington Square College—my first class was at 11:00—go to classes through to maybe 2:00 or 3:00, then get a White Tower hamburger for about a nickel and an orange drink for another nickel, and back in the office by 3:30 and work till 10:00 or 11:00 at night, then go home and study. And for two years—for one month, I kept track—I got four hours of sleep a night. And I did this for two years.

My God.

It damned near killed me.

He had some very complicated and large international accounts. The biggest one was the prosecution of the Black Tom and Kingsman sabotage cases that came out of World War I, and he and the famous John McCloy worked with him; between them, they represented the Canadian Car and Foundry Company, Bethlehem Steel, and about 125 insurance companies.

And he had worked on this one case for, I don't know, fifteen years, I guess, and lost. It had been tried in The Hague, it had been tried in London, it had been tried in Washington, it had been tried in New York, and he'd lost, and he kept on trying. And one reason he kept on trying was that during the war, because this case had not been settled, the Alien Property Custodian had sequestered something like $20,000,000 of German property to pay this case, in case it was ever won. So he had his eye on this.

It was a pretty good target.

And every time he lost, he raised the percentage of his take. And he finally won the damn thing, and he made a bundle! And so did McCloy.

And he had another regular practice. He wasn't making any money on this; so he had a regular practice to keep body and soul together while he went after the big one. He was a great education for me. He said to me, "Eddie, if you're going to make it in New York, you have got to work and work and work and work and work a lot harder than anybody else. That's the only way." "Because," he said, "it's full of smart people; you've got all the competition in the world; but there's one thing you can do that they won't do, and that's work. If you work hard enough, you'll make it."

Good advice.

It was good advice. Another thing he said; he would sit there, dictating and rewriting briefs until midnight, 1:00 in the morning; he would keep two or three secretaries going. And he said, "You know, I never consider a brief finished until I have re-written it at least seventeen times." I never re-wrote things seventeen times, but I re-wrote a lot of things two or three times more than I would have otherwise. And that stood me in good stead in the ad business later on, I think.

Anyhow, I did that for two years, until I thought I was going to die, I really just did. And I was walking down Fifth Avenue in front of Rockefeller Center one day, and I saw a guy in a Navy-looking uniform, gray pants and blue jacket and blue hat, and there were a bunch of people following along behind him. He was a guide. So on the spur of the moment, I just turned and went into the RCA Building, and hunted around and found the guided tour lounge, and I walked in and asked for the boss. The boss turned out to be a woman. And I said, "At this time of year, in the spring, you must need a lot more guides, with all those tourists coming in." And she said, "Yeah, we do." And I said, "Well, how about a job? I'd like to do that." And she said, "Yeah, you and —" and she opened this file drawer and said, "You and all these people in this file drawer two feet long." I said, "Yeah, but they're in the file drawer and I'm here." To make a long story short, she hired me, right on the spot.

That was a fun job. And I made more money than I'd ever made in my life, by far; I made $75 one week.

I did that that summer, and then I decided that I was going to postpone going back to school to get those dozen or so credits I needed for a degree. I was going to do it someday. But during my time in school, I had been exposed, in a *very* peripheral way, to advertising. And I'd heard—I guess it was through this uncle of mine—I'd heard of an agency called Kenyon & Eckhardt. The job had dried up because of the tourist season at Rockefeller Center, and so I looked in the telephone book, found Kenyon & Eckhardt, 247 Park Avenue, went over, and asked for the Personnel Department, which turned out to be one woman. And I said, "I want a job," and after an interview, she said the "Don't call us, we'll call you" sort of thing. And I thanked her and left, and hitchhiked down to the farm. And so I went home, and figured, "Now I'd better sit around and figure out what the hell I'm going to do." Because it never occurred to me that I'd get a job at K&E. But damn it, about a week later, I got a telegram: "Report to work Monday."

No kidding!

And as to what I was going to do, I didn't have the slightest idea. But I went up at the appointed time, and found myself a room for $8 a week, and reported to work in the mail room.

What year was this, do you recall?

I think it was 1936. It was September, and I started working in the mail room, you know, distributing the mail around.

I know well. I did it at Benton & Bowles.

And after a couple of months of that, I was moved into what was called the Facts Department. It was a department of five of us adjacent to Otis Kenyon's office. We had our own door into his office. He was the Chairman, Henry Eckhardt was the President. See, Otie Kenyon was an engineer. He was a hell of an engineer and mathematician. He'd studied under Steinmetz. And his interest in advertising was in industrials. We had Mergenthaler Linotype Company and Permutit Water Softening Systems and stuff like that. He was a smart cookie, and he said, "You know, the big money is in the consumer stuff, so I've got to get a consumer guy." So he got Henry Eckhardt in. Eckhardt had had experience in consumer goods and in the rag business, and almost right off the bat, made him President. And then we started going for consumer products. We had some Kellogg's, Munsingwear, and stuff like that.

But anyway, Otie Kenyon had this little Facts Department.

And he used us to do anything he wanted done, and it was a fascinating job, because we would be researching all kinds of different things. And you know, I didn't know sheep shit from parched barley, but I was learning a lot. We made new business presentations, we researched every facet of some businesses, we made our own charts, we wrote speeches, we did everything. And it was an interesting experience. But we had fun. We worked hard; we worked our asses off, we really did.

And we were working right with the boss, and whenever we put things together, numbers especially, they had to be right; because he had a circular slide rule on his desk, and man, he would run that thing, he'd just heat that thing up, that was spinning all day!

But then, after maybe a year, I was probably making close to $36 a week.

Wow!

And then I was transferred into Account Management, and was in that until I was drafted into the Army in 1941. This was before we were in the war, in August. I was drafted for one year. But I had worked on Munsingwear, Abercrombie & Fitch, and several others.

I've got to tell you one thing about an ad that we put together. In a little agency like that was then, you were sort of a jack-of-all-trades, you did a little bit of everything. I never was officially a copywriter, but I was always writing copy.

If I couldn't get the lazy copywriters to write it, and it was due, I'd write it myself. You know, take it over, sell it, then go set the type and get the artwork done; the next morning I'd have a proof. You know, we'd grind out ads overnight.

You learned the business that way.

You really learned it. And Abercrombie's had a new product, a flea killer for dogs, and they wanted a newspaper ad for that. So a copywriter and I put together what I thought was a hell of an ad. The headline was, "If Your Bitch Has The Itch, See Abercrombie & Fitch." And I couldn't sell the damn thing!

Today it would go. But I took that over to Walt Haynes, who was the ad director of Abercrombie's then. And he couldn't buy it. He thought it was good, but he couldn't buy it.

It was beneath their dignity.

Yeah. Anyhow, the war came, and I left, expecting to go back, if I lived through the war. I was down in Camp Croft, South Carolina, when the war broke out at Pearl Harbor. I hadn't seen any of my family since I had left in August, and this was December, of course. And it just happened that my mother and father decided to come down to see me *that* weekend.

And we were in the car Sunday morning, when it came on the radio, and the local radio station said all Army personnel were to report to their posts, So I headed for Camp Croft, and as we went in the gate, the guard leaned in the car to my mother and father, and said, "You'd better say good-bye good, 'cause you ain't gonna see this boy no more!"

So, I was nearly five years in the Army, being stuck in the thing; and they asked me to go to OCS, so I went to Fort Benning, and wound up in the 45th Division, and went to Africa and the Sicilian landing and so forth. Then I got banged up a little bit, and wound up in the hospital in a town called Mateur in Tunisia, which we appropriately called manure. I was unable to go back into combat, so they sent me to Eisenhower's headquarters in Algiers. I was there for a year, and then was sent back here to the Pentagon, where I spent about the last year of the war.

While I was there, I met two chaps in the advertising business, named Curtis G. Pratt and Bryan Houston. They both had been vice-presidents of Young & Rubicam, and they said, "What are you going to do when you get out of the Army?" I said, "Well, I guess I'm going to go back to K&E. I guess they've got to take me back, under the law, whether they want to or not." And they said, "Well, when you're going to get out, and you know you're going to get out, get in touch. We'd like to talk to you."

So, when I got out, I called them up, and wrote something, and went up to see them. And at this point, Bryan had left Y&R and was executive vice-president of Pepsi-Cola, under Walter Mack, in those days. Boy, has it changed since! So, anyhow, I saw Curt Pratt, and Curt said—I called him "Colonel" then—he said, "I want you to interview some people." So he set up a whole bunch of interviews around the agency, and I went around from one to another, and finally I wound up being interviewed by a guy named Harry Carpenter, who lived in Greenwich; and Harry was, and I guess still is, a very thoughtful, knowledgeable, exacting taskmaster. And he grilled me; he didn't interview me, he grilled me about what I knew about the advertising business.

And the fact of the matter is, I didn't know a damn thing about the advertising business. I knew how to get an ad produced and that was about it. But as for marketing, and real knowledge, I had damned little knowledge. I had learned more in Otie Kenyon's Facts Department than I did anywhere else, and that was precious little. So after this grilling by Harry, I went back to Curt's office, and I said, "Colonel, thanks very much, but let's forget this; this just isn't going to work." I said, "I just laid the biggest brilliant egg you ever saw with Carpenter. Carpenter thinks I know something about the advertising business, and it's a fact that I don't know anything." And he said, "Wait a minute." He disappeared, and he came back, and he said, "I want you to meet one more guy." And he took me in to Lou Brockway's office. Well, there was a man you could talk to, I'll tell you. Did you know Brockway?

Wonderful man.

Wonderful guy, and he was not grilling. He had a different way of doing things. Anyhow, for some reason I never will understand, they hired me! They hired me for $6,000 a year. Well, I had to still get out of the Army; it took me several months, and I guess I got out in April of '46.

And the first day I reported to work they did something that—I would have murdered for Curt Pratt and Young & Rubicam. They said, "Your starting salary is going to be $7,000 a year." This was before I had done a day's work. You know, how to make a guy really go.

Psychologically very smart.

Oh, it was a smart thing. I don't know whether they engineered it with that sort of psychology in mind, but whatever, it was really something. I started working on a small piece of the Pepsi-Cola business we had, a product called "Evervess," which was a sparkling water. It never got off the ground. But we did some fun things.

I've got to tell one story about Walter Mack.

The Pepsi-Cola advertising director used to send me in to get stuff approved by Mack. I guess he was a little afraid of Walter. I'll never forget; we had an ad that had a painting, and I had the mechanical and the copy set and the painting, and this was just final approval. We'd spent a lot of money on this thing. So I took it in to Walter Mack, with a certain trepidation, and he looked at it, read the copy, and then looked at the picture, and he said, "If I could draw, I could draw better than that!" I never got over it.

I don't think he realized what a non sequitur it was. But you know, it was one of my first, if not my first, real tests of salesmanship and fast thinking. I couldn't go back to *anybody* and say, "I didn't sell it." I just couldn't; it was impossible. I would have had to drown myself in the East River, which I had to cross to get back to Y&R. So I thought, "Well, I've got to talk this guy somehow into putting his initials on this painting." And I did. Finally, he said, "I still don't like it, but I'll buy it."

I had given him a lot of stuff about how his people and our people had thought this through very carefully, and it was this particular kind of drawing because it fitted into the psychological portrait, and on and on. I guess, just to get me out of there, he initialed it.

Let's go on. I want to know whose backs you climbed over to get to the top.

I haven't even started yet. Well, you know, you say that, and I can say, honestly, as far as I know, I never did. I never wanted the job, particularly. I never sought it. You know, I was working on accounts. And I did remember what this old uncle of mine had said; he said, you know, "If you're going to make it in New York, you've got to work harder than anybody else." And that's the one thing I did do. I never thought that I was any smarter than anybody else—in fact, I knew there were a hell of a lot of people smarter than I was. But I defy anybody to say that anybody worked any harder than I did, because there were weeks and weeks and weeks that I worked, you know, till 10:00 or 11:00 at night, all night sometimes. If I had a plan to write, I wrote that mother over and over again, and if I didn't, Ed Barnes, who worked on some of my accounts, made me, because *he* was a taskmaster.

He was a great plan conceiver and plan writer, and I worked for years under him. And that was a great education. I was on piddly little accounts for the first year or two, and one day I was walking by Barnes' office. Barnes had one of the front offices, a two-window front office on Madison Avenue. So you knew he was not just a vice-president, he was a *big* vice-president. And as I came by his open door, he said, "Hey, you, come in here!"

Well, I didn't know him. I'd met him, but he was tough. And he said, "How'd you like to get into the big time?" I said, "What do you mean, Mr. Barnes?" He said, "I mean you've been working on this crappy little stuff. How'd you like to work on something really important, something really big? How'd you like to work on the Lipton business?" We then had Lipton Tea and Lipton Soups. I said "That'd be great, that'd be wonderful! I'd love to do that!"

He said, "Well, just keep it under your hat. Don't tell those other bastards. I'll get this worked out; we'll have it worked out." That's the way he worked. He was tough; he'd walk all over anybody to get what he wanted, and he usually got it, too. He would stomp on anybody, grind his heel in their innards. It took him a couple of months, but sure enough, suddenly I was put on the Lipton Tea and Soups.

Account Exec?

Yeah, Account Exec, and he was the Account Supervisor. And that was an education.

Barnes was a real marketer, he was the best. He had good accounts. He was on Goodyear, he was on Lipton, he was on Remington—I forget what else. I worked with him on Lipton Tea and Soups, and Remington. We became great friends, and I'm sure I learned more about the advertising business from Ed Barnes than from any other single person, because I worked longer with him.

And he was, as I say, a great conceiver and a great plan writer; and surprisingly, although he was gruff and tough and irascible, the creative people respected him. I don't think they liked him very much, but they respected him, and they would work with him. And he's the last guy you'd think the creative people would really like, because of his directness and gruffness.

Another one I learned a fair amount from, an entirely different kind of account, was Chef Boy-Ar-Dee.

An American Home product.

All accounts have their politics, but boy, they really had their politics in that one! Lipton did, too, but the weirdest thing—you know, the intramural jealousies were just incredible in those businesses, as you know just as well as I do.

Clients all try to climb over each other's back, and they're trying to use the agency to help them get up a notch. And I would get my arse in the middle of things. I got in one once, at American Home, that I didn't think I'd ever get out of. For some reason, I got involved with the head office, the parent company, with Bill Stedman and Walter Silbersack. Walter Silbersack was the President and Chairman, and Bill Stedman was the Director of Advertising for the whole shmear. And Stedman took a fancy to me, and Walter took a fancy to me. Well, that was fine, but it got me in trouble all the time with the guys in the Foods Division, because they hated my guts; because they couldn't open their trap without saying, "Well, that guy's going to go running to Silbersack." Well, I wasn't doing that, but they thought I was. And finally, they tried to get me thrown off the account.

And they did; they got me thrown off.

And ten minutes later, Walter Silbersack was on the phone, and he said, "I hear those bastards down in Foods have tried to get you off the business." And I said, "Yeah, Walter, they have; they've got me off." He said, "Don't move; you'll be back on in five minutes." And I was! He called Brock or somebody, and I was back on the business. What a nice situation to be in!

I lived through it; I don't know how, but I lived through it. I had the same kind of problems with Lipton. I was always getting into these terrible political things. I did get thrown off Lipton after ten years. I got in between the old management and the new management. The old management said, "Do it this way," the new management said, "Do it that way." And I was caught in between, on an Arthur Godfrey matter. I had to work with Arthur, which is about as difficult as anything could be, but I got along with Arthur. I could stand Arthur, and almost like him, for about an hour, an hour and a half, and then things started to go. But anyhow, I got caught in the middle, and got tossed off of that one.

How did you get up into management?

Well, I don't know, I honestly don't know. I had apparently done a successful job on important accounts, and in those days we had a system, like I guess other agencies do, where we had a Department Head and a Department Manager. Harry Harding was the Head of the Account Management Department—Contact Department, as it was then called—and he asked me to be his Manager, Manager of the Department. I had previously become a Vice-President at some point—that's a weird story.

I was over at Lipton one day, and I got a call from Ed Barnes, and he asked me to come back to the office by 5 o'clock, and he went and got Harry Harding. He said to Harry, "Now, tell Ed what I told you to tell him." And Harding said, "Well, we're announcing some new Vice-Presidents tomorrow, and you're not going to be one of them; but you are going to be on the next list of Vice-Presidents made." And Barnes said, "All right, that's all, go."

Somewhere along in there, Sig retired [Sigurd Larmon, President of the agency]. We had begun to think he never was going to retire, because he'd gone way past his own mandatory retirement age. I suspect that he felt there was nobody who could possibly run the agency once he was gone. But eventually, he decided that George Gribbin maybe would be able to swing it.

So at some point, I became Senior Vice-President, and then Executive Vice-President and General Manager, where I had everything under me except the Creative Departments, and Grib had all the Creative Departments under him, and we sort of split things.

He was President. But I don't think Grib ever liked the management end of the business very much. He was pretty good at it when he wanted to be, but he really didn't want to be very much, I don't think. He and I both, if we did anything that was of lasting importance in the agency, it was to begin the expansion of Y&R internationally.

It was important. You see, Sig had not wanted to. He didn't want to grow internationally very much. He wanted—and for his time, he was right, up to a point—he wanted to have important, big, profitable accounts, and a relatively limited number of them, here, where it was easy for him to keep his eye on them.

In his time, there wasn't much wrong with it. But as it became apparent to Grib and me and others that the international business was going to represent a big opportunity for long-term growth because there is a limit (at least I used to think there was) to domestic growth, under our system where you can't handle competitive accounts. This was before the multiple-merger kind of syndrome took over.

The Interpublic idea.

Yeah. So Grib and I—well, even before Sig left, I remember one of the first big, important things that happened in this area, as far as I'm concerned, was that I had been working on the Remington business for a number of years, Remington Shavers, and became very good friends with Henry Landsiedel, who was the President of the Shaver Division of Sperry-Rand.

Henry said that he had quite a bit of business in Europe, and he said, "We're going to have to get a new agency in Italy. We have good business there, and it's a good account, and if you will open a shop in Italy, you'll have our business." And I said, "Well, we certainly ought to be in Italy, and we have tried to get started there, and we've been having problems with Sig on it. But I'll go to work on it."

So I went back and got Grib, and said, "You know, we've got to do this, and we've got to do it fast, because this is what we need. We've got a nut right there, now, in our hot little hands, and this is the time to do it." So we tried; we bearded Sig, and he turned us down. Well, we kept after him until he finally agreed, and that was the beginning of our Italian business. Sig had limited our overseas business to Canada, in Ottawa and Montreal, and London and San Juan and Venezuela. That was all we had. J. Walter Thompson, you know, they were in 80,000 countries, and losing their tail in a lot of them, I know that; they were in a lot more countries than they wanted to be in, or should have been in.

And McCann was, too.

But that was the beginning of our rapid growth, and it was quite rapid. Of course, we had a pretty good office in London. But we went into England, France, Spain, Austria, all of the Scandinavian countries one after another; partly at the behest of, and interest of, Procter & Gamble. And we, as you know, had a lot of Procter business. We had more Procter business in Europe, by far, than anybody else. And typically—

You had more in Europe than you had in the U.S.

Yeah, we did. And typically, as soon as their business got big, they started taking it away from us. And we'd lose our butts in these little countries where you'd build up to handle the business, and then they'd cut us off at the knees. I'd get so mad sometimes I'd want to go down to Cincinnati and kill the bastards. But you know, you can't have everything, what the hell. But we broke all the Procter rules in Europe for a long while. We had competitive stuff, and it was only because the rule was all right to break as long as it was good for them. Once it was no longer good for them to break it—then you couldn't do it. And we had many of those cases. I have taken their names in vain many times. But they're smart, and they're good.

I don't remember the timing or all that stuff, but eventually, I made Ed Ney the head of International, and Steve Frankfurt the head of Domestic. And after a relatively short time, it was pretty clear that the set-up was fine, but I don't think the people were right in those respective jobs, and something had to give. And I had wanted for some time to take early retirement. I had done everything that I figured I could do. I could have worked another three or four years, and I'd have had a hell of a lot more money, but I don't think if I had a lot more money I would have led a different lifestyle. It's just not my dish of tea. So, the logical thing, it seemed to me, out of the choices I had, was to put Ney in charge of the whole thing; which, it has turned out, was a pretty good decision. He's done his thing very well. I think he's done a great job.

And the proof that it was right, I guess, is that he's done it in a way that I never would have done it. I wouldn't have done the things that he did. One thing he didn't do that I was certain he was going to do; I was sure he was going to go public. I know they did a study after I retired, not whether they were going to go public, but how and when, and after they did the study, they finally said, "This is not for us." Which made me feel good, because there'd been a lot of pressure internally on me to go public.

And I said, "No way, not so long as I'm running it. You guys can do whatever you want when I quit." Again, if I had gone public, if we had gone public, I would have made a bundle. And sometimes I say, "What a fool, you fool, you!" But I really don't feel badly about it.

I went through the same thing, Ed.

I guess some of the agencies that went public are glad they did, but some of them aren't, I'm sure.

Ogilvy's certainly very pleased about it, and I think Interpublic is very pleased about it. I don't know about all of them. Grey seems to be happy about it. Of course, they've grown so, these agencies.

And inflation's had something to do with it, but God, if you're not a billion dollars today, you're nothing!

That's right. You know, I was looking in a crystal ball then to the day when we might reach a billion dollars. It didn't take long!

Why did you want to get out early?

I guess the biggest single reason was one that I've never talked very much about; it's a personal reason. I have two wonderful daughters, and both of them had terrible problems, just terrible problems. And I guess there was a certain amount of guilt—

Because you were working so damn hard?

There were times when we just didn't know what was going to be next. I don't know whether having both parents around helped or not. I like to think it did. Anyhow, that was the biggest single reason.

So I just quietly did it; and I thought, you know, to be honest about it, I was pretty damned good as an Account Manager, I did a pretty damned good job. But I was never convinced I was terribly good as the head of an agency. I never was really convinced of it. Maybe I was better than I thought I was, but I never thought I was very good. And all these things were stirring around in me, and so I said, you know, "It's time to pull the string." And I don't regret it. I've had a marvelous time since.

Are you enjoying retirement?

147

With my motorcycle and my golf and shooting and all—and a computer, my God, I spend more time with a computer than anything else, especially in the wintertime. I love it.

April 30, 1982

PAUL FOLEY

Paul Foley retired in 1982 as a Director and Chairman of the Finance Committee of The Interpublic Group of Companies, Inc., the largest world-wide advertising-marketing communications organization. He had been associated with Interpublic's largest advertising agency, McCann-Erickson, Inc., since 1955. He was elected Chairman of the Board in 1964; and in November, 1968, also became Chief Executive Officer. In January, 1969, Mr. Foley was elected to the Board of Directors of the parent company, Interpublic; in April 1971, he became its President and Chief Executive Officer; in April, 1973, he also became Chairman. Mr. Foley relinquished his title of Chairman and CEO at Interpublic on December 31, 1979. He died October 30, 1983.

Following his graduation in 1937, with a B.A. in Journalism, magna cum laude, from the University of Notre Dame, he worked for several newspapers. During World War II, Mr. Foley served the U.S. Office of War Information in Istanbul, Turkey.

In 1946 he joined MacManus, John & Adams, Inc., Detroit, as a copywriter and left there as Executive Vice-President and member of the Board.

Mr. Foley was a Director of the Advertising Council and the International Executive Service Corps; a member of The American Academy of Advertising; and a member of The Newcomen Society in North America.

Mr. Foley received the 1973 Human Relations Award of the American Jewish Committee; the 1973 "For New York Award" from The City Club of New York; the 1976 Advertising Man of the Year Award from the Association for the Help of Retarded Children; in 1977 an "Outstanding Executive" award from *Financial World*; and a 1977 "Salute to New York" Silver Apple Award from Boys' Towns of Italy.

He was a member of the Board of Trustees of The University of Notre Dame and a recipient of its honorary degree of Doctor of Laws in 1976. In 1979 the Art Center College of Design in Pasadena conferred on him the honorary degree of Doctor of Humane Letters.

His book, *Fresh Views of the American Revolution*, was published July 1, 1976.

He was elected to the Advertising Hall of Fame in 1983.

PAUL FOLEY

Interview

I grew up in Pontiac, Mich. My father was the managing editor of the *Pontiac Daily Press*. He had been a writer most of his life. He started out writing little things for boys' magazines, and he was in newspapers for quite a while. Then, just as the war years were coming on, a young senator by the name of Truman came up, and tried to find out how people were going to live out at Willow Run where they were building all those big airplanes.

He got various reactions from various people, but it was my father's plan that he adopted, and they did indeed go ahead and build housing out there, and they built it on the premise that it would still be there after a war, assuming it wasn't blasted off with bombs.

That was part of the Federal Housing Administration's beginning. So that's how he slid into government. Then when that was over with, he went to Washington as the first Federal Housing Administrator.

He and my mother were there nearly 20 years. And I still have one little memento that I'm going to keep forever: a very fancy invitation from the White House to my mother and father for dinner, and on the back my mother had written her shopping list!

Just recently, the Truman Library called upon me and my sister to give them some more of our father's papers. He had sent them some before he died, but he had apparently not sent them too much of anything. So we went to work on that project not long ago. He had sent to me, four or five years ago, a whole packing case with a lot of papers in it, which I had just barely gone through. But we went through that and got it all set, and it's all down at the Truman Library.

I went to school in Pontiac—Catholic schools there—and at

one point I won some kind of a scholarship. But in any event, my family moved into Grosse Pointe, and I went to St. Paul's School there, a little Catholic school, and then I went down to Notre Dame. But that was in the Depression years—in the '30s. And when the first year was over with, there was no more money. I went back to Detroit and went to work. I worked in the County Building, doing tax things, etc. Three years later, I did get back to Notre Dame.

So I was a little older than the average freshman by that time, which turned out to give me confidence. So I went through Notre Dame; I was really involved in communications. And Hearst, at the time I graduated, was recruiting from colleges. I went directly from the campus to the *Chicago American,* a late and unlamented newspaper.

I worked there about three years, when a friend called me and said, "Hey, we're looking for writers here in Detroit." One of the agencies, MacManus John & Adams, was looking for writers. I said, "What are they paying?" and they said, "$9,000." I said, "Damn, I'll be there Monday."

What year was this?

I graduated from Notre Dame in '37, so this would be '39. And I went out and worked at MacManus, John & Adams.

As a copywriter?

Yeah, a copywriter. And old man Adams was still alive then, of course. He was running the place. He was a character, I tell you, he was something else. Big, big fat man. He never would go to his clients; the clients would have to come to him.

He was a writer?

He was a writer. Jim Adams was the guy who had the Cadillac and Pontiac accounts.

Chuck Adams' father, right? [Chuck Adams is currently Washington executive vice-president of the American Assn. of Advertising Agencies.]

That's right and he was quite a character. He wouldn't fly in airplanes. He always took the train. And even there, he was pretty big for the train seat. But he was very good to young guys like myself, if they had anything they could offer. He didn't try to keep it all in the family. There was quite a lot of family around. But on the creative side of the business, the writers and the people who were making the advertising, they didn't have to be cousins. The cousins and people were mainly on the account, business side. I liked Jim very much; he was a good man. I came down here to New York several times with him, on the train; he was always very fascinating. But from there, the war years came on very rapidly.

Jim Linen, later CEO of Time Inc., who was a space peddler in Detroit, was in New York with the Office of War Information, and asked me to come down. I was too old to be drafted and had a wife and child, so I went to work with the OWI.

Along with Thurmond L. Bernard and company?

Oh, yes. And for some reason, he sent me to the Bretton Woods Monetary Conference run by British economist John Maynard Keynes, even though I protested that I didn't know how to make change out of a dollar! And he said, "You just listen to people, they'll tell you." And it got to be pretty interesting. And when the conference was over—it lasted over two months—Jim Linen called me and said, "All right, you did a good job with this." So he sent me to Turkey, where I stayed for a couple of years.

When the war was over, I came back to New York and went directly to work for the Associated Press. And I got a call from a friend, who said MacManus John & Adams was looking for writers. And I said, "What are they paying?" "$9,000." "Damn, I'll be there Monday morning." And that was it. And I was in Mac-Manus John & Adams for about—

Wait a minute, Paul, I'm misunderstanding you. You went from the newspaper in Chicago to MacManus—

Yes.

And then after the war, you went with MacManus.

Yes.

Twice?

Twice.

Well, if they were paying $9,000 the first time, they must have been paying more the second time.

Well, they were paying maybe $10,000. But in any event, that's where I went. And I must say, I learned a good deal in that agency, because it was a little narrow track, that is, we were entirely dependent upon the automobile industry.

General Motors.

153

General Motors—Pontiac and Cadillac. I'll never forget Jim when I said, "You know, you haven't called up your clients very much." He called up—there was a new guy sent in to be director/manager of the Cadillac group. So Jim called him and said, "You've got some advertising here. Why don't you come on over to the agency on Wednesday (or whenever it was), and have lunch, and we'll talk about advertising." And this guy knew nothing about advertising: he was an engineer. So he came over, and Jim went through it with both feet—he had very meticulous hands for a big fat man—and he'd show him: "Here's this and that, and here's how we're going to do this, that and that," and when he gets down to where it says, "Here's what the cost will be, it'll be $3,000,000." And this little guy says, "THREE MILLION DOLLARS: Jesus!" He said, "Think of the engineering building I could build with that!" Jim says, "Don't worry. We'll build it for you."

Jim Adams could be pretty tough to work with sometimes, but essentially, he knew what he was doing. And he really believed in the superb Cadillac. To him, that was just like the Hope Diamond. And it was honest; he wasn't making it up just to get 15%; if they'd only given him 10% he would have done the same thing, probably. But that was a pretty interesting place to be.

Did he do any radio, or was he strictly print?

He was pretty much print, but by the time I was there, these other media were involved. As a matter of fact, I could do some of that, you see, which he didn't want to do, or others of us could do that. Ernie Jones (later president of the agency) was there, but Jones was never a writer; he was a salesman's salesman.

But I learned a good deal there as to what you can and cannot do. I was—I've forgotten how the hell I happened to get to New York. No, I don't either. We were down around the Fisher Building somewhere, as I remember. I got a call from someplace saying, "McCann-Erickson is opening an office in Detroit, and they need somebody that knows something about the automobile business to help them out." And what with one thing and another I became the guy. And I joined that company on the very same day that McCann got the Coca-Cola account. I figured, "Holy Toledo! I've fallen right into the biggest account you can possibly fall into." Let's see—this was about 1952 or 1953.

I didn't stay too long in Detroit. I was there about four years. Then I was moved into McCann in New York.

As a writer?

Always as a writer. And I spent nine or ten years over there. For about seven or eight of those years, I was chairman of the place, if there can be a chairman of an advertising agency, and I'm not sure there can. I was in charge of it, for whatever it was worth.

How did that happen, Paul? That's one of the things I'd like to probe on a little bit. You were a writer, and you had a group of guys supporting you.

The basis of McCann is Esso/Exxon. That's pretty close to automobiles. And they didn't have enough people that knew that, or felt that kind of a relationship. And I think there was a time when Esso wanted somebody in there who knew something about the automobile business. That's what they were living off of. H. K. McCann was the advertising manager of Standard Oil Company when the dissolution of that company took place, and somebody said to him, "Harry, if you'll open an agency, we'll give you the account." So he did, and we've still got it 60 years later. But still, it had to be more than just that one client; that was the problem they were having over there. Most of the people there had grown up on Esso/Exxon; and with the new media coming—television, radio, this, that and the other—you needed a wider span, so they were looking around for people, writers for television. I never got very much into television when I was there, other than to write things for it. I never was involved in producing it.

I was there nine years, something like that, when Armando Sarmento of Interpublic came over to me and said, "Look, Marion Harper's leaving, you've got to come over." I'd never been over there. I really didn't even know it existed. But he said, "You've just got to be there, you've got to go over." Harper had gone, trailing all his problems behind him. "Somebody's got to go over there, and we've got to go public," Sarmento said. "And if we're going to go public, we've got to have somebody with some visibility in the advertising agency business, some background that people will understand, and you're the guy to do it." I said, "All right, but why me?" Well, you're a writer, you're writing the advertising, and I think it would be an easier transition than if we picked out

155

somebody who's a technician or lawyer or something." And after considerable pulling and hauling, I said, "All right, I'll give it a go."

So where was Bob Healy at this point? Because he had retired and came back.

He came back, yes, and it was also on the same premise that I just mentioned. Sarmento got to him, too. He, of course, was not interested, was not involved in the creative process at all; he was a good financial man, and knew the territory, and had great credibility with clients, and was a tower of strength at that time. But, as I say, when I came over here, Jesus, I had to get rid of about fifteen people. I didn't even know who the hell they were.

Well, you know Marion; he just loaded them by the dozen.

The Bob Durham crowd was still here, and we had to sweep that out pretty fast. It wasn't all fun, I must say.

Sarmento was right; in order to go public, we had to have some kind of a package to sell. So what we did finally was, when we decided that we were going to go public, and got that done technically, then we visited all kinds of people in the financial communities as to what advertising was about, because they didn't believe in it at all.

As an investment, they certainly didn't.

Too flimsy, as an investment. But we worked hard at it, and I think we gave them some good ideas about it. At least it worked.

Well, did Bob Healy come in as the chairman when he came back?

He was chairman for a while, I guess, before I came over.

But I didn't come over as chairman, at the beginning; I came over as president. But Healy said, "You do it, you are a contemporary guy, you do it. I'll back you up, you know, anything you want me to do." Which he sure did, and he was a good financial man, which I am not. And of course, Bill Hogan, we got him on the board. When we went public, we had to have a board.

And then we brought in these guys. And we had one woman, who we still keep around here.

She formerly had been a Catholic nun. She ran Hunter College for a while—Jacqueline Wexler.

But anyhow, that's how I came over here. I'd never been in the building before, but it was not all that difficult, because what we had to do was new anyhow. It had not been done before. So we could start from that point, that is, going public.

That was after Harper, you went public. You had very little truck with him?

No, he was still around. I had quite a lot of truck with him. He called me at one point and said: "You kind of talk to the guys over here and tell them to cut this thing out, they're going to ruin everything. Tell them to shut up." You know, he was trying to get back, but gee, he had done so many things so strangely. The guy had a genius, there's no question about it. But he had absolutely no respect for money. None! There he buys this goddam airplane, you know. And a Viennese boy with a fancy suit walking around with the booze and everything.

And then he bought a whole company with airplanes up in Westchester.

Yeah, well, Healy stayed on, of course, and it worked out well, it worked out just fine, that's my point. But I was hesitant, because what the hell am I going to do with a typewriter over here? You know, I'm not going to make any ads over here!

How long have you had that typewriter?

Got it in MacManus, from the Pontiac Group. It says right here, "To Paul Foley from the Pontiac Group, 1955." They gave it to me.

And it was old when you got it.

Oh, yes, it was an old thing. "Through these rollers passed the most beautiful words in the world."

I think one of the things that a book of the kind you are planning can do, and undoubtedly will do, is to get rid of some of these shibboleths of people coming and going, and everything falling apart. The advertising agency business is a good solid business.

You bet it is. And wonderful people.

The only real assets you've got are the people, and therefore you try to get the best you can. And you're not in a situation like saying, "Well, people with two or three slides into second base, we're going to fire 'em."

You don't do that.

You don't do that, because that's all you've got. And the cry and need for them is becoming bigger and more eager. You pretty much have to be very much people-oriented, internally as well as externally. And when you get right down to it, that's all you've got is people, and of course, you've got clients. If you don't have clients, you don't have any of the people you want.

Well, you're very modest about your assignment as the head of Interpublic, but my God, here you were, the chief executive of the biggest conglomerate of advertising agencies and communication groups in the world, and it must have been interesting to run, it must have been complex; you must have had a lot of problems, and a lot of opportunities. You make it sound very simple.

There were problems, but they were pretty much the same problems that agencies have, except bigger. The fact that we are not an agency here, that we don't make any advertising here, makes a very big difference in how you function. It took me a hell of a long time to get over that. I didn't tend to see that, and I've found it, now, in Geier [Philip Geier, chairman of Interpublic], a little bit. He also wants to not only run the corporation, he wants to run every agency in the thing, and that just won't work. It may work once in a while, but unless you're called upon by them, there's no reason why you should be monkeying around with them.

For example, when we bought Campbell-Ewald, that was an interesting story, and I'll tell you about it, because I was in Europe doing some work on the Opel account, and I went up to one of the guys who was running that business at General Motors. And all of a sudden this Opel executive reaches into his desk drawer and pulls out a whole stack of business cards, maybe 20, and spreads them all out for me. From various ad agencies—and Tom Adams' is one of them. And here's what he wants me to do: he wants me to have all these 15 agencies. And I said, "Now you know I can't do that."

And that was the first hint I had that Tom Adams (Campbell-Ewald chairman) wanted to get overseas. It didn't surprise me much, because it was getting more and more difficult to get top-grade people to work on one account in one city. So that's when I decided we ought to go and see if he would join this organization. We could take him, the company, to whatever he wanted to do; we certainly could take him overseas; and it took a year and a half to get that wrapped up.

And he has been with us; they are overseas, very well overseas. But more than anything else, he can get much better people now, because they have much more variety to offer people than before. He opened in New York, you know as well as I, four or five times, and went clunk, clunk, clunk. Because he just couldn't attract the people to that one account. And when we finally got the deal done, and got him overseas, I think it was a whole new ballgame for him. And for us, it was a very good thing.

It's worked out very well. Tom has changed quite a bit. He's not quite that—well, he still is Mr. Detroit of the agency business, but he's got a much broader horizon than he had.

He even comes to New York once in a while now. Which he hates.

Yeah, he hates New York, but he's here quite a bit. But you couldn't possibly get this whole thing done without some kind of problems here and there. And he's had some, and we've had some, but nothing of any great seriousness. For a while, we were diving a little, but he and Geier were not seeing eye to eye. But that's pretty well changed. I think we're in a pretty healthy state now, because I got after Tom, and I said, "Look, you've got to make the change." He was sitting up at the end of it. And it worked out fine. He enjoys the business a little bit more than he used to, I think, but still, he's a Detroiter, and that's fine. I think that's great.

Well, you've got two terrific guys in Tom Adams and Al Seaman of SSC&B and the people behind them.

Of course, the Seaman thing grew out of this—whatever it is— the big companies still in Europe. Lintas of Unilever. This was one reason I was interested. McCann-Erickson, by and large, has never really been very big on the consumer items that are on the shelf.

That's right. They never have been a packaged goods agency.

No, not really. They had some little odds and ends here and there. But they didn't have that background, which is getting to be more and more important all the time.

So we had to have somebody in this system that had those skills. And it was Geier, of course, because of his time in Europe, that knew how to get that one done, that knew that that company was interested in getting it done. So that's worked out very well, and Al's has been a great group to have around.

Well, did you bring Phil Geier into the business?

Yeah, in a way, I did. He never would say it that way; he was already involved, he'd been hired by someone out in Cleveland, I think. He was in our Cleveland office for a while. But that was too narrow-based for him, basically. Yes, I was the only one who knew him, as a matter of fact. He was in McCann and then came over here to Interpublic. But he really has a more contemporary point of view about the money side of this business, that whole aspect of it, and he's a hell of a hard worker. As a matter of fact, that's one of his main problems.

Works all the time.

Yeah, a workaholic.

Well, it's nice to have a guy like that running the show, though.

He has to do it with a little finesse. He's had some problems between himself and McNamara once in a while, because McNamara is a lawyer, and he's a very easy, cool guy, and Geier's in there saying, "Look, we've got to get this done by 2:00!" But that's calmed down quite a bit now. He's doing well, and he's well regarded in the business, as far as I know. So it's been an interesting time, I must say.

Well, where does Interpublic go from here, Paul, as you see it? I guess you could still take on more agencies.

Well, what we can do, as we have done recently, is put three or four agencies in the same country—like in France, for example. There are places in the world where we have done that—Latin America, particularly—where we have four or five agencies. But in Latin America, where I think there's a great deal yet to be done, we're doing very well. I would have thought the age was going to be pretty tough for this business, or anybody's business. But business has been surprisingly good, which I think has something to say about advertising as no longer kind of a special thing.

They don't stop spending like they used to when things get tough. I think, as a matter of fact, the smart guys keep the spending up, and even increase it a little bit sometimes.

That's happened to us in Brazil, and of course, Brazil is a hell of a big country, and that could be overlooked.

That could be one of the big countries of the future, I think.

And Geier's international experience was considerable; he was in London quite a long time, and not only just in London, but in

Europe. So he has a pretty good grasp of that; a more contemporary grasp probably, than the others.

Tell me, Paul, what's your philosophy about the advertising business?

I say that there was a time when *homo sapiens* began to be able to talk. Now I think we have to say it's *homo communicato,* man in communication with all other people. That concept is right down the alley of communications, and while we can't use that word in the same sense that others might, it is what we're doing. Communication.

We're communicators. And we're communicators expecting something to happen, which not all communicators are. So that when we communicate, we want something to happen.

Let me ask you what your thoughts are on advertising education, what you think about it, what you know about it. Is it important, or isn't it?

I think it's on an upbeat now. For a while, even those who were teaching it were not all that up-to-date, and there were professors who thought it was a little beneath them. Now, where the university has a marketing school, advertising is part of that. Whether that's happening on a large scale or not, I don't know, but it seems to be happening.

It's growing.

I find at Notre Dame, for example, now people say, "Notre Dame doesn't need any publicity, they've got all the publicity in the world!" Yeah, it's all football. Academically it's a very, very good school, and far better than it ever was before. So they're teaching communications, and even dipping into media these days, because that's what these kids want to know. They'll take all the usual Latin or whatever they have to take, but more and more, most universities, even those with the very high motives, are really preparing people for their careers.

That's what they're supposed to do, and they can't do it just by following their old policy over and over again. The fact that you went to Yale doesn't mean that you can go over and get a job any place. It doesn't work today. Guys say, "Well, what can you *do?*" Don't tell them you went to Yale, but what can you do? Now, they don't want to get to be just schools that turn out plumbers or something. I can understand that all right. But they do have to understand that they are responsible, to some degree, to make these young people—the bright ones and the not-so-bright ones—capable of doing things that need to be done, not simply have a degree and then sit around on a bench all the time and go back to the alumni affairs. And I think even the most testy of them all have come out for that point of view.

It used to be, and you know as well as I do, to get into some of those types of schools like Princeton or some place or other, you had to have two or three grandfathers that had been there, or some way of getting in, and they were good universities, no question about it. But they were a little bit outside the norm. Take Detroit, for example. The University of Detroit, when run by the Jesuits, was not doing too damn well. They were kind of specialized; I've forgotten what their specialty was. But finally they got wise; they've got to go in for the practical business of educating people for a life and a career, instead of just the liberal arts. Liberal arts are fine, but you've got to have more than that. You can't make a living with it any more.

It's interesting, Paul, these girls that we're all hiring in the business today, going right into jobs as account executives. We've had them for years in media and research.

That's right. And we thought that's where they should be.

Yes, but now they've gone into copy and production of TV, and my God, I'll tell you, our account management department, over half of them are women today, and they are so competitive with these young fellows they're making some of them look sick.

Well, look at this Mean Joe Green commercial for Coca-Cola. That was done by a woman, a couple of women. And damn, I'm telling you that was a blockbuster. And I must say that in the case of McCann, right now, their creative department—probably among the best talent they have are these women.

That's right. That's what we find.

And I said, "Well, hang on to them! Don't let them go!"

We've had women in creative for quite some time. But the thing that has developed over the last few years is the women that are in account management, running the accounts. They're doing a hell of a job.

Yes, they are. As a matter of fact, most clients like it. We've got a couple of women sitting over here right now who are red-hot, and we'll have a lot more women, I hope. Ten or fifteen years ago, you'd have had no woman that she could talk to at the client. But now that's changed, too. Plus which, she doesn't have to talk to women, she can talk to men.

Let me ask you just one more question. What are your plans for the future? I know you're here for a while, but I mean, what do you see ahead for you?

Well, I think I'm going to do at least another book. I've been thinking, toying with it. I'm thinking of doing a book which has nothing to do with the advertising business at all: *The Fountains of New York.*

We've got *The Fountains of Rome* already. *The Fountains of New York.* And it shouldn't be too difficult to get the data from the Parks Department. What caused me to think about this was, in my apartment—870, right over the East River—there's this big fountain you see going all the time.

How long will you be sitting in Interpublic? Forever, do you want to?

No, I was asked to stay for three years. I'm about halfway through. And I don't have to come in here every day, unless I feel like it. On the other hand, I like the idea that I can come back in. But, you know, I think I'm going to get working on that book.

I will stay on the board, probably. Even longer than that three years. The three years thing was set up just to see that nothing went screwy with the new group. And that's how things have gone, but that's pretty much over with.

October 8, 1981

ARTHUR C. FATT

Arthur C. Fatt joined Grey Advertising at age 17, while continuing his education at New York University. He has been with Grey ever since, and from 1956 to 1961 he was President and Chief Executive Officer.

From 1961 to 1970, he was Chairman of the Executive Committee, assuming the title of Founder-Chairman on January 1, 1970, which title he holds currently.

During this 62-year period, Grey grew from a one-room office to the fifth largest domestic agency and the ninth largest international agency in the world, with offices in nineteen countries. Mr. Fatt has played a major role in the expansion of Grey abroad.

Mr. Fatt is a native New Yorker, and attended the city's primary schools, continuing his studies at New York University.

He plays an active role in many charitable institutions, both local and national; is a Trustee of Brandeis University; Vice-President of Hillside Hospital and a member of the Board of Trustees of Long Island Jewish-Hillside Medical Center; a member of the Board of Federation of Jewish Philanthropies and Anti-Defamation League; and a Member at Large, National Council, Boy Scouts of America.

Mr. Fatt served on the executive committee of the National Marketing Advisory Committee of the U.S. Department of Commerce. He is a former Director of the Harvard University Seminar for advertising and marketing executives and has been the recipient of many awards from the advertising industry.

Additionally, Mr. Fatt is author of *How to Sell To and Through Department Stores*.

ARTHUR C. FATT

Interview

I was born on 83rd Street in Manhattan. I live on 81st Street now. I have two homes out of the country: one in Barbados, and one in Mallorca, Spain. I was too young for World War I and too old for World War II. And every night of my life, I have had an apartment on Manhattan Island, which I think is unique.

I went to public school here, and then to the High School of Commerce, where I was editor of the weekly newspaper, called the *Commerce Courier,* and the monthly magazine, called the *Commerce Caravel;* and I also was a reporter for the *New York Globe,* which was an important newspaper at that time, writing school news; so that, when I was graduated from high school, I decided I would go to work, and wanted to take courses at New York University, some during the day, and some during the night. And when I looked for a job, I had in mind that I was writing, and it seemed to me that something connected with writing made sense.

And so I think when I was offered two jobs in 1921—one by Standard Oil Company of New Jersey at $29 a week—and one by the Grey Studio at $15 a week, I took the Grey Studio job, feeling it had more connection with writing and with advertising.

Now the fact of the matter is, it was not then an advertising agency; they didn't have a single account. And the man I went to work for, Larry Valenstein, was located in a tenement house on East 29th Street, and I walked up three flights of stairs into a two-room office. One was a bedroom occupied by a homosexual artist, who slept there; the other was a much smaller room, containing two desks, one occupied by a man by the name of William Hedler, and the other by Larry Valenstein. So all I had was a chair.

How old was Larry then, Arthur?

He was 22. I have often wondered why I took the job, it must

167

have really been fate. And while I don't believe in fate, it was a job that anybody with good judgment would probably not have accepted. That's how I got into the business.

Now Larry's business, at that time, was syndicating direct mail to fur stores. Actually, he issued a series twice a year, once for August fur sales and once for storage, so that there were two mailings a year; and that was his whole business.

How long had he been in that business?

Probably three or four years. He was a youngster. The first week when I was on the job, I wasn't occupied a great deal, so I walked up Broadway with these announcements, and the first store I called on was a store called S. Aranow, and I got an order for $278. Larry had promised me 15% commission on the business I did, so I made almost two weeks' salary on that first day. As a consequence of my ability to sell these things, I went around New York City and sold them; then I took trips to Philadelphia, Baltimore, Washington, Chicago, and sold them quite extensively and quite successfully.

That gave us some capital. Now, interestingly enough, Bart, on the train going from Chicago to St. Paul, I was in an upper berth —going with the purpose of calling on fur stores to sell these announcements. And I didn't sleep very well, and I thought during the night, "Why the hell do we get out only two a year? Why not get out a magazine, called *Furs and Fashions?*" I named it in bed and I even took some paper out and made a dummy, so that when I got to St. Paul the next morning, I had a little dummy of what I called *Furs and Fashions;* and I explained it to a young lady whose name was Eva Hope. She worked for a fur store called F. Victor Ekholm.

And she said, if we turned it out, she would buy it. When I got back to New York and explained it to Larry, he said, "Go ahead and do it." So we turned out *Furs and Fashions,* and then I travelled all over the United States, selling it only to one store in a city; but on the basis of the business that we did on *Furs and Fashions,* we made enough capital to get some people to move our offices to bigger space, and to hire more professional advertising people. Now, as a result of the background that we had in furs, Larry went out and got the A. Hollander & Son account, which at that time was the largest fur dyer and dresser. But they weren't doing any national advertising; they were doing trade advertising. And I got the Mendoza Beaver account, and our first national advertisement was placed in the *Ladies' Home Journal* of August 1926. At that time, you needed American Newspaper Publishers Assn. recognition, Periodical Publishers Assn. recognition, and Curtis was separate. The first ad we placed with Curtis was placed before we got recognition. They gave us recognition immediately thereafter, but they never paid us the commission on that first August ad. And I tried to get it for years and years, but I was never successful in getting them to pay that commission.

So that was the beginning of my involvement with Grey Studios; and after we got the Hollander account and the Mendoza Beaver account, we turned our minds toward becoming an advertising agency and changed the name of the company from Grey Studios to Grey Advertising Service. Subsequently it was changed again, to Grey Advertising Agency, but that was the transition at that time.

Very interesting. Okay, now you'd moved to better quarters, and you started hiring a few skilled people. Now tell me about how you started building this agency. You were Mr. Outside and Larry was Mr. Inside, is that what you were?

Well, pretty much. I was the salesman, so to speak, and we moved first from East 29th Street to 25 East 30th Street, but that, too, was a residence, a larger apartment. And Larry's artist, at that time—he was not an art director—his name was Charlie Cullen, and he slept in the quarters where we had the office. And we were there for a couple of years, and got a few additional accounts, mostly ready-to-wear.

From 25 East 30th Street we moved to the Greeley Arcade Building at 128 West 31st Street, where there was a resident buying firm on the seventh and eighth floors, and we occupied part of the ninth floor. This resident buying firm had a group of stores for whom they bought certain apparel, and they had a trade name called Carolyn, and they were beginning to advertise. I heard about it, and I walked from the ninth floor to the seventh and eighth floors and called on a man named John Block, who was the head of Kirby, Block & Fischer, and the head of this Carolyn Modes—that was a subsidiary firm of theirs. And I think largely because of proximity, because it certainly wasn't experience, he gave us the Carolyn account.

And that, too, helped us in what then was the ready-to-wear field. Again, I walked up Seventh Avenue, because we were close by, at 31st Street between Sixth Avenue and Seventh Avenue, and I would call from one floor to another on ready-to-wear companies; and I succeeded in getting a few companies, one called Little Lady Coats—actually, the name of the firm was Knobel & Bloom, and their trademark was Little Lady Coats—and that became a fairly active account at that time. And as a result of the proximity to Seventh Avenue, and the little business we had, our first business, almost entirely, was ready-to-wear. We had a Noxal Blouse Company, a hosiery company, Mojud Hosiery—and other things related to ready-to-wear.

Shortly thereafter, we hired a fellow by the name of Ed Weiss, who was working on *Printers' Ink*. And he joined us and started to publish *Grey Matter,* which is a publication which we still issue, but in those days we issued it nine months a year, and now we don't issue it quite as frequently. In those days it was four pages, and today sometimes an edition might be twelve pages. It's a more sophisticated house organ today than it was then. But interestingly enough, shortly after the third or fourth edition went out, two men walked into our office, named Sem Deitrich and Lou Bonham, and they said they were with the Mennen Company. Mennen was then very important; shaving cream, hair tonic, things of that nature. And by the time they left the office, they had given me—I was the one that interviewed them—our first packaged goods account.

What year was that, roughly?

I would say 35 years ago, or more. Let's see—I would say 45 years ago. And we've had the Mennen account ever since. From that first exposure to a packaged goods account, and with *Grey Matter* giving us more publicity, we expanded our efforts to get business in the packaged goods field, and one by one, we grew.

Good fortune has to play a part in almost every firm's activities. And you may remember a fellow by the name of Mortimer Berkowitz, who was the head of *American Weekly.*

I certainly do—One of the great salesmen of all time, in my judgment.

That's right. And he was retiring from *American Weekly*, and came to see Larry and myself, and we decided to give him a job as a salesman for Grey. One day he said to me, "Arthur, I have an appointment at Procter & Gamble, with a man whose name is Clem Uhling." A name you probably remember.

Sure. C. C. Uhling. I know him well.

And I said, "Mort, I'd like to go with you," because I didn't think that he knew enough about Grey Advertising to call on as important an advertiser as Procter & Gamble. He consented to my going with him, and we went out and had this interview together with Clem Uhling. It seemed like a pretty nice interview, but nothing evolved from that meeting. We were back only a few weeks, and lo and behold, the Biow Agency closed. And almost within days, Clem Uhling called us and gave us a couple of assignments from Procter & Gamble; one was Lilt Home Permanent, and another was Shasta Shampoo. And from that beginning with Procter & Gamble, we really entered the big time field of advertising.

As important as getting the Procter & Gamble business, we got about seven people from the Biow Agency that closed, some of their top people, and a few of them are still with us; and as a matter of fact, our present chief executive officer, Ed Meyer, was one of those people, and he has obviously contributed very importantly from the time that he was president to today, where we have grown from reasonably humble circumstances to one of the top ten agencies, and while we today have 25 offices throughout the world, our total billing will aggregate a billion dollars this year.

One of the other good things that happened to us is that we got an account called Soft-Light Lens Co., and they had connections with Bausch & Lomb; and a chap by the name of Herbert Strauss was working for Bausch & Lomb, and he came to work for Soft-Light Lens Co. We became friendly, and then he went off to World War II, and when he came back, we hired him for Grey Advertising. And that was a splendid addition, because he was not only a great man, he succeeded me as president of the agency. And he was a magnificent human being, in addition to being a fine businessman. Unfortunately, he died prematurely.

One other interesting and lucky event occurred, which I think I might mention here. I was in Paris, and I went to the concierge at the hotel, and asked for a couple of tickets to the *Folies Bergere*. And he got me a couple of tickets, and they were in the box alongside of the stage. During the course of the program, a couple of almost-nude chorus girls came up and took me by the hand, and put me on the stage, and I was not reluctant to comply. And I stood there, doing nothing.

Came intermission, I went in to the lobby, and a chap came along and said to me, "You're Arthur Fatt, aren't you?" And I said, "Yes." He said, "I'm Sam Dalsimer. We met a number of years ago at a charitable affair." And I said, "What are you doing, Sam?" He said, "I'm with the firm of Cecil & Presbrey"—then, a reasonably important advertising agency. We talked in the theater, and came back to New York, and then I read that Cecil & Presbrey closed their doors. So I called Sam Dalsimer, and said, "Sam, remember, we met at the *Folies Bergere*?" He said, "Of course I remember, Arthur." I said, "I hear your firm is closing. How about talking with us?" And he was handling the Block Drug Company, which was a multi-national advertiser, and I succeeded in convincing Sam that he should come with us; and he did, and brought the Block Drug account with him. And that's an account we still have with us to this day, and it bills in the multi-millions of dollars; and, again, we have had this piece of business, which actually I don't believe would have occurred if I hadn't met Sam Dalsimer in Paris.

A wonderful man, Sam. I knew Sam and Herb both very well. They were great guys, Arthur, both of them.

I referred to them in the talk I made at our 60th anniversary as being among Grey's greatest alumni. Unfortunately, they both died prematurely, and they both must have had premonitions, because they came to me separately and asked to retire. I persuaded both of them to stay on with the company on a reduced work schedule, anything that they wanted to pursue, because they were both such magnificent men, and I don't believe in the history of Grey Advertising that we ever had two better performers, and two better advertising men.

Herb went into semi-retirement, bought a house down in St. Thomas, and had a heart attack entering his apartment building in St. Thomas, and died on the spot. Sam came to me after he was on some sort of a reduced schedule, and said that he had been offered—I think it was the presidency of the Anti-Defamation League. And I said to him, "Sam, if you wanted to leave Grey because of the intensity of work, you're going to take on two or three times as much activity at Anti-Defamation League." But that was a burning interest in him, and he took the job, and on one of the trips travelling around the country for Anti-Defamation, Sam died. Both of them, as I said, had come to me separately, and I repeat: they were splendid people who had a great deal to do with the growth of Grey. Actually, when we got the Procter & Gamble business, Sam was the account supervisor for the total account.

And one of the fellows that came from Biow whose name was Jerry Stolzoff was the account executive on the Lilt and Shasta business. Now today we represent Procter & Gamble all over the world, and I would presume, though this isn't official and it's a pure guess on my part, that worldwide we probably do $100 million worth of business with Procter & Gamble, in all of the countries where they are and we are.

And the people that came to us from Biow were some very important creative people, Ben Alcock and Bernie Kahn, who were creative directors with us for quite a time until they retired. I frankly don't have any idea where they are today. They're not any longer connected with us. But of the original people that came to us from Biow, Larry Deckinger [media director] is still with us; a girl by the name of Betty Coumbe, she's vice-president for spot broadcasting; and of course, the most tremendous individual was Ed Meyer, who became our chief executive officer after Herb Strauss, and who has done so very, very much in building the agency to its present position. I call him a workaholic. He just works all the time; and he's smart, dedicated, and very capable. So he has all the combinations that one needs.

Tell me, Arthur, in your relationship with Larry, as the agency grew and got into all these different phases of business, with so many prominent clients, you were the guy who got most of this business, or opened the doors ...

In the early days, that was true.

Larry ran the inside of the business. While he was not a creative director by himself, he supervised the inside running of the agency. I would say that Larry's abilities were: his executive ability, and money affairs, and his good relationship with people. Actually, in the 60 years that we have been together, we have never had an unpleasant word.

For heaven's sake!

I went to work for Larry as an office boy, and I would say it wasn't seven years before we were equal partners, and have remained equal partners throughout the years. Of course, when we sold the majority of our stock in Grey to other employees, our ownership, which at one time was 50-50, diminished considerably; but I think it's interesting that the man I went to work for as an office boy ended up as my friend and my partner. And even to this day, we are very close friends, and so are our wives. They get along together as well as we do. [Larry Valenstein died in September, 1982, at the age of 83.]

That's wonderful. Now let me ask you some things specifically. You're going to do about $1,000,000,000. Now, that requires a lot of very smart people, and I'm sure you must do some recruiting among the colleges. Can you tell me a little bit about how you do that, and what you look for, and what you think of advertising education—or don't you think it's important?

I think it's very important. The fact of the matter is, we are constantly recruiting; we have, I think 1,200 people in our New York office, and obviously that grew from Larry Valenstein, Bill Hedler, Charlie Cullen and myself. So the progress has been rather dramatic. I'm inclined to think that very few of the advertising agencies that are important today grew from such humble beginnings as we did, because it was not an advertising agency at the beginning; it just evolved into one.

You know, I doubt if there is any other major agency that, today, is run by the founders. I can't think of one.

It would be unfair to say that we run it today. We don't. I wish I could say that I was active in the firm's activities today. That would be an exaggeration. I'm delighted to say that at the age of 77, I'm still permitted to come here and occupy quarters, delightful quarters, alongside of my partner, Larry Valenstein; and my contacts are mostly with clients that I brought into the agency, and today they're mostly social contacts, because I've been with Grey for 60 years, and obviously I didn't start at the age of two, so I'm

77 years of age now, and that's hardly an age where people want active account supervisors.

But we do periodic solicitation at various universities. Now, that's a part of the job that I have never been involved in, so I know less about it than I know about other phases of the business.

I was just wondering what your attitude is. As I've talked with people, some people think that advertising education is a very important thing, and that we ought to try to improve it; there are others that feel very strongly that it is a waste of time, and they will tell you, "Give me some bright person, woman or man, that gets out of college, that has had a liberal arts education, is a good writer, has a good mind, knows how to think; we'll train them in our business."

It's hard to make a positive decision one way or the other. I have been encouraging the School of Commerce at New York University, where I indicated to you I'm involved.

Do you do some lecturing?

No, I'm not doing any lecturing; but I'm on the board of directors of part of the university, not the entire university, and I've been encouraging them to have more advertising courses, because it seemed to me that they have so many more accounting courses, and, of course, law and other things, but they haven't been as progressive with advertising courses as I think is warranted. And they're improving the number of courses, and variety.

But I'm no longer involved, really, with soliciting new people in the agency; nor am I involved with the progress that is being made at universities around the country, other than at New York University. I do know that our personnel people interview at a number of different universities each year, soliciting whom they consider the most able, brightest, most promising young folks to join the agency. That's an important and continuing effort, and I suspect that it will get even more important as time goes on, because as the universities increase the intensity of their courses, and more young people take advertising courses, and as the demand of advertising for personnel increases, as it has been increasing and will increase, we will need to find more and more potential employees.

No question about it. It's happening all the time. We need them. Okay. You've had, I think, personally, and your company, a very fine relationship with the trade press, the advertising trade press. Do you have any comments you'd like to make about the trade press, what you think they contribute to our business? Do they help it or hurt it?

When you speak about the advertising trade press, it seems to me you're talking about *Advertising Age*, today.

At one time, *Printers' Ink* was the Bible, our No. 1 periodical. But *Advertising Age* is so all-inclusive today; as a matter of fact, I try to go through each issue, and I find I take it home; it takes me almost a whole evening just to go through it! Now, I don't read every article, but there is enough current news about what's going on in the advertising business that interests me, obviously, having spent 60 years in advertising and today with quite a variety of accounts. And having been a salesman at heart, I watch the movement of accounts with more than passing interest, so that my only trade publication that I pay any attention to is *Advertising Age*.

Of course, I look at *Forbes* and other regular magazines, and I'm a subscriber to a great many newsletters; however, they're mostly financial newsletters. And I'm always amused that one newsletter will say, "Buy," and the next one you read will say, "Sell." So that you can't get any strong opinion one way or the other from reading these newsletters. If anything, you get confusion.

Tell me what you think of comparative advertising, which is a relatively new thing in our industry. What's your reaction to it?

Well, in some respects, it surprises me. For a company to come out and clearly say, "We are better than A, B, C, D . . ."—obviously, those are challenging statements. I guess they must provide the periodicals, the media, with some substantiation to make comparative statements like that. And all I can say is, they surprise me, because they're persuasive, and yet I can't completely bring myself to the belief that that's the best course for advertising to take. I think the consumer is importantly influenced by that. But it would seem to me that, brought up as I was, the best thing to do is extol your own virtues, rather than take cracks at the competition. And I wouldn't be surprised if those comparisons will, one day soon, be ruled out.

You think so?

Well, I'm not sure. But it's an interesting development, and we have to keep our eyes open as to what will develop.

One of the things I wonder about, myself is, I wonder if there is anybody else in the advertising business that has been employed in one company for 60 years.

I doubt it.

I suspect, If I had not been a founder of the business, and a principal stockholder, that I would have had to retire at an earlier age. The agency doesn't have mandatory retirement, but it doesn't look with favor on people staying over 65. Well, here I am, 77, and Larry Valenstein's 82, and while it's hard to say that we're active, at least I'm down here every day that I'm in the country. And then I travel a great deal around the world. I think it's fair to say that I started Grey International.

Yes, you did, and you built it.

Well, strangely, our first company was Canada, which seemed like a natural and easy move from the United States. But then after a while I went to Larry Valenstein and said to him, "Larry, don't you think we ought to be abroad?" And he said, "Yes."

When did you actually start going overseas?

That would be in '62. We went to Jere Patterson [a consultant on foreign business and advertising] when we decided to go abroad, because we didn't know the name of a single advertising agency at that time. He gave me the names of the first four or five companies that I did business with. The first one I called on was Nicholas Kaye, of Charles Hobson agency in London. And I made an arrangement to buy an interest in his business, and since then, he is out of the business, and we own it 100%. That was in '62. In '64 I called on Jacques Hirsch in Paris, and he had the Dorland agency in both Paris and Brussels, and we bought an interest with him.

Then, the next year, I went to Germany and called on Mr. Gramm of the Gramm Agency, again a reference from Jere Patterson, and Mr. Gramm was not very anxious to do business with us. But he had two younger men working for him, Theo Breidenbach and Chris Kleinau, and both of those were even younger than I, and they persuaded Mr. Gramm to join forces with us; and we have been together with Gramm ever since, and Gramm, today— it's Gramm-Grey—is one of the largest agencies in Germany.

But being all over the world today, I had, for example, a hand in calling on Australia, making the first contact there, and South

Africa. And interestingly enough, South Africa today is one of our most profitable, if not the most profitable, international office. Interestingly enough, when I was on my way to South Africa from Europe, I received a wire from the executive committee suggesting that I not go to South Africa, and I think that their prejudice about South Africa is almost the same as the prejudice that exists today because of apartheid. But I was the chief executive officer, and I said, "I'll go," and I made an arrangement which has been very highly successful for both of us.

Is that wholly owned, or a partnership thing?

A partnership. We own a number of the agencies by ourselves, but the pattern in Grey has always been to share ownership with employees; and Grey today is a public corporation, but I would say that the majority of stock is held by employees of Grey.

November 19, 1981

ARTHUR W. SCHULTZ

Arthur W. Schultz was born in White Plains, N.Y., in 1922, where he attended public school. His family moved to Chicago in 1940. He is a graduate of the University of Chicago. He served in the U.S. Army Air Force in World War II.

Mr. Schultz retired as Chief Executive Officer of Foote, Cone & Belding Communications after thirty-four years service in January, 1982, having joined Foote, Cone & Belding as a trainee in 1948. He served successively as an Account Executive, General Manager of the Chicago Office and Executive Vice President, before being named Chairman of the Board and Chief Executive Officer in 1970.

He was active in his industry's affairs, serving as President of the Chicago Council, Chairman of the Central Region of the American Association of Advertising Agencies and as Director-at-Large.

He has served as President of the Welfare Council of Metropolitan Chicago, President of the Cook County School of Nursing, and as a Director of the Jewel Companies, Chicago Crime Commission, Community Fund, Lyric Opera, Better Business Bureau of Chicago and Barrington Hills Plan Commission.

Currently, in addition to being Chairman of the Board of Trustees of The Art Institute of Chicago, Schultz is a Trustee of The University of Chicago and Chicago Public Television/WTTW. He is a Director of Paxall, Inc., Springs Mills, Inc., and Chicago Council on Foreign Relations.

ARTHUR W. SCHULTZ

Interview

I'm one of the few New Yorkers who ended up in the advertising business. You, more than most, know that most of the people who have emerged as the leaders of our business are Midwesterners, and that's because all the advertising schools are in the Midwest. There are no advertising schools in the East. In the Midwest there are Illinois (where you went), Northwestern, Missouri, Michigan State, etc.

I was born in New York City, at the Fifth Avenue Hospital, in 1922. I graduated from White Plains High School, in White Plains, N.Y., and was raised in Westchester County most of that time. My family moved to Chicago. My father was an architect. And I went to the University of Chicago.

How old were you when you moved?

Eighteen years old. I went to the University of Chicago, went to the war, then returned to the University of Chicago, finally finished up my undergraduate work there, and stayed in Chicago. It was one of those fortunate things, because Chicago's been wonderful to me. Now I'm retired, and I'm staying in Chicago.

Sure. You're working for Chicago.

Yes, I'm working for Chicago, and I love it. It's been great to me.

Did you start in advertising?

No, I was an economics major, and went to work for the United States Gypsum Co. One weekend, on a visit to the Merchandise Mart, I came upon a friend (a manufacturers' representative) and he had just had one of his customers reject an order for 100 gross of all-metal rustproof clothespins.

Like that one right there. And I said, "Gee, I'll bet I could sell those." He said he'd give them to me at half price. So I became the owner of 100 gross of all-metal clothespins.

I was going to try to sell them by mail order. I wrote an ad and ran it in a local suburban paper—the *Palatine Times.* When I placed the ad, I went to the advertising manager's office, and just gave him the advertisement—I'd never written an ad before. I paid him the money, he ran the ad, and I got one order. The order was from his wife, who was in the office when he asked me, "What is that thing?" and I explained it to him. She was so interested in it that she sent her dollar in for three dozen of the hold-tight rust-proof clothespins.

So I was in the hole. I had paid the man for the clothespins and wasted the money on the advertising and said, "Now what am I going to do?" So, in one of the eventful happenings of my life, I sold the clothespins door-to-door, and in the process, I learned how to sell. I really got to know the consumer. In eighteen months I was the largest distributor of all-metal rustproof clothespins in the United States. I was spending $7,500 a week on advertising: radio mail order, newspaper mail order, direct mail—doing it all out of my parents' garage. I was living with them. I had just come back from the war. And I quit the U.S. Gypsum Company.

Then, in 1948, Harry Truman had a shoot-out with the steel unions, and the steel unions went out on the biggest steel strike in history of this country, and my little supplier went out of business when he couldn't get any more steel. But he didn't tell me about it, hoping, thinking, wishing that the strike would be over. In the meantime, I was getting thousands of gross orders and had no clothespins.

I was in bad shape financially and had to pay a remittance on the orders. And I had finally talked Elizabeth, whom I'd met at the University of Chicago, into marrying me. When I paid the remittance, I was broke. A business like that has a certain momentum. I was disappointing distributors—and disappointing the women's clubs who were selling them for me. I just couldn't fill orders—it was a very traumatic time in my life.

I said, "I have to go out and get a job." So I thought to myself, "Where would this experience be most merchandisable?" Well I supposed, an advertising agency. I remember calling on Young & Rubicam, a small operation in Chicago, and they didn't want anybody. I went to the Leo Burnett Company, saw a couple of people, and they didn't want anybody. I went to Foote, Cone & Belding, got in to see the manager, told my story, and finally got to see a man by the name of Leo Rosenberg.

Oh, I know Leo. A great guy. He must be 86 or 87 now.

I still see him. We communicate, and we are very dear friends. And Leo said, "Well, I'm sure you've got some ability; I'm sure you've got some guts, but I haven't got anything. Go to see Forrest. He's the office manager." So I went to see Forrest. Three weeks later, they called up and said, "You can have a job as a trainee in the research department." And they called on the Wednesday following the national election, when Truman beat Dewey. So that's when I went to work—November 8, 1948.

Then, six months later, I went in to see the general manager of the office, a fellow by the name of J. Hugh E. Davis. I said, "Mr. Davis, I've only worked here six months, but I'd like two weeks' vacation, because I'm going to get married." And he said, "OK, kid, you only get married once." And then he thought, well, he'd been married many times, and he said: "Well, you don't get married very often." So that's how I got into the business. And when I talk to young people, in colleges, or when they come in, or my kids, I say that in any field there are so many opportunities, you're going to have so many chances, that all you have to worry about is preparing yourself to take advantage of them. Don't worry about not being able to find something to do. Worry about getting yourself in shape to take advantage of all the opportunities you are going to have.

OK, now let's take a few minutes—from being an assistant in the research department up to the point where the agency was sort of dumped in your lap. Did you continue in research very long?

About a year. And then I became the assistant account executive on Hallmark; then the account executive on the First National Bank; then the account executive on Minneapolis-Honeywell. And I worked on the General Foods business out here—Good Seasons Salad Dressing. I digested that, and became the senior account man on General Foods—Kool-Aid, Good Seasons and S.O.S.

And then, rather traumatically, General Foods built their headquarters in White Plains, and consolidated everything there, including moving their Midwest staff East. We transferred the account to our New York office. Our people wanted me to go because I was the senior guy on the account. I went home and talked it over with Elizabeth, and we agreed we would stay in Chicago.

Then Fax [Fairfax Cone, head of the office] said, "Well we're going to get a new account," and we got it, and gradually I came back. I think, looking back, it was a healthy year, but it was one of the hardest.

But it bears out what I said earlier—that I feel you should get yourself in shape for opportunities. And then I gradually moved up. I became manager of the Chicago office—it's always been our largest—and then Fax was getting ready to pull out. The company was troubled. So, finally, they turned it over to a few of us.

You and O'Toole.

Yeah—O'Toole, Scott, Trump and myself.

You mentioned Fax Cone—What part did he play in your career?

One of the great strokes of fortune was to work for Fax Cone and to learn the business from him. He had been taught the business by Albert Lasker, and so I was an inheritor of those great lessons and experiences, so to speak.

Fax not only knew his trade exceptionally well, but he felt good about the business. He was proud to be working in advertising. There was no cynicism in his makeup or in his feelings about our business. One of the great lessons he taught me was to always put the clients' interest first. If they took advantage of that position, then you could resign them.

He also taught me that you could run an advertising agency without a single compromise on principle. Because of that, I found I could tell the young college graduates whom we interviewed for jobs that in the thirty-odd years working for Foote, Cone & Belding I was never asked to do anything I didn't want to do—never asked to compromise a basic principle.

So as I retire from the business I, too, have a very good feeling about it and toward it. I owe that to Fax most of all.

As I recall, when you took over, the agency was having a tough time. You had lost a lot of business. FCB had gone public in 1963. The large stockholders had made a killing and apparently their incentives were gone. So when you became CEO, what did you do to straighten out the agency so successfully?

I went to see a man who was a professor at the University of Chicago, Dr. John Jeuck (pronounced Yoick), dean of the Business School. We had lunch together, and I told him about our problem. Professor Jeuck asked, "What is the most successful company since the industrial revolution? The answer is IBM. The reason is discipline." He identified discipline as being "the single most important reason for corporate success." He said, "In every category of business you'll find the most disciplined company is always the most successful."

That makes a lot of sense. What was the result of your meeting with the professor?

I asked him to work with us as a consultant, and fortunately, he accepted. He talked to 45 of our people—in our offices in New York, Los Angeles, as well as Chicago. He also talked to some of our clients. When he had completed his investigation, he said, "Art, you're right. You really are in trouble. Morale is very bad. People are leaving or trying to leave. You've got to build confidence in your new management—and in a hurry."

So what did you do?

Together with Professor Jeuck, John O'Toole and Lou Scott, we put together a plan to reinstate the philosophy of Albert Lasker, who had built the agency when it was known as Lord & Thomas. Under Lasker, the agency had operated under a disciplined framework for years, and it was our goal to return to these same fundamentals.

John O'Toole was put in charge of our creative product, and John agreed that *discipline* would be the key to strengthening our creative output. We looked at every other facet of our business—media, research, account management, financial management. I felt we had to become the most disciplined agency in the business. We zeroed in on planning—set corporate goals—developed plans for creative training, new business, research and media. We spent untold hours reviewing our new disciplined management program. Ultimately, we developed a five-point program. Then we published a series of booklets which became our library—our sacred writings, so to speak.

First, and perhaps most important, is WRITTEN POSITION

STATEMENTS. These are precise statements dealing with the major functions of our business. Writing them is a sharp discipline in itself.

Second, regular management meetings of all FCB offices to review, discuss and strengthen our disciplines. This we do at least once a year, and more frequently when necessary.

Third, training our own people through a formalized program translates into tutoring that corrects, molds, strengthens and perfects; recruiting the kind of people we think best suit our needs; attracting top talent from outside to obtain new ideas and greater drive.

Fourth, outside appraisal for the broader perspective that only outside counsel can give. We employ an outside management firm that specializes in compensation; an outside research firm that tells us what others really think of us; outside directors who candidly appraise us and help shape our policies.

Fifth, short and long-range plans for all our activities. This requires each office manager to prepare a three-year plan, updated annually, that covers financial projections and a comprehensive analysis of new business, client status, department functions, public relations, recruiting, hiring and training.

Your program of multiple disciplines is not only interesting, it is truly brilliant. What results have been achieved by it over the past decade?

The progress has been gratifying. In the '70s our net income grew 547%. Our clients increased from about 350 to 1,050, and *Ad Age* figures show us as No. 1 in growth among the top ten agencies worldwide for the latest five-year period.

What a marvelous achievement, Art. You and your management team are to be congratulated. Wasn't it difficult to persuade your employees to accept your "discipline" concept?

Yes, it is difficult. Policing is necessary, for you must stay with the disciplines constantly, or the program erodes.

Conversely, disciplines should not be confused with conservatism. We have not been overly cautious, afraid to take chances. We have taken chances, and as a result, we've been burned a few times. But altogether, we are way ahead. The costs of maintaining our standards are high. However, they are worth every dollar and the effort.

I'd like to have your thoughts on advertising education. Do you think it's of any value to youngsters in college, if they're going to come into this business—versus those that just take plain liberal arts, or whatever?

Well, I think you ought to take both. I think that a liberal arts education is good for anyone. Your first obligation is to become an educated human being.

Right. Read and write.

And know something about the history of man, and how and why people react in different ways, and their cultures. No matter what you're going to do.

Now, is advertising education helpful or useful? Immensely. In my own case, it's been a tremendous help. The University of Chicago doesn't teach a single advertising course, so I went to night school at Northwestern.

Did you? This I didn't realize.

Took every advertising course they offered.

And this was when you were at Foote, Cone?

When I was a trainee. My advice to young people is learn everything you can while you're young and have the energy. Learn more about this business than anybody else. Because it'll do two things for you: It'll give you self-confidence. And it'll allow you to become more expert.

You have a hell of a record, Art. You have something to be very proud of.

I feel good about what we were able to accomplish as a disciplined team.

I'll bet you do. Have you severed all connections?

Yes, I get off the payroll February 1.

Are you still on the board?

I'm still on the board, but won't stand for re-election at the annual meeting this spring. I believe that you should get out completely.

January 22, 1982

NEAL GILLIATT

Neal Gilliatt retired April 1, 1982, as Chairman of the Executive Committee of The Interpublic Group of Companies, Inc., the corporate parent of the world's largest advertising group, in New York.

He joined the Chicago office of McCann-Erickson, Inc., an agency of the Interpublic Group, in 1945, as Associate Research Director and was named a Vice-President and Account Supervisor in 1952. He was transferred to New York in 1955, appointed Senior Vice-President in 1960 and Vice-Chairman in 1964. In January 1966, he moved to Interpublic, the parent company of McCann-Erickson, as Executive Vice-President, becoming Vice-Chairman and then Chairman, Executive Committee.

Mr. Gilliatt attended the public schools of Washington, Ind., graduating from Washington High School in 1935. He graduated with a B.S. degree from Indiana University and an M.B.A. "with honors" from Northwestern University. He attended the Harvard Advanced Management Program in 1960.

He has been active in the affairs of Indiana University as a member of the Board of the I.U. Foundation; recipient of the Beta Gamma Sigma Award for business leadership in 1963; recipient of the Distinguished Alumni Service Award for Indiana University in 1970; member of Sigma Alpha Epsilon.

Mr. Gilliatt is a member of the boards of Chemed Corporation, Omnicare, Inc. and the Kubin-Nicholson Corporation; a director and past President and Chairman of the Epilepsy Foundation of America; Chairman of the Board of the Institutes of Religion and Health; recipient of the Human Relations Award of the American Jewish Committee in 1969; a Trustee of Millikin University in Decatur, Ill.; a Director of the Silver Hill Foundation, The Boys' Clubs of America, Religion in American Life, the Philharmonic Symphony Society of New York, Inc. and Technoserve, Inc.

NEAL GILLIATT

Interview

I was born in a little town of about 400 people called Plainville, Ind. My father was a partner in a small tomato canning business. As his business prospered and when I was about six years old, we moved to the county seat when he moved his office to Washington, Ind., a big city of about 9,000 people. That's where I grew up and went to the local high school and from there to Indiana University.

A good friend of mine who still practices law in Washington, Ind., and I were (I guess one would say) the "scholars" in the class. We did a lot of things in high school—we resurrected the high school annual for one thing. We also got the school to permit our class to have a prom, which had not ever before been done in Washington, Ind. I was the business manager and promoter and my friend was the editor of the high school annual and the two of us put it out and we made money for them. That was in 1935. . . .

You sold ads to all the local merchants . . .

That's the ticket. I got my father to buy a new car so I could get a double-page spread from the automobile dealer, I remember that.

Was that fair?

Yeah, I thought it was a fair deal—my father was kind of amused about the whole thing. I went to Indiana U. because it was only 50 miles away. It never really occurred to me to go anyplace else—it was an easy place to go. And my father's business wasn't prospering in those days so money was important. It was very simple. I hitched a ride with a friend of mine—my father gave me $50—and a group of us went up to Indiana and stood in line in the proper place and registered—paid whatever the fees were in those days—$35 a semester or something like that.

My family weren't rich but they weren't quite that poor, so I didn't really work until I was in graduate school. Instead I joined a fraternity and became very active in outside University affairs. I was the business manager of the University theater; I was not an athlete, but I was an athletic manager and got my "I" as a swimming manager; I was involved in politics on campus; I was a member of the board of AEONS, which in those days was the highest student governing body on campus, made up of only eight people.

I did a lot of work for a variety of other activities in terms mostly of promotion and selling.

I graduated in '39 and I went then to Northwestern for a Master's degree in what they then called the School of Commerce. I went to NW because they had the best scholarship—my father's business by that time was really bad and he subsequently died while I was there. I went to NW for a year and got a Master's degree in 1940. Then my plan was to come back to Indiana and to get a doctorate in economics and business, which was a new program at the University at that time; I was the first candidate for the combined degree of the School of Business and the School of Arts & Sciences for a Ph.D.

But you may recall in 1941 we had a little altercation and so the faculty and myself and everybody else went off to war. I did not go to the service, but I went to the OPA in Chicago following the head of the economics department in Indiana with whom I was doing graduate work who opened up the OPA office in Chicago as head of the Price Division in the midwest area, and I stayed in that office during the war.

Were you still single?

I was married—I met my wife when I went back to Indiana from NW to take graduate work. We were married in February '43.

During that period I was asked by NW to come and help them out because there was a shortage of faculty and they were also doing a big naval program there, so I was asked to come and help teach in their night school, which I did. I did that for about 10 years—teaching in a night school. I taught sales management, I taught a basic course in marketing, and I did have some courses in retailing. When I got my Master's degree I worked at Carson's on a special type of intern program that they had at Northwestern so I did have some experience in retailing.

NEAL GILLIATT

This was always at night?

Yes, my teaching at NW was always at night because I was working full time at the OPA in the daytime.

I had quite an interesting decision to make as the war began to draw to a close, and the OPA began to fold its tent. It was quite clear that I wasn't going to go back to the university life—the OPA had kind of opened some wider horizons for me.

I started looking around and talking to some people that I knew. One of those persons was an ex-faculty member from Indiana who had joined the Standard Oil Company of Indiana as an economist in their marketing research department. He had become very much interested in advertising and advertising research and advertising measurement. He told me that Standard Oil's advertising agency, McCann-Erickson, really needed somebody in their research department. So why didn't I talk to Homer Havermale, who was the manager of the McCann office in Chicago. I did, and he interviewed me very quickly and hired me almost on the spot.

I came to find out later that my friend at Standard Oil was causing the agency enormous problems and was not very popular with the agency; so there was a great deal in my hiring of "maybe this guy would help to manage that guy" in the Standard Oil Company.

But it was quite clear when I joined the agency that research was not something which I most enjoyed, and I certainly was not technically enough oriented. I'd worked on some studies on research both for Swift & Co. and for Standard of Indiana, and I gradually moved over into account work on both of those accounts.

I think of an interesting story about my really first account executive assignment: They came to me early in 1946 and said that a young man had rejoined the Standard Oil advertising department—he had come back from the service, and he was a very restless, questioning, difficult kind of a guy, and he and I had similar backgrounds—he also had a Master's from NW—and maybe I could get to know him and do some work with him. That young man was Stuart Watson [subsequently head of Heublein], who's been a close friend with whom I'm now getting to be associated in the consulting business.

193

I stayed at McCann-Erickson in Chicago for ten years from '45 until '55, and I was made a Vice-President (I think the year was 1952) and account supervisor. My major account at that time was the Maytag account, which was a good account then as it still remains today.

In 1955 McCann-Erickson had the opportunity to take all of the consumer products from Westinghouse, and so one bright day in 1955 I discovered that McCann had to resign my client out from under me. My first experience with the management of conflict in the agency business!

At that time McCann also was soliciting the Coca-Cola account. So McCann was obviously bringing in, as you would expect, a wide variety of odd people from different parts of the country to work on that solicitation. Because they had to resign the Maytag account I had some time, and also they'd found out that I was the only person at McCann in those days who really knew a Coca-Cola bottler. I knew my local hometown bottler very well—they were close personal family friends—so I started working on the Coca-Cola account and I was involved in the part of the solicitation having to do with the servicing of Coca-Cola bottlers, and I spent a lot of time in the summer of 1955 working on the Coke presentation.

In the meantime Marion Harper called me up one day and said that he wanted to take the central research department of McCann-Erickson and make it a separate division—separate subsidiary. This was in the early days of learning how to build an advertising agency business with separate profit centers and it was his idea that the first profit center would be the central research department. We had a very big one in those days—many of the top research people who are still around in New York were in that department in those days—and he asked me to come down to New York to head up the central research department—not to be the technical research head, but to be the person who set it up as a new business. And then to move from there into major account service, and we both agreed that if we by any chance got the Coca-Cola account that I would start working on the Coke account. So in the summer of 1955 I moved to New York and began to learn my way around the research department at McCann and also around the research business as it existed at that time. In

October McCann was awarded the Coca-Cola account and I instantly left my research life and started working on the Coca-Cola account.

My part of the Coca-Cola account at that time was to be the account supervisor on making the advertising. We divided the account really into three parts, one the national, one the U.S. bottlers and the other part of the account was the advertising part and that was my responsibility. The account was organized originally by Bob Healy, who was then Executive Vice-President of McCann, and he spent a year or so in getting the account set up. Then the top responsibility on the account as far as the management was concerned was given to George Giese, who had been head of McCann-Erickson International and handled the international part and had been very instrumental in getting the account; and then unfortunately George had a heart attack. So that catapulted me into the top job on the account.

Coca-Cola played a big part in your career.

I spent most of my career at McCann and Interpublic. I also supported the Coca-Cola account and also out of my experience on the central research department, moving gradually to what we eventually called MARPLAN, and became a part of the gradual evolution of McCann-Erickson into what became Interpublic. The Coca-Cola account was one instrument.

When we started soliciting local Coca-Cola bottlers (in those days many of the bottlers had their own agencies, and some of them had large, well-known agencies; the Coca-Cola Bottling Company of New York, for example, used Esty) we felt that we probably would maybe not have much success in soliciting that account for McCann-Erickson because bottlers wanted to remain independent of the parent company. So we elected to solicit the account for Marschalk. Marschalk was an industrial agency, known as Marschalk & Pratt originally, which was bought by McCann-Erickson in 1954. It was bought by McCann because Harry Marschalk was getting older and he discovered, as many entrepreneurs have, that he didn't have any way to get his money out of the agency business and it would disappear out from under him. He was a good friend of Harry McCann's, but also he had a piece of the Esso business which McCann obviously wanted to get back. He had sold Esso on a radio show called the Esso Reporter, a new show, so for a variety of reasons it was advisable for McCann to buy that business. But all the accounts other than Esso were in one way or another competitive—industrial accounts, they were in a specialized kind of business—so McCann elected to keep that agency as a separate agency.

A year later when we were soliciting Coca-Cola it was a separate agency, and I was part of the idea of well, let's solicit the New York bottler guys with Marschalk, which we did. In the meantime we enticed Stuart Watson to come aboard, and he became head of Marschalk and that's been the beginning of the development of Marschalk as a separate, competitive agency to McCann-Erickson. Then, shortly thereafter as the Coca-Cola company diversified into other soft drink brands, they solicited and got those brands, most of which they still have, like Sprite, etc.

Stu Watson came from S. C. Johnson....

That's correct. Stu Watson went from Standard Oil of Indiana to S. C. Johnson—sometime in the early 1950s, and then he came to Interpublic in, I believe, 1955.

And he did a good job there.

Oh he did indeed. He came first into McCann-Erickson in a marketing type position but very quickly moved into Marschalk as the chairman/president and he built that agency—changed it from an industrial agency into what Marschalk is today. And then one of Marschalk's big clients enticed him and he could not turn down the job of being Chairman of Heublein.

I came to New York in 1955 and have been here ever since. And I was in McCann-Erickson in NY from 1955 until 1966 and then I moved to Interpublic. The reason for moving to Interpublic was that the Coca-Cola account worldwide became a multi-agency account—multi-agency within the Interpublic system. We were trying to build Marschalk and trying to build the other non-Coca-Cola brands. The Coca-Cola company has about three divisions. In 1960 Marschalk took the business which they still have. It became clear that supervising all the aspects of that account out of McCann-Erickson, while we were trying to foster the independence and competitiveness of Marschalk, wasn't going to work.

So I moved to Interpublic and supervised all of the Coca-Cola account out of Interpublic. However, I did move very quickly to place responsibility over the various brands in the agency and I then became much more involved in corporate Interpublic management and overall client management of Coca-Cola and then later some other multi-national accounts and moved out of the direct supervision. In fact, we hired Bill Mackey, who is now head of McCann-Erickson Worldwide, at about that time to come into McCann and take over as the head of the Coca-Cola brand account. I had known Bill Mackey, who was a client of mine back in Swift & Co. when I first started working as an account executive in the 1940s.

I guess that's about all there is to my career. I was involved in '66 and '67 with the problems of Mr. Harper and the problems of saving Interpublic—I became vice-chairman of Interpublic and later chairman of the executive committee . . .

And were you still keeping your hand on Coca-Cola all through this?

Well I did, but in most recent years I deliberately pulled out of it simply because as you look forward to the facts of age and retirement, it seemed to me that one had to make sure there was a successor there, and I could pull out. I did not want to go into the situaton of suddenly being the supervisor and keeping my hand on everything and then suddenly retiring some day, leaving the agency high and dry. John Bergin then moved into that spot where he is now.

Going back a little bit to that difficult period that Interpublic had—here you have this man that is literally a genius, who is still looked upon by many of you guys with great affection—who kind of went off the deep end. It must have been a very difficult period to go through, because here was the guy who was sort of the father of the whole thing, and yet he was also the cause of the problem. It must have been a hell of a tough thing to go through.

It was indeed. We struggled over a period of several years in the early and middle 1960s to try to get Marion [Harper] to put the company on a sound basis. But unfortunately Marion went in the other direction. I thought a good deal about this. Obviously Marion was a man of enormous ego; a genius like that and a leader is always a man of enormous ego. When he was focusing that ego on building accounts and focusing on the account, focusing on the advertising problem, focusing on the subject of how do you make better advertising, and trying to understand research and advertising and advertising strategy in which you made such really significant contributions to the thinking of the entire business—he was great.

Until Mr. McCann died, McCann-Erickson and then Interpublic was a profitable and well-financed business because Mr. McCann owned 98% of the voting stock of the business until the time he died. He controlled the business and he was "near with the buck" as we used to say. He was also, however, a man willing to invest and innovate, and he supported Marion. They made a super team, because they always made money on what Marion did; they had to have a P&L to it.

But Mr. McCann, unfortunately, was killed with Mrs. McCann in an automobile accident and he had set it up in such a way that the company was left in the hands of Marion, who was the obvious chief executive officer. Marion was President of the company when Mr. McCann was killed.

The chief financial officer that Mr. McCann left in the company—Bert Stilson—finally couldn't take Marion any longer; they clashed, and Bert just walked out one bright day and went to Florida and retired to play golf. That's where he is today.

After Bert left, the financial affairs of the company really went downhill very fast. Marion's ego became transposed from the business that he was in—that is, making great advertising and serving clients—into building a monument to himself. Building a business which would be a monument to himself, and then living and acting accordingly. He decided that he should live as well as some of his major clients, even though the advertising business doesn't support that unless you happen to own the business, which Marion did not.

So the financial problems of the business were caused essentially in two ways, because of Marion's wild seeking for new ideas and new enterprises. He would hire a group of people to set up a sales promotion business, which we did. Rather than setting it up in an orderly fashion and getting clients and making a little money and then building on that, he decided to go into the sales promotion business. And so he hired a group of people, set up some fancy offices, and set up the business; he incurred the expense before getting the revenue. He did that on several other pieces of business

—he even had a merger and acquisition business going at one time with some character who subsequently ended up in prison for securities fraud.

Marion was unfortunately easily taken in by people like that. And interestingly enough, that was true of his own personal business affairs, as well as in the company business affairs. Marion was always personally out of money, completely bankrupt. He decided to be a gentleman farmer down in Virginia, and he got in the hands of a man down there and he lost enormous amounts of money, none of which he had, and also incurred a very large IRS bill, which bill has still not yet been paid completely.

McCann was always profitable in this period, never lost any money and was always well managed. He did not particularly affect the operation of McCann-Erickson under people like Armando Sarmento and Paul Foley; they ran a very good business. He just took all that money and spent it at the corporate level.

I can remember years in which the earnings on the Coca-Cola account were two or three times greater than the earnings of the total corporation, so you can see what the man was doing. Then, as he began to be aware of the trouble he was in financially, he desperately struck out for the great new account that was going to save everything. He spent enormous amounts of money and made himself ridiculous by going around to major businesses and putting on *very* expensive solicitations with no hope of getting the business.

Trying to get him out was an interesting problem because there were people in the company of course who were loyal to him on the board of directors—it was a continually fluctuating board. Other people who were running the business and making money in the business were never on the board, or we were on the board for a very short period of time and then rotated off.

And I gather that was at his whim?

That's correct. And Marion on the face of it owned 20% of the company. The rest of the stock of the company was owned by the employees, all scattered around among all of us, so with that amount of shares and with the way he controlled the board, things had to become very, very serious; only when Don McNamara, the then chief counsel, and today President of Interpublic, really began to understand the seriousness of the problem and began telling the directors their fiscal responsibility to shareholders, and that some of the actions that were taken were really criminal actions, that we were able to get enough votes on the board. I went on the board in 1967, shortly before we got rid of Harper—and some others, Sarmento was on the board—and we were able to get enough votes one day, with the banks screaming on our backs to dismiss Mr. Harper.

I had the pleasure of telling Mr. Harper, which was a very interesting experience I will never forget, over in the old Fifth Avenue Club in the Steuben Glass Building, telling him that the board was going to meet and suggesting he not come because he was going to be dismissed, and that's the way it was going to be. The company was bankrupt.

How did he react—did he believe you?

By that time he was acting as if he did not believe—that nobody could do this—he had built the business—he was a petulant and distressed guy, who knew that that was what was going to happen, but on the surface kept up this facade of the guy who was being tossed out by a group of people beneath his stature and dignity. I think he also had some understanding although I'm not sure how much understanding he clearly had, but he also had some understanding of his own personal financial situation, because not only was the company bankrupt, but he was bankrupt and was in deep trouble with the IRS.

When you dismissed him, Neal, was he actually fired from the company?

He was fired as an employee of the company. We however made a deal with him. He was fired from the company and then we made a deal with him for his stock. We paid quite a bit of money to get rid of him, and to get back his stock. The company bought his stock. I don't need to go into the legalities of it, but the fact of the matter was that his stock—he never really owned the stock actually—I mean, for most of it he had not paid the company, and then he had taken that stock and hocked it for personal loans, so it was a very complicated and difficult kind of problem.

Bob Healy had been brought back, really by Marion because of pressure by the banks, I guess maybe a year before or six or eight months to come back and try to straighten out the financial affairs of the company. So Bob was the obvious choice and the unanimous choice of all of us to come in and take over as chief executive officer—Bob had retired before this time, but Bob's strength and his knowledge of the company made him absolutely the ideal man.

The company was saved financially—that is, we were able to keep from either going bankrupt or having to give up the majority ownership of the company to outside financial interests, because of three clients who loaned the company money. That expression of confidence on the part of Coca-Cola, Heublein and Carnation enabled us to go to the banks; and we employed Bill Hogan—a man with enormous reputation as chief financial officer—as the company's chief financial officer and with Bob Healy and the fact that McCann-Erickson and Marschalk were both profitable operating companies helped solve our problems.

Do I recall that Bryan Houston was helpful with Chase ...

He was very helpful. Bryan had come in—he was the Heublein guy—he was at Interpublic doing the kind of overall job with Heublein, account management supervision for Heublein. He did have friends at Chase and he did make the introduction, and he was very helpful.

Well you fellows did a helluva job in saving that thing. And everybody was awfully happy it was saved. I think it would have been a tragic thing for the advertising agency business if it had gone under.

Other agencies were very supportive. We did not have a run on our accounts by a large number of agencies suddenly descending upon all of our major accounts to try to solicit those accounts (not to say that we didn't have competition as we always had) but nevertheless the agency business was extremely helpful, very supportive. It would have been a really tough problem if we had failed. We were so big, and the company was in such bad shape financially, that the losses to media and the impact on the business would have been terrible, to say nothing of the impact on people. Some of us of course could have left that company and taken accounts and made a lot more money personally by dividing up the company, but nobody did. We lost only one major account and that was Miles Laboratories.

As Vice-chairman of Interpublic and working your way away from the Coca-Cola business gradually, what was your function, what were your responsibilities?

Well, my activity has been in the corporate office—always was —in what one might call the professional area. I was the man in the business in the corporate office focused on accounts on advertising professional performance. I was never the person in the corporate office who spent time and was thoroughly involved in the management of offices or management of agencies.

Are you skillful in the area of appraising advertising?

Yes, I think so. I've done a great deal of it—I have travelled the world for years as the one member of the Interpublic management group who would go into an office and look at the professional work and understand the client's work and understand where the business was as a business. Whereas other people from the corporate office would be conferring about money and bank accounts and the lease on their property and that sort of thing.

But because of my position on Coca-Cola and concern on other major accounts, I was able to go in from that background and that's what I did—so I audited the business worldwide and travelled very extensively. My life then was trying to understand where we were as an advertising business. I spent a lot of time with some of the new agencies that we bought—I tried to understand those agencies and what they had and understanding our own management people.

So that's what I did. I set up the awards and managed the professional awards and looked at people and looked at other agencies to buy and had a very strong feeling about which agencies were doing well and which were not, and why they were doing well and why they were not. I suppose I was the philosopher and the guru and the professional person at Interpublic for a long time.

Since Interpublic bought Campbell-Ewald, what's your impression of Tom Adams? I think you're aware that he and I are very close personal friends.

Oh, yes. I know that. Well, Tom's a good friend. When we were able to get Paul Foley to come to Interpublic from McCann-Erickson, he had a lot of management responsibilities and he shared the responsibilities for advertising—he being an advertising man. The relationships of Tom Adams and Paul were very close, going back to their own personal friendship, and Paul's background in the automobile business.

I see you have some notes on certain aspects and standards and functions of the business.

Yes, I've called them the lessons that I've learned about this business. I always emphasize the fact that there's nothing new in this. Perhaps, what might be significant to someone like you is the fact that what I say and what others have said are so similar, the basics, etc.

My *Lesson No. 1:* the business of an advertising agency is not making ads. The business of an advertising agency is to help clients build brands, enhance company value, communicate ideas. As I said to you earlier, I spent many years auditing the professional performance of Interpublic agencies worldwide. Today Interpublic has about 200 offices worldwide and I've been in more of those offices than any other single person at Interpublic, except maybe the internal auditors.

When I go into an office and the office people start making presentations to this character from New York—when I hear them talking about ads, about awards for ads, about techniques, I know that office is headed for trouble. When I go into an office and I hear them talking about clients' problems, about strategies for building clients' brands, about changes in share of market, about changes in attitudes, then I know that that's an agency office that will grow. That's why I say the business of an agency is not making ads.

My *Lesson No. 2* is that the agency business is a business; and some of us at Interpublic learned that lesson the hard way. It's a business with all that means in terms of good fiscal management, getting paid properly for what you do, and all of those aspects of good financial management that any business knows. But it seems to me very important also, it's understanding how you make better advertising at lower cost. The buzz word today of course is productivity, but I really think there is much to be learned by all of us in the advertising business on how to retain innovativeness and creativity and focus on clients' businesses and improve the productivity of our business; and I spent a lot of time at Interpublic on that particular problem.

Lesson No. 3 is that there is no substitute for service. This is a service business. Now I'm not talking about entertaining clients and meeting clients' wives at airports, I'm talking about a deep involvement in the client's business and serving that client fully in the areas of expertise which you happen to have or decide to have.

Lesson No. 4 is that in the world of persuasive communication, there is no No. 2 worth having. Only great advertising pays off. There's too much competition today; advertising, all communications, are too expensive to be satisfied with the tourist class performance. Unfortunately, I think that many clients have become satisfied with less than first-class performance, but my observation is that they are the ones whose brands decline and whose market position is soft.

Lesson No. 5 is that there's no such thing as great advertising without great strategy. There is no great advertising campaign unless it's talking about the right thing. I think this is one of the lessons that Marion taught.

Lesson No. 6: A great agency has to be master of its own destiny. Now that may seem a very trite thing to say, and I suppose in a way it comes out of Interpublic experience in which I'm trying to teach individual Interpublic agencies to stand up for what they want to be and what they want to believe, but nevertheless decide to look at the business and understand that this is a business of serving clients. I have observed the agencies that shift their own positions, shift what they want to be in order to get a client or hold onto a client, and my observation is that an agency that does that is an agency that is going to go down the hill. The great agencies are the ones that carve out a position for themselves: what they believe in, what they want to be, and they stay with that position. Unfortunately, I think too many agencies have tried to and are trying to reach out to be too many things to too many people.

And my last point is *No. 7*—that we always have to remember that this is a very personal business. That friendship and pride and cooperation and concern are the hallmarks of a great agency. A great agency is full of great friends—good friends.

So those are my rules for a great agency.

Let's talk a little bit about young people who want to come into the business—what kind of an education you think they ought to have.

Well, I'm a product of a school of business, I'm not a product of an art education, and I think that has always been a problem as far as I'm concerned. Obviously this business has to be made of many different kinds of people, that is, we certainly have to have chief financial officers with financial backgrounds and financial training, but for the professional aspects of the business, whether account management or creative, the education has to be such in my opinion that people focus on the consumer and on people and on persuasion, as well as on language, communication, etc.

I think that's very important. I think that I haven't quite overcome that, not because of my educational background but what I have learned on my own and what I have done in my leisure time. For example, I'm a director of the Philharmonic, have been for a long time. Now I think all of that is very important.

I don't mean that somebody has to come out of the arts college with an arts degree. I just think that because somebody else knows how to put together a profit and loss statement and how to do accounting and understands client concerns for making a profit— all these things have to be put together—these are really renaissance people in that use of that word in this business.

I am not one who wants to go out and hire the best or highest ranking of the Harvard MBAs; I want to see that MBA who also maybe helped with a home talent show, or played in the band, or something human, because it is that sort of a business. It is a very human business; and you yourself have observed agencies where the financial people, the business people, have taken over. I can think of one today, and I think it has lost a great deal.

I'm sure you've talked to a lot of youngsters over your career, so what were you looking for? Was there anything in particular or was it a question of them selling you?

Well, I was interested in what they did in their summer jobs. I was interested in courses that they took beyond just the required kind of courses. I was interested in their outside activities in college. I think that so many of our people who have done well in the advertising business are people that did that—I did it when I was in college and I know you did, and I know so many others did, but I was also looking for good academic performance because this is an intellectual business. Could be another one of the lessons that I could have made specifically an item because you're thinking about strategy and persuasion. You do not get that out of a book.

You're dealing with human behavior.

Exactly, which is what Marion learned way back when he started working with Paul Lazarsfeld. It was so exciting to be in that kind of an atmosphere—the research departments of

McCann-Erickson were the core, the very life of the agency in a way that few agencies today have. I kind of slid from research into account management, but always had a foot in the research door. I spent time in the 1950s and '40s in the Chicago office on what today are called focus group sessions; we didn't call them that in those days. I used to set them up myself.

I still remember the development of the current Maytag dependability advertising—we started that at McCann-Erickson. Pete Peterson and Chet Posey and I developed a basic stance, a strategy for that business, and we had to give up the business and Leo Burnett took it. They kept the same strategy—they haven't changed it one iota—and Maytag is today a very successful business because they have not changed that basic dependability strategy. And I remember going out to the countryside, out in Wisconsin, and we called on new purchasers of Maytag washing machines, sat in their kitchens and on their back porches, and talked to them. Now I'm interested in hiring people that when you talk to them you get the feeling that they're willing to do that. That they like to go into stores and they like to see how people buy, and they like to do all of these things.

You can tell that if they get their kicks out of looking at a sheet of figures or spread sheets—if they get their kicks out of intellectual parsing out of Shakespeare or something—I think this business is not for them.

Well, you can put them in a different area of the business.

You probably can, but if I'm trying to interview people, I interview the type of people that I think are going to handle accounts and be at the top of the business. Creative people can handle accounts, or art directors or actually account executives. McCann-Erickson is just starting today a young man that I found and hired who falls into this category. He's on my mind because he called me to say that he's starting at a summer job at McCann on Monday. He comes out of a business school background, but we're starting him at McCann with McCann's creative director in the New York office in the creative department; that's what I like to do and he's the kind of a guy that will do it.

Do you have any great concerns about the future of our business?

No, because I see whereas certain agencies are going in a direction which I think will be a disaster for them in terms of their intense business orientation and their moving away from the form and from the innovation and creativity that is really the life's blood of this business, I see on the other hand new businesses coming along and new people coming into the business that I see doing that.

My concern, I guess, about the business is really the concern I've already expressed, a concern about American business itself—where are the new Mr. Woodruffs [the man who built Coca-Cola] coming from? He was a businessman par excellence and made enormous amounts of money—but he worked very hard at advertising and marketing. He had a strategy for building the Coca-Cola brand. He had people that did do it—that he listened to.

Now I don't find as many such marketing oriented leaders in American business today as I would like to see. I find some Japanese names among the marketing oriented leaders, but I don't find as many American names as I would like. I see too many great companies, RCA for example, or you could go down the list, so many food companies—the many great brands that we used to care for and feed and were very, very special—whatever happened to those great Lifesaver ads, what is Lifesaver today? Do you remember what it was?

I've been very, very fortunate. It's a fascinating business. The fact that I fell into the business is what is fascinating to me because I did not plan to go into it—I might have been an economist, and I'd have been a lousy economist.

Well, almost all economists are.

June 11, 1982

WILLIAM A. MARSTELLER

William A. Marsteller was born in Champaign, Ill., Feb. 23, 1914, and received his education in the local schools, graduating with a B.S. in Journalism from the University of Illinois in 1937.

He served as a reporter on the *Champaign News-Gazette* from 1932, while still in high school, until 1937, all through his college days. He was a group supervisor for Massachusetts Mutual Life Insurance Co., Chicago, from 1937 to 1941, when he left to join Edward Valve, Inc., East Chicago, Ind., as advertising and sales promotion manager, subsequently becoming secretary of the company and being named Vice-President and Director in 1945.

Mr. Marsteller became manager of advertising, public relations and market research of Rockwell International Corp. Pittsburgh, in 1945, and was elected a Vice-President of the company in 1949.

His advertising agency career began when he founded Marsteller Research and Marsteller Inc., in 1951, companies which he served as President, Chairman or Chairman of the Executive Committee until he retired as Founder-Chairman, in 1980. The agency and Burson-Marsteller, its public relations affiliate, became affiliated with the Young & Rubicam group in 1982.

Mr. Marsteller is a present or former trustee, director or officer of the Whitney Museum of American Art, Barnard College, University of Illinois Foundation, the American Assn. of Advertising Agencies, the James Webb Young Fund, Marsteller Foundation, and others. He is also a founder member of the Football Writers Assn. of America, a member of the American Assn. of University Professors and the Albert Gallatin Associates of New York University.

He is the recipient of the University of Illinois Achievement Award (1973) and the President's Award (1976); the Barnard Medal of Distinction (1979), the G. D. Crain Award (1979); and the American Academy of Advertising Service Award (1981). He was elected to the Advertising Hall of Fame in 1978.

Mr. Marsteller is the author of "The Wonderful World of Words" (1972), and "Creative Management" (1981).

WILLIAM A. MARSTELLER

Interview

I grew up in Champaign, Ill., and when I was still in high school, I started working part-time at the *Champaign News-Gazette*, really covering minor Champaign High School sports, so we didn't have to bother to send anybody out there. This was, of course, in the bottom of the Depression, and the newspaper staff was just a skeleton. From that, when I went on to the University of Illinois, the first year, when I was a freshman, I took a full 15-hour schedule; but after that I only took 10 or 12 hours of credits each semester. And as a consequence, I went to school for five years. But I worked all that time, on the newspaper.

The *News-Gazette* was a seven-day-a-week paper, the evening paper except on Sunday morning. So, until the Wages and Hours Act was passed, the staff went to work Saturday morning at 7:30, and worked straight through till 1:00 Sunday morning, putting out two editions. And when the Wages and Hours Act was passed, then the Saturday evening paper—which didn't amount to a hell of a lot, but they wanted to keep the franchise going—was put out by the senior staff people, who came to work late Saturday afternoon to do the Sunday morning paper.

(I was the cheapest available hand, a junior in the journalism school) and we put out the Saturday evening paper. We used a part-time staff, who were the professors of the University of Illinois School of Journalism, so they were my professors five days a week, and worked for me on Saturdays; and as a consequence, I didn't have very much grade trouble in my last two years in school. And to be perfectly honest, I never even bothered to buy a textbook, and sometimes didn't bother to go to class. But those were greatly relaxed days compared to the agency business.

Also, I was an editorial major in journalism school, but I took a

211

minor in advertising. Those advertising courses were pretty primitive; the required course was one semester of advertising layout, and one semester of advertising copy; and in that copy class, you were supposed to take a mythical client and do a whole semester's worth of campaigns for them.

And I thought, "What the hell, I might as well get a real client," and I went over to a men's store on the campus, and said, "Look, I've got to do this thing, and I'll write your ads for the next six months." They were doing them themselves, and not very well. "And I'll write your ads for the next six months, and you'll give me a suit, or something like that, from time to time."

How long did you stick with it?

I wound up doing it for a couple of years, even after I was out of the thing, taking it out in trade; and by the time I had graduated, first of all, I made a little money along the way, and secondly, I had the best wardrobe I had for 40 years. It took 40 years to get back to where I was when I graduated!

I had been making in total, I suppose, $35 or $40 a week by the time I left Champaign, which was a hell of a lot of money at the time. But I didn't want to just stay there forever; I didn't see any future there at all. So I went to the *Chicago Daily News*, which was the only place I could catch on, and wound up getting $20 a week; and, since I was very anxious to get married, and didn't think I could live in Chicago on $20 a week, through a mutual friend, I got a part-time job selling life insurance for the Massachusetts Mutual Life Insurance Co. And by the time I had sold a $1,000 policy to the parents of any friends that I had, they offered me a full-time job—in essence, recruiting and training young agents. And that, again, was very good experience. I really didn't like the work that much but I stayed there four years, until the war.

I was 4-F, but the life insurance business was certainly nothing to be in during World War II, and I got a job at a manufacturing plant in East Chicago, Ind.—the Edward Valve Company, where I worked straight through the war. I went out there as the advertising manager, because their advertising manager had gotten drafted. But right after that, the sales manager, who was in the Reserves, went off to war, and since really our only customer was the government, I took over the sales department, which really meant dealing with the government. It really meant handling the mail, and handling the government expediters who came in, and so forth.

But then, ultimately, I wound up with the personnel responsibility, too, which was extremely useful later on; we had about 500 employees then. I negotiated a couple of labor contracts with the Steelworkers Union (all the plants around there were being unionized at the time), and at the end of the war, our company was bought by what's now Rockwell International.

The name of the company, at that time, was the Pittsburgh Equitable Meter Company, and when Al Rockwell, whose father started the company, came back from the service, he said, "God, Dad, we've got to change the name of this company, it's really terrible!"

They called three or four advertising managers in from several subsidiaries that they had, and said, "We'd like to have sort of a skull session here to come up with a new name." And the secret to my success was that, immediately, I said, "I think they ought to call it Rockwell Manufacturing Co." And Mr. Rockwell, Sr., and Mr. Rockwell, Jr., thought that was a brilliant idea!

A month or so after that, I was given the assignment of putting together the first corporate advertising program they ever had, and the first corporate public relations effort they ever had; and as a result of that, I became, finally, a vice-president of Rockwell Manufacturing, and ultimately had all the marketing.

Where were you located?

I was in Chicago. However, they were in Pittsburgh.

So from 1945 to 1951, I went to Pittsburgh every second week, at least, for a good share of the week. So I didn't want to move there, not for the customary reasons that people don't want to move to Pittsburgh, but all the time I just felt that sooner or later, I had to get out of there. Because basically, in those days, it was totally a family company. Col. Rockwell was chairman of the board, his son was president; he had four daughters, and three of their husbands were vice-presidents of Rockwell; there were six vice-presidents, only two of whom had no family connection. And Col. Rockwell always sent out a Christmas card which was his family tree in pictures, with him and his wife at the top, and his kids below, and then an increasing number of grandchildren coming down the line; and I just felt that, about the time I was 50 or

55, I was going to be working for the grandchildren, and the Rock-wells really owned the company.

And so, how I got into the advertising agency business involved no great plan at all. In the summer of 1950, I told Al Rockwell I thought I really wanted to go out on my own, and I'd give him plenty of time—we were very good friends, he was exactly the same age I was, and we had sort of come into the Rockwell picture together, right after World War II. So he said, "Fine." I said, "What I think I really want to do is to buy a trade paper; I think there's a lot of money to be made in a trade paper."

I talked to a half a dozen trade paper publishers, and I came within one weekend of buying the plumbers' magazine, which was called *Domestic Engineering*; and over the weekend I went to a lawyer to get it into legal form, and he looked at me and said, "Jesus Christ, do you really want to go to plumbers' conventions the rest of your life?" And I went home and told my wife what he'd said, and she said, "Well, if you do go, you'll go alone; I'll tell you, I'm not going to go." Anyway, I backed out of the damn thing.

We had, at Rockwell, started a market research department, which was a fairly new function, certainly in the industrial field. There were a few in the consumer field, but not much in the industrial field. And because I had tried, for Rockwell, to buy some market research services; and whenever you said, "We want to know what the market is for water flood meters," they said, "Goodbye," because nobody had any idea what to do about this. So we started to develop this on our own.

To get a staff on this, it seemed to me the only hope was to go out to the three or four colleges that, in their business schools, were teaching market research; Penn State, Duke and Northwestern were three of them. And ultimately, I decided to go to each of the professors there and say, "Who's your brightest graduating student?" And I hired one out of each of those three schools; the one out of Northwestern is Dick Christian; the one out of Penn State is a fellow named Clark Daugherty, who later became president of Rockwell, and after that became President of Mallory, and is now retired and lives in John's Island; and the third one now runs a plastics company of his own out in Ohio.

They all did pretty well, and they were probably the only three people in the country that knew much about what they were doing at the time, because they were learning, just learning as we went.

So, when I came up to the end of 1950, I told Al Rockwell that I'd decided there was a future for a small market research firm to serve industrial companies. And he said, "Well, we'll give you enough business to keep you going for a few months," and so forth. I said, "I'd like to take one of the three along." And he said, "Well, which one do you want?" And I said, "Well, I don't know; I feel strange about this, because I think very highly of all three of them. But since I'm going to be located in Chicago, and Dick Christian went to Northwestern, why, he's probably the most logical one." Al said, "Okay."

Al had a cocktail party for us at his house shortly before Christmas 1950, sort of to say goodbye, and in the course of it, Col. Rockwell, who'd had a couple of Scotches, said to me, "You're nuts. This market research is not going to be around in another three years. It's just a fad—I've seen dozens of these things come and go. Why the hell don't you start an advertising agency?"

And he added, "I thought you were nuts all the time to have four agencies for our accounts; if you put them all together in one, you've got $500,000 worth of business. Why don't you start an advertising agency, and take our business with you?" And he said, "That isn't any harder to do, I don't think, than to start a market research firm."

Well, I went back to Chicago; there was an agency called Gebhardt & Brockson. They had handled the Edward Valve advertising, and I knew that Brockson was dead and Gebhardt was past 60, and it was a small agency; and I went to him and said, "Geb, what are you going to do with your agency?" and he said, "God, it's a real problem; I thought maybe my son would take over, but he just isn't interested in that." So I said, "Well, you've got a going business here, you've got 15 people or so. We'll buy you out over a five-year period or something like that; you'll get your money out of the business." And he said, "That sounds good."

So then I got hold of a man named T. T. McCarty, who ran a fine agency on the West Coast; and for one reason or another, he had opened a series of offices here, and he had a little one in Chicago, a little one in Michigan somewhere, and one in Pittsburgh, that he set up when Rockwell bought a company out on the West Coast and moved it to Pittsburgh, and he had a little three-man service office there. He, too, was in his sixties, and he had talked to me several times about how he wished he hadn't started all these damned little branch offices. So I asked him: "How would you like to get rid of your little Pittsburgh office; we'll pay you out over a period of a few years?" And we did.

Gebhardt brought along with him the Clark Equipment account, and of course we had the Rockwell business, and the two of those were 85% of our billing in 1951, which was just about $800,-000 total. And what we did, in both cases, was to give them a decreasing percent of all the commissions on those accounts over a five-year period. In the meantime, they both stayed around and helped service them for a while. McCarty, it was a long way back, but he just came out once a year or so, and it didn't make very much difference. Gebhardt stayed working on that Clark Equipment Company until he died. But they were our real start.

I think our first breakthrough came from General Motors. General Motors hadn't changed an agency, in any division, in a good many years; and Kudner had a lot of that business. And at the end of World War II, there was a great resurgence of the railroads in the United States, and the Electro-Motive Division at General Motors had become a huge business. They had Kudner, and Kudner wasn't interested in that industrially-oriented business, and they just didn't give a damn.

So the guy at Electro-Motive got permission to change agencies, and I think the account was perhaps $250,000, but the scramble for it was just enormous, because it was General Motors, and everybody thought it was a foot in the door, which, of course, it turned out not to really be; it was a separate kind of a thing. But in any event—it was 1953—we got a chance to pitch that, and finally, they got it down to two agencies, ourselves and Campbell-Ewald, who had a lot of General Motors business at the time.

Well, we just naturally assumed that Campbell-Ewald had a big office in Chicago, and these two last meetings were to be held in the agencies' offices, and we had a skinny little office with 25 or 30 people by then. So we got the office in the building in which we were located to put a bunch of ladders and paint buckets and everything else just outside our door, so that when the people from Electro-Motive came, we said, "We're so glad you could come today; we're just starting to rip out the walls, because we're expanding greatly here." After we'd gotten the account, we found out that Campbell-Ewald only had three or four people in Chicago, and we were big by comparison! We had no idea of that.

The other thing, I think, that was interesting in our early days, was how we got into the public relations business, which has become a huge part of our business. Today, it's slightly over half of our total business, and has been profitable right from the start. That, too, was an accident, in a way; and it was traceable to the Rockwells.

Col. Rockwell did not like having plants in big industrial centers. He liked his manufacturing plants in places like Uniontown, Pa.; Leetonia, O.; Russellville, Ky.; and so forth. Now, one of the problems was getting executives into those places. You either had to drive all night, or fly to someplace 150 miles away.

A lot of time gets wasted.

Al got the idea that he was going to buy a helicopter, and they would run a regular shuttle service around and land in the plant parking lots. He called me on the phone one day, and told me what he was going to do, and he said, "Jesus, it's great—we ought to get a lot of publicity on this." He said, "I think it could wind up on the cover of *Life* Magazine, or *Saturday Evening Post,* or something like that; big stories, I'm thinking." And he said, "Well, you guys can handle that, can't you?"

Like many small agencies, we wrote an occasional news release, but I knew this was going to fail, and I just didn't want it failing with us, because the stakes were too great on other things. So I got in touch with a couple of people I knew in New York and asked them if they had any suggestions. Then I got the names of three or four very small, mostly one-man public relations firms, with the theory that if it went sour, we'd just give them whatever they could get out of it; if it went sour, they went down the drain, not us.

Well, the first one of the several I wrote a letter to was Harold Burson; instead of replying he just got on a train and came to Chicago to see us. And at that point, Harold, who had also been in the service, and when he came back out had started in public relations, was just eking out a living in New York in mostly personalized public relations—one man on a job at a time—and he used a graduate student at Columbia, and one girl, and that was it.

Well, anyway, he looked as good as anybody, as innocuous as anybody else; so, we met, and we said, "Harold, we'll meet you in Pittsburgh, and introduce you, and whatever you can get out of it, you're welcome to it."

So we went to Pittsburgh, and it was agreed that he'd get $2,000 for doing this whole thing. Fortunately, Sikorsky went on a nine-month strike, and the helicopter wasn't delivered for nine months. And then Bell took three months to equip it, and it was a year before they got it, and Harold was getting nothing of his $2,000. So he went back to Pittsburgh and talked to us, just to see if there was something else that we could do something with in the mean-time.

One of Rockwell's divisions made home workshop tools, the Delta Power Tool Company. And Harold was talking to somebody there, and they showed him some of the pictures they had taken at the Wisconsin School for the Blind, where they were teaching blind students to operate these power tools. Well, by God, Harold got three pages of pictures in *Life* of these blind students running these things. Rockwell made millions of reprints—it was a safety story, you know—and the dealers all loved it.

Then, on the heels of this, Harold talked to Col. Rockwell about his philosophy about acquisitions. Col. Rockwell had been buying some companies and selling off some, too; he was really an early conglomerator, so to speak. Well, Harold got a story on Col. Rockwell placed in *Fortune* and I remember the title very well, because the Colonel had it framed and hung in his office: it was "Cool Col. Rockwell and the Companies He Keeps."

Anyway, by the time the helicopter was delivered nobody paid much attention to it! It didn't make a hell of a lot of difference, because Harold was in good shape there. Well, in the meantime, I'd introduced him to the people at Clark Equipment, and to a couple of our other clients, and I began to notice something that I thought was kind of upsetting. After Harold had been around a little while, he was doing business with the Chairman of the Board, the President, the chief financial officer, or whatever; Dick and I were doing business with the advertising manager, the sales manager, and as we began to get a few consumer accounts, the product manager, etc.

And I got to thinking, "This is nuts!" So I said to Harold,

"Look, we're your New Business Department up to now," and we were very good friends, so I said, "What do you say we put these two businesses together?" And at that time, we were just in the throes of setting up our first profit-sharing plan, and Harold's business had grown, mostly thanks to us, to 10 people or so, and I said, "We can't have two people on Rockwell accounts, a PR guy and an advertising guy, making a different amount of money on a profit-sharing plan." So we just called it Burson-Marsteller, and turned it into first a subsidiary, and ultimately a division.

And, of course, it thrived very well. I like to think that we had a big effect on the public relations business, because at the time we got started, the typical PR firm acted as if it was a law firm or a public accounting firm, and the idea of making "a new business presentation" as such—they would go in and show some loose clippings and talk about what they'd done for somebody else—and Harold Burson and Buck Buchwald and some of those guys who participated in joint presentations visualized an entirely different kind of thing. And I'll never forget, Harold and I had lunch one day with John Hill of Hill & Knowlton, who, in a fatherly and very kindly, mild way, sort of gave us a little lecture on professionalism.

I remember he said: "I've heard that you people even come to these presentations with a magic lantern! And show slides and things!" He thought this was pretty unseemly; but in the meantime, we were getting a lot of business. And at that point, you know, the advertising agencies, by and large, were trying to avoid the business; David Ogilvy made a speech in which he said they never should be together. And David had a very successful PR operation going in London, which he made them live off of, as he said. But only Ketchum, MacLeod and Grove and ourselves and Thompson, with a public relations operation that really was about as much of a service department to the accounts as the media department or something, were really into PR.

It was a very fortuitous thing, wasn't it?

Yes, it was. And what really took us to New York, from Chicago and Pittsburgh, was the fact that our public relations operation, which was there, was getting big, and it was developing clients of its own, and we sort of decided it was time to repay the new business activity, and have them help the advertising part of it.

219

So we started looking to buy a small agency there; we were still, essentially, an industrial agency, and I'd talked to half a dozen small industrial agencies; one which shall remain nameless and is now nameless. It's long since gone, but it was one of the most prominent industrial agencies in the country, and at one of the first Four A's conventions I went to at the Greenbrier, I talked to the president and the chairman of this agency about a merger. And at that point, our billing was about one-third theirs, but we had exchanged just enough figures so that it developed that they were taking everything out of it that they could, and we were leaving it in, and our net worth was three times theirs! So they were perfectly willing to make a merger on the basis of billings. We wanted to make a merger on the basis of money in the bank, fixed assets and so forth. Nothing came of it.

Ultimately, we bought Rickard & Co., in 1955!

We were four years old at the time we went to New York. By that time, Harold's operation had moved twice within the *Daily News* building, and was getting bigger. And Rickard was in a loft on 36th Street, between 5th and Madison, and you would think that you were going into something designed by Charles Dickens. That office was so old and so quiet, and so unkempt, really; and the three men who ran it, lovely old gentlemen, who never knew that several young people whom they had there called them "Wynken, Blynken and Nod"—they were all over 65, and in a position of "what the hell are we going to do with the agency?" And once again, we bought it out over a several-year period; it didn't have very much value, but they did have several accounts which went back to right after World War I.

And allegedly, Bill Rickard, who started it, was one of the great copywriters. He had come out of Westinghouse, General Electric, one of those companies. But during the 1920s, it was the number-one industrial agency in the country, and it slowly diminished in its activity, and it slowly lost superb clients. There is a book on the history of the N W Ayer advertising agency which has a section about the Bok awards, set up at Harvard by the Bok family—the *Saturday Evening Post* family. For the Best Advertising of the Year, you got a silver cup, etc. Rickard & Co., among all the agencies, was No. 3 in number of Bok Awards. Needless to say, ·Ayer was No. 1, and as I recall it, Thompson was No. 2, but Rickard was

No. 3. And one of the assets that they wanted to mark up, because they were carried on the balance sheet as zero, were about ten silver loving cups that they had on a chair rail in the board room! Tarnished as hell!

Anyway, that's how we got started in New York. I moved to New York in 1960, partly because that office was growing the fastest, partly because we quickly found that New York advertisers will not buy a branch operation. And in 1960, IBM fired Benton & Bowles, and talked to, originally, I guess 15 or 20 agencies, and ultimately it was cut down to 6 or 8. We were not on the original list, and I got somebody up there and said, "You know, really, what you've got is an industrial product. You ought to talk to the No. 1 industrial agency in the country." So we got added to the list, and you know, luck plays so much of a part in life.

I think we were originally scheduled to be the third agency pitching, and would have been lost in the middle of the fracas, but as it happened, something came up; they had to cancel ours, and we were put on last accidentally. Our presentation went off very well, we'd worked very hard on it; and we got the IBM account,

I'd already been thinking about moving to New York, and I promised that I would move to New York, and would stay active on it for at least the first year or so. And that was very important, because they were bringing out the first of a whole series we brought out for them, the 1040, and then in the middle 1960s, the 360, which was their big, huge success; and I think we learned as much from them, seriously, as anybody.

Well, that's great.

It was a great learning experience for many of our people, certainly for me.

Also, in late 1960, Harold Burson said some of our clients were beginning to set up marketing offices or European headquarters, partly for tax purposes, partly because this was going to be the big deal; the European Common Market was in the making, etc. And Harold had spent a lot of time overseas during the war and immediately after that, and he was hot to start a European operation. And I grew up, as you did, in Illinois, and read the *Chicago Tribune* every day, and by nature was an isolationist, I think. And we went over to Europe.

We had hired Jere Patterson as a consultant for this purpose, and he and Harold and I went over on one of the early 707's, and they put me in the middle so I couldn't get away before we got there, because I thought the whole thing was ridiculous. And we were so naive; we were trying to decide, "Well, should we put our office in London, where we know the language, or in Switzerland, which is the best tax haven, or in Brussels, where there's going to be the European Common Market?" Thinking that we could handle all of Europe in one place. And of course, that was a learning experience.

Yeah, we all learned that one.

Originally, our idea was to have one man over there, and then get into joint ventures and minority interests, and we did a little of all of that. And it was universally unsuccessful. And after we'd been there, in the middle '60s, we began to realize the folly of this, and we began to either start all over again, totally on our own— which in most cases, we did—or in a couple of cases, to buy out a small agency. We bought a PR operation in London, we bought a small agency in Stuttgart.

But mostly, we started our own operations, and in each case we sent some people over initially. We had a series of Americans in Brussels, because they were dealing largely with American companies there. We sent two people over—we sent a total of three people over to manage the Swiss operation in Geneva; first, one man who had both advertising and PR, and then as soon as it built a little, we sent two people over for advertising and public relations. They've both been there nearly 15 years now, and are Swiss citizens.

One of them was born in Germany, and his wife was German, and although he was an American, he is totally a citizen of that country, and doesn't think of himself really as an American at all. The other one, who has been there a year or so less, wanted to live in Europe, wanted to all the time; he loves to ski and everything else, and he thinks living in Geneva is as near as you can be to heaven. And he's a hell of a long way from anybody looking over his shoulder, too, you know.

The other thing about that is, year after year after year, on the basis of profit percentage per dollar of billing or income, it's the most profitable office we have anywhere in the world.

That's interesting.

Different offices have done better or worse; the Belgium office, the Brussels office, has had periods of great success, and then, the nature of our business changed.

Starting several years ago, Bob Leaf, who was doing international work in New York, was sent over there, first in Brussels and then to London, and was made President of Marsteller International. As that business has grown, too, and as we now have offices in the Far East and Australia and one South American office and so forth, his job has been split, and he's President of Burson-Marsteller; he was originally a PR guy. And a fellow named Chris Norgaard is President of Marsteller Advertising International, and he's in Brussels. But both of them, by the nature of their jobs, now travel I suppose 50% of the time.

Tell me, how did you get into package goods?

Well, you know, you finally run into yourself in any field, and in the industrial field we were beginning to have real conflict problems. We worked for two or three chemical companies, but in all cases, we couldn't take all their product line, because they were competing. And you get one materials handling company, one computer company, and you're out of the business.

And also, it looked to us like, on the public relations front, the PR agencies that were into consumer publicity, by and large, did better than those that were doing industrial publicity, because basic industrial publicity didn't amount to a hell of a lot.

Corporate financial publicity is something entirely different, and is very good and quite lucrative. Companies will spend for that, as they'll spend for annual reports; but for a catalog, they want to keep the price down as low as they can. So, we concluded that if we were going to continue to grow, we were going to have to branch out, and our feeling was that we were really going to have to buy a television reel, buy a way in, to some extent. And after exploring dozens of agencies, we made a deal. We bought the Zlowe Company. They were doing about $15 million worth of billing, and it was damn good work, high quality work, starting with Dannon Yogurt, which they'd had from the start—a wonderul story of building that up. They had some National Distilleries business, Louis Sherry Ice Cream, and it was a total consumer operation. None of the accounts were huge, but they were doing very, very well with all of them. It was good advertising. You've got a ready-made reel; you've got a ready-made creative director, Milt Sutton, who was very good indeed; and they had some soft goods business. But it was a well-rounded, small consumer business. This was in 1972.

We'd been chasing business futilely in that field for a long time. But, you know, it was getting back to saying, "Now, if you hire us, we'll show you what we can do." And it was very hard to compete. I remember somebody told me, "Well, you can always get some business at American Home Products, and you'll learn a hell of a lot, and"—

You'll lose your shirt.

But anyway, we talked to people—a guy that you must have known, Wil Shelton, for instance, who was at American Home—

I knew him very well. He was the president of Compton for a while.

Anyway, Wil Shelton said, "I don't know why you would want this business, but if you go out and get yourself a little reputation as somebody that can do something, I'll give you this business." And after we got Zlowe, I went back to Wil, and he gave us a couple of accounts which we had for two years; and finally, I was down here over the Christmas vacation, and one of my daughters said to me, "Are you going to make any New Year's resolutions?" And I said, "Only one; the first thing I'm going to do after the first of January is to go see Wil Shelton and say, "Wil, you're damn nice people and thank you, but we've learned all we're going to; we can't afford to continue, the tuition is too high.' "

But, with Zlowe, we'd begun to get our foot in the door. The other thing that we did, Bart, that was helpful; we decided that the food service business would at least get you introduced to some of the food companies. And we hired a man with good experience in that field, and started out after that kind of business; and in relatively short order, we'd gotten half a dozen accounts, because there weren't too many agencies that really were trying to specialize to any extent.

And we got the Armour Food Service business, and a paper goods account, Ft. Howard Paper, and some others; and in many of those cases like R.T. French, they ultimately got us into some consumer business, or at least, you could show, even if they were food service ads, you had some ads on products that were really consumer-oriented.

From that start, Burson-Marsteller also bought a public relations agency called Theodore R. Sills, which was one of the two real food public relations agencies; the other would be Dudley Anderson Yutze. And they had a great test kitchen; a beautiful test kitchen. We bought that business, which was maybe $15 million, all women, and ultimately moved them in alongside our other business. And we had a test kitchen on our premises now, so that when you talked to a consumer account you tried to get them to come to the office, and it's good for consumer business.

But also, they brought along some accounts in the food business that helped us get our foot in the door on advertising food.

But nowadays, while our advertising and public relations businesses have a good many joint accounts, they have more and more been kept quite separate. They just go straight up to the board of directors as separate disciplines; nobody in the PR business reports to anybody in the advertising business, or vice versa. And the reason for that, of course, is that as we've gotten into much bigger companies—multi-division, multi-product companies—where there may be two or three advertising agencies, and sometimes several public relations agencies, it's just a hell of a lot more comfortable for the client to have those businesses clearly separated. So there's no intermingling anywhere in any of our offices. They're kept totally separate, much as Ogilvy does with Scali, and as Compton is doing, and as many others are now doing.

How does your business break up between industrial and package goods business at this point?

Well, the consumer products are not entirely package goods, but consumer products are now about 55–60% of our total business. And of the remaining 40–45%, today, in terms of billing or income, way over half of that is what we would call corporate or financial. For instance, Colt Industries, which is a client of ours, is a totally industrial company; we don't handle any of their industrial products, but we do their corporate advertising etc.

In a sense, it's industrial, but it really is a different kind of thing—you have different kinds of writers on it, different kinds of account men working on it, etc.

Bill, you no longer are independent. You want to talk about that?

Sure. Over the years, Bart, going back to the early Sixties, we'd been approached many, many times.

Almost invariably it was because somebody was frustrated with the fact that they either had to handle the industrial end of their account and couldn't make any money on it, or because they wanted our public relations business; because somebody was really concerned about the fact that a PR company was getting in there and talking to the president—same problem we ran into in our own early days, when Harold was talking to chairmen and we were talking to ad managers. At any rate, over the years, Young & Rubicam; Ogilvy; Foote, Cone & Belding; Thompson; just about everybody approached us, and mostly we just discouraged them completely. The only one I ever really talked to very seriously was Foote, Cone & Belding, soon after they went public. And then everybody thought, "Gee, this is the great thing," and Bob Carney came over to see me, and ultimately we had a couple of meetings with him and Rol Taylor and Fax Cone; we finally said "No," for the same old reasons.

They weren't even much interested in our PR business; but they had some Minneapolis-Honeywell business, and they had International Harvester Trucks and Scout and all, but along with that, they had to handle a couple of materials handling products and similar products that they were losing their shirt on.

Chuck Winston, who ran the Chicago office, was getting beat up by the guys in New York for this, and he said, "Well, goddamn it, why don't you buy Marsteller and turn all the crap over to them?" But you know, as was typical in those days, they didn't charge for layouts on any of those accounts; and we grew up in the industrial business, and we would have starved if we didn't charge for them. So we charged for everything, and our clients normally expected it. And I said, "I just don't think that International Harvester is suddenly going to start paying for things that they've been getting for free. Anyway, we don't want to be your second-string office."

But the other thing was, Bart, it was about the time that I said—Harry Paster [VP of the American Assn. of Advertising Agencies] really said to me, "Bill, you've got to start planning." Gebhardt had died, and I'd gotten all of his stock, and Rod Reed, who ran our Pittsburgh office, died and I had bought his stock; and I had about 75% of our stock at the time.

Harry said, "That's a dangerous thing, and you've got to start thinking about it and doing something about it." And so I started selling a little bit of stock to other employees each year, and selling it back to the Company, and then a Board decision was made as to who got it and so forth.

But at that point, I still had enough of the stock so that, on the proposal which Foote, Cone & Belding made, I would have been the largest stockholder in Foote, Cone & Belding; and when they did the arithmetic, I think that slowed them down a little bit, too.

They weren't necessarily interested in that. Although Fax didn't give a damn but I think, some of the others did. Anyway, that's the only one we ever got at all serious about. Mostly, we just said, "No." Over the years, Bart, the most persistent suitor was Ed Ney, who started in 1971, soon after he became president of Young & Rubicam. He took me to lunch, and he used to have lunch with me a couple of times a year, and breakfast with Harold Burson a couple of times a year. And at the time we finally made this deal, I explained to the Y&R senior executives, a couple of hundred of them who were brought together, that I made the deal for two reasons.

The first one was that in 1939 or '40, after I'd been out of school a couple of years, I'd wanted to get out of the life insurance business and decided that what I really would like to do, where I could make some money, and not go back to the newspaper business, would be the advertising agency business. I went to the Y&R office, which was then managed by Art Tatham, and he told me to go get a job someplace as an advertising manager for six months, and then get a job selling door-to-door for six months, and then come see him. And it looked to me like the only way I could get a job at Y&R was to sell our business to them!

But the second reason was that I had just absolutely gotten fed up having lunch with Ed Ney, and Harold thought it was a nuisance to come in from Scarsdale to have breakfast with him, too. But Ed stayed after us.

There was and is another connection there. We tried to operate our business, although it was a private company, along the principles of what a public company was. And since the middle Fifties, we put our first outside director on the Board, Mel Anshen, and Mel learned the advertising agency business serving on our Board.

By the time we sold out to Y&R, we had Bill Cole, who was the dean of the Medill School of Journalism at Northwestern; Jim Hays, the president of the American Management Assn.; Mel Anshen; Bill McNeil, who is an attorney in Chicago who special-izes in advertising law; and Joe Wilkerson, who had taken early retirement from Y&R.

Joe's a naturally enthusiastic man; he just gets all charged up about things. And he got all charged up about our business. He is really mostly in London; he has had an enormous impact on our London office.

We just gave him an office in London. We had a hell of a hard time getting him ever to take anything; for so long, he said, "Oh, I enjoy it so much." But he kept telling Ed Ney, and the people at Y&R, "God, you know, those guys, that's a different kind of business, and it's been so long since Y&R had to do some of the things that they do, and——." As a result of Joe, mostly when Ed and I were together, we would talk about my learning something about what a big agency did, and his trying to learn something about how we would try to deal with some of the petty problems, especially where they were adding smaller, non-integrated offices. It was a new world for them. So we became very good friends.

Meanwhile, I had become extremely close to Jock Elliott. And Jock and a couple of people from Ogilvy talked to us, Shelby Page and others, several times. And we exchanged the financial data. But I wasn't really interested, because I just didn't think that, if I was going to continue to work, I was going to get along with David Ogilvy. I thought he was too strong a person. And he'd been cynical from time to time. He and I had served on a couple of 4A's committees, I think he thought I was some kind of a country jerk with small industrial business. I just didn't think it was going to work. I think Jock realized that, too.

Great fellow, Jock.

I think, Bart, his contribution to Ogilvy has been greatly under-estimated. I don't think David would have ever done anything near what he did without Jock. I think his internal and external effects have just been great.

At any rate, I knew him because one of our daughters went to

Barnard, and ultimately I wound up on the Barnard board, and Elly Elliott was the longtime chairman of the board. They lived a couple of blocks from us, so we got to know them very well. And Jock and I had talked about retirement several times.

We had promised both Ed Ney and Jock Elliott that if we ever were serious, we would talk to them. And so we did, because I was 65 in February of 1979, and I had sworn that I was going to quit at the end of '79. So in mid-1979, we talked to both of them again.

By the time, however, Ogilvy had bought Scali. As a public company, they were very concerned about paying us on a basis that would not dilute their shareholders' equity. And they've got a couple of important stockholders who are out of the business. So that's as far as it went.

Then we started talking to Young & Rubicam, and in essence, we said, "This is what it would take to interest us," and in essence, they came back the next day and said, "Okay." And the negotiations were very easy and simple. And we did as most agencies, I think, that are in a position to do so did; as you probably know, they had a five-man board, which was expanded to seven, and Dick Christian and Harold Burson went on it. We had an agreement where we'd keep names and keep identities and so forth, and it's been very successful. Harold and Dick have been quite active, really, in the overall management of Young & Rubicam.

I know Ed's very happy about it.

Well, Jim Mortinson, until he retired, was on our Board, as is Art Klein; and now, the new financial man who came from Chemical Bank, who replaced Mortinson, is on the Board, too, but for all practical purposes, is an outside director. And the real connection between the two companies is Dick and Harold, and to some extent, Art Klein.

So, let's get into advertising education, Bill. You've done so much for it.

I think we got interested in it, really, because of selfish motives. I thought that if we were going to act like big boys, we ought to do proper recruiting at the college level, and our early efforts were sure a waste of time and money. We went to Harvard, and to Northwestern, and various places like USC, and nobody knew who we were, or cared.

At a company that I knew very well in Chicago—Chicago

229

Bridge & Iron—almost everybody came from Purdue. What they had done was give Purdue a lot of money, and gotten very close to the engineering professors, and they kept sending them their best people, and saying to the best people, "This is a great place to work." And I said, "Well, why can't we do the same damn thing? Let's just adopt two or three schools and get close to them, so that when we go recruiting on those campuses, we've got somebody there who's been working for us all year long." So we concentrated originally on Illinois and Northwestern, where we had a pretty good in; Dick went to one, and I went to the other. They both had good journalism schools, or advertising courses, and we started there. Ultimately, we wanted to do something on the West Coast; we did the same thing at USC. And in the East, we began with somewhat less success, but we began at Penn State and a couple of other places.

Anyway, one day, at one of those 4A's meetings in Chicago that they have the educators come in for, I was sitting with two or three of them, and they said, "You know, what we really need is more case histories for teaching, so that we get more real life things. Do you think we could get a couple of agencies, for example, to make a new business presentation next year at this meeting?" Anyway, we had started, in the late '50s, to take over Sterling Forest Conference Center for a week, and we would run, side by side, a sort of broad, concentrated week for younger account executives that had been with us for a year, but generally less than two or three—sort of a post-graduate refresher—and then we ran an advanced seminar for people who had been promoted to an account supervisor level or above, in all disciplines; art, media, everything else. And in that advanced group, we used outside professors, or outside people, a lot, because we were talking about people management. That's how we got a hold of Jim Hays, who became a director, from the American Management Assn.

Anyway, Vernon Fryburger at Northwestern had been at those, and he had just, as an observer, sat in on some of our basic seminar sessions. He said, "I've got an idea. How would you like to run one of those week-long basic advertising educational seminars for a bunch of educators?" And he said, "I don't know how much they could afford to pay," and I said, "I'll tell you what; why don't we make a grant to Northwestern—I don't want to be picking professors out to go to this—turn it over to you, and with that money, you can then pay the bills as a non-profit organization, and you can set up a steering committee and pick the people, and we'll do for them exactly what we do with our young people." And so that's how that started.

That's an annual event?

No, not any more, because we ran out of key professors, and we were taking the key people; then we'd give them the material so that they could go back and use it. We've done three of those. But because public relations was so much a part of our business I said to Fryburger, "When half of our money is earned by the PR business, and they want to get to know the people who are teaching PR in a few places, this has got to be a combined thing. We combine our PR and advertising people, and teaching communications." So that's what was done.

As a consequence, Burson-Marsteller has some kind of relationship with Syracuse, with the University of Florida, with Texas Christian . . .

The result of this, is that our recruiting has been greatly helped everywhere. Also, of course, as we've gotten to know so many people in the field, we get so many more requests, that a lot of it makes sense. So we've given the University of Southern California a fair amount of money, and Illinois, and Northwestern, Syracuse, Florida—I saw the other day, American University in Washington, in their foreign service, they are teaching government kind of public relations. I noticed that we've made a scholarship grant to them, because we had a hell of a time getting people for our Washington PR office. It's very hard to find anybody. But we did try to keep all that one step removed, just to set up a corporate foundation, and have kept a couple of outsiders on that, so that it's differentiated from contributions to the Man of the Year in the airplane industry.

You've been very generous to these universities, I know.

I think it's paid off.

Well, sure, but you know, look what you've done for the James Webb Young Fund. It's been a wonderful thing.

Well, yes. Of course, when Sandy [C. H. Sandage, long-time professor of advertising at U. of Illinois] had that idea, he got me and G. D. Crain and Leo Burnett, and a few other people that he knew in Chicago, and proposed this, and—we all agreed to give him $1,000 the first year. G. D. Crain only wanted to give $500, but they got it off and running.

They're giving every year now, but they give a little more than that. They've been very good to us.

By the way, I owed G. D. Crain a lot. When Dick and I were leaving Rockwell to start that market research business, which we did start in January 1951, the agency—it took us three months or so to really get it all put together, and we didn't start till May, 1951; and we got the research operation going, and it still continues as a separate division operation. It has never made us a hell of a lot of money, mainly because the rest of our business grew so much faster that we just lost the time and the interest in putting in on that part. But we were trying to get started, in January of 1951, and the first client we got was G. D. Crain [publisher of *Advertising Age*] who gave us a couple of research assignments; one to see, with regard to a hospital publication they used to have, what would the future of that really be, and should they sell it, or carry it on? And we also did a research study on whether or not they should start a buyers' guide for the advertising field, for advertising services. But those were two of the very first market research problems we ever got, we got them from him.

April 5, 1982

RAYMOND O. MITHUN

A 1930 graduate of the University of Minnesota with a B.A. in journalism, Ray Mithun began his career as an advertising agency executive on April 1, 1933. That was the day Campbell-Mithun opened its doors—and President Roosevelt closed the banks.

Despite its inauspicious opening date and total billings of $197,-000 in its inaugural year, the agency became the largest west of Chicago 20 years later; broke the $100 million barrier in 1973, and had reached the $250 million mark by 1982, when it became part of Ted Bates Worldwide while still operating separately.

Currently Mr. Mithun holds the title of Founder/Chairman of Campbell-Mithun, Inc. He is also Director of International Dairy Queen; Chairman and Director of Northstar Bank Corp., and Director of the Minneapolis Foundation.

He had been a Director of Northwestern National Bank, Minneapolis Chamber of Commerce, Minnesota Orchestral Assn., United Hospital Fund, United Fund of Hennepin County, National Outdoor Advertising Bureau, American Association of Advertising Agencies, and President, St. Barnabas Hospital Board.

Mr. Mithun pioneered use of the fee system in agency compensation, and was the first Four A agency to announce the acquisition of a medium.

Mr. Mithun has been active in educational efforts to stimulate interest in and understanding of advertising. In 1962, he established an advertising scholarship at the Minneapolis College of Art & Design, and in 1974 he set up an advertising scholarship for black, Chicano and Native American students at the University of Minnesota.

He has been given the Outstanding Alumni Achievement Award from the University of Minnesota, the Minnesota Advertising Club's Man-of-the-Year Award, and has been elected to the Minnesota Business Hall of Fame.

RAYMOND O. MITHUN

Interview

My father ran away from Norway at the age of fifteen and came to the United States to make his fortune. That was back in the 1890s. And he quickly learned that it was inadvisable to be ignorant, so he put himself through college. He became a schoolteacher, then a county superintendent of schools, and eventually a newspaper publisher.

All this was in Buffalo, Minn.—a beautiful little suburban town close to Minneapolis. But he became fairly powerful in the Republican Party, a delegate to national conventions, and died at the ripe age of forty. He died at the time that all the banks in the country were closing. He left my mother with money in three banks. Then all three banks went bankrupt, closed, and she went to work and published the newspaper. She was left penniless. One of the banks eventually reopened.

So at the age of ten, I didn't have a father, and I had a younger brother, and we learned to work right away.

This put you back into the early '20s, then, didn't it?

That's right. I started working on the newspaper, cut off my thumb when I was six years old in the paper cutter; learned how to set type and run the linotype machine and run the presses; and eventually became editor of the competing paper in Buffalo, Minn., at the age of fifteen. The *Wright County Press* was a large competitor, and I convinced the board of directors to merge the paper with the newspaper my mother was publishing. So that became my first business deal, to consolidate two newspapers, the largest two newspapers in the county. I went to school, graduated, and wanted a job, and when I got out—

Now wait a minute. You went to the University of Minnesota. What did you take when you went there?

235

Business and Journalism, 50–50; I had a degree in both, or enough courses in both.

And you got out of there when?

1930. And the Depression was on; I wanted a job in a newspaper, and the newspapers weren't hiring; they were letting people go. But I wound up down in Mankato as city editor of the *Mankato Free Press*. And every weekend, on Saturday or Sunday, I would drive up to Minneapolis and call on BBD&O, and knock on the door, and they'd be working over the weekend, and I'd ask them for a job. And after six months of that, they gave up and hired me as a copywriter.

I worked there for about a year and a half, and Roy Durstine, who was running BBD&O, came out to learn why it was that we were the only office in BBD&O that was making money. All the rest were losing. And Durstine decided that it was because we had food accounts, and the other branches had very little food business.

Who was running the office?

Ralph Campbell. And Durstine ordered Ralph Campbell, then, to move to New York to establish a Food Division for BBD&O. Ralph refused to move, and they got in a squabble, and Durstine called it gross insubordination; and so then Ralph Campbell turned to me, and he said, "I think I'm going to start an advertising agency of my own here in town. Why don't you come with me?" I said, "Why, that'd be fine, if you let me run the business; and on what basis are you going to let me get started with you?" He said, "50–50." Well, he was 47 years old, and I was 22 or 23, and it just seemed to me like it was Utopia.

And so I borrowed $1,500, and he already had $1,500, and we went down to the Northwestern Bank to see Mr. Decker, who was the head of the bank, to see if we could get some space in the building. When we got to the building, it was closed. Roosevelt had closed the banks. And we asked the guard if we could see Mr. Decker.

The guard said, "Well, Mr. Decker is in his office, crying." But he said, "You can go see him." I didn't know Decker, but Ralph Campbell, being the older man, knew him. We got in to see Decker, and we told him we wanted to start a business, and he

236

leaned back in his chair and he laughed and said, "You guys must be crazy." Finally, we convinced him we wanted to start, and we asked him if he had any space. He laughed and he said, "80% of this building up above is unoccupied; go help youself."

As we were leaving, he said, "Have you got any furniture?" We said, "No." He said, "Well, on the fourth floor, we've got a bunch of desks all piled up from people we've had to let go. Go help yourself." And because of his helping us get started in business, we've remained loyal to that bank all the years we've been in business, and they eventually gave us their advertising account, which was a big one at that time; it was $25,000 a year. And I finally got on their board of directors, and have been involved with the Northwestern National Bank, which is the largest bank in the Ninth Federal Reserve System, and the bank corporation all my business life.

That's great. How did you build the business?

Well, we dunced along step by step. We started with five people. We resolved, on day one, that we would never go call on any of the big clients in Minneapolis or St. Paul, because they thought that you couldn't get any good agency service in Minneapolis; all the important accounts were being serviced in New York or Chicago. So we resolved we would never call on one. We would earn their respect so that they would come to us. And by George, that happened. Over a period of years and years, about one big account a year would knock on our door and say, "Would you like to work with us?" And that's how we got Honeywell, Land O'Lakes, Northwest Airlines, Hamm's Beer, every one of them.

Now, from day one, we decided that we would involve our employees in ownership of the business. Ralph Campbell took 40% of the business and I took 40%, and we arranged for 20% to be available to other employees, to be our partners. But times were tough, and they didn't have the money to buy the stock; and very early on, Ralph Campbell died of a heart attack.

From overworking?

Between halves at an Iowa-Minnesota football game. The reason that he took me on as an equal partner is sort of interesting. He said to me frankly, "I'm a lazy man, I don't want to do a lot of work." And he said, "I know you like to work like hell." And so he said, "You can do all the work, and I'll provide the grey hair." And that's how we got started.

We didn't grow very fast, but we plowed everything back into the business. After Ralph died, I bought out his interest at book value, and then I made an offer to his widow, who was left without anything. I paid her every month until she died. No written agreements or anything like that; it just worked that way. And we just worked hard, that's all. Times were tough; it was the Depression days. Our total billing the first year was $197,000. For six months, we didn't pay ourselves a dime. We finally were making $1,000–$5,000 a year, and I decided that we had to have some real good talent, and we had to plow the money into the business. So I went down to New York and hired a copywriter for $25,000, and brought him out there to go to work for us. His name was Dan Casey.

Gradually, the businessmen in town began to recognize that we meant business, as we decided that we would build that business and try to cement the good people into the organization. So as soon as Ralph died, I went to our attorney and asked him to devise a stock option plan, and at that time you could give people ten years to pay up an option; and everybody was offered stock at current book value. They didn't have to put in a dime; they could wait until ten years were up and the day before the option expired, they could pay for the stock. And every year we grew. The philosophy was to build instead of milk. We never milked the business. So everybody who has ever owned stock in the agency, and everybody who has retired, has made a capital gain, has made a profit.

Do you have some sort of a profit-sharing plan?

We have had a profit-sharing plan almost from day one.

How long was Ralph with you before he died?

About ten, eleven, twelve years.

I was scared stiff when he died. I didn't know whether I could make it go. And that's why, of course, I so urged our people to become involved, and make that stock option plan available.

Now, as we worked on that stock option plan, we attracted people like a man that you know, Al Whitman, and others; and it might be interesting for me to explain how we extended the agency over a period of years. As we began to make more money than we needed in the daily activity of the business, we began to invest in our clients, the clients that we knew had good products and good management.

Buying their stock?

Buying their stock. And eventually we had such a large stock portfolio that, of course, the IRS began to complain. That's when we decided that we'd better get into some other operating businesses.

Is that why you went into that outdoor advertising business?

That's exactly right. I know some other agencies have gone into businesses where they have not been successful. But we decided that, rather than pay the money to the government, due to excess accumulation of funds—we decided that we would get into some businesses that we knew something about. And we first got one outdoor advertising plant, then a second one, then a third one, and then we bought a couple of radio stations, and finally we bought a manufacturing business, so that we had quite a few things going. Plus, the investment in the stock of various companies.

Today, I noticed in the *New York Times,* there was an article about the International Dairy Queen Company, and the value of their stock and how it's gone up. As an illustration, we bought one of the areas of Dairy Queen. We owned 300 stores, had 300 stores in the Dairy Queen business; eventually we sold them to the mother company. After stock splits and so forth, I suppose our stock cost per share would probably be about 50¢ or 40¢ in Dairy Queen. Well, today the stock is quoted at $22 per share.

And when people retired, like Al Whitman as an example, we would say, "Do you want cash or would you like to exchange your stock for some of these blue chips that are in our portfolios?" We bought out Al Whitman almost 100% with exchange of stock, which was tax-free to him, and on which we didn't have to pay any capital gain. So it was a benefit to both parties.

Whitman worked with us for maybe 21 years and he's been retired for about eleven years. And like myself, he's become involved in some other businesses. He's director of several companies, and incidentally, he's the greatest partner anybody ever could have had. Absolutely honest man, and a hard worker.

It took a number of sessions until Al was sure that our philosophies were the same. I told Al that the job is the boss. Not Mithun. You just do a job for the client and everything takes care of itself. Our philosophy was that you're never satisfied; you're always going to make it better. You're always going to do better and better for the clients. You're going to create better advertising. You're not going to worry about whether you're getting paid—I mean, you worry if somebody can't pay their bills, but you're not going to worry about whether you're making enough money off of them.

It was very tough attracting people to Minneapolis for many years, because most advertising people think New York is the Mecca, and in the early days nobody knew whether we ever were going to amount to anything or whether we were going to die on the vine, and they were afraid of moving to Minneapolis for fear it would be Siberia, that they would get out of the main stream.

For many years it was very difficult. We'd get a lot of castoffs, reformed alcoholics who'd turn into alcoholics when they got to Minneapolis. But as times have changed, and as we have become recognized as a pretty good house, it now is not really a problem to attract people to Minneapolis. They love it. And I have never known anybody who came to work there who wanted to leave.

How do you recruit your people and how do you judge them?

I believe we have been fairly creative in two ways in our personnel activity. First in recruitment efforts—and second, in screening our people.

Because this business depends almost 100% on people, I wanted to improve on our guesswork in hiring. So I asked a firm of industrial psychologists to help us. First, they studied our industry. Next, they studied Campbell-Mithun. Finally, they said they thought they could help us.

So next we decided to test the testers. I asked them to judge the top 25 men in Campbell-Mithun. After years of working with all 25, I knew their various qualifications. Lo and behold, the psychologists came up with the right answers 24 out of 25 times.

This gave us confidence. So we hired them to pre-screen all our major prospects. We were not looking for duplicates in Brooks Brothers suits. We wanted the mavericks with the right mental and emotional talents to fit into this high-strung business.

After many years of success in this area, I was asked to present our methods at the 4A convention in Greenbrier. It soon became evident that most of the agency executives were not interested. They knew the answers. But our method really works. For example, we hired several people from Europe. Artists—who instinctively know a lot more about symbolism than American artists. They have been brought up in a society where the Bible stories were told on cathedral walls when most people were illiterate.

We hired a superb Indian artist. He was great with Hamm's TV animals. We hired Cleo Hovel fresh out of the Army. He was a genius. He could draw—paint—sketch—write—and *think*. I brought him the rhythm of the voodoo dancers from Haiti. Then he created the music and the creative pattern of Hamm's beer.

. Leo Burnett wanted a beer account. So he hired Cleo to solicit Schlitz. Cleo worked on Schlitz—then Green Giant, P&G and other accounts—until Leo made him his creative director. But Cleo missed the spirit at C-M. So he came back to us as creative director. Sad to say—he died at an early age—sitting in our apartment in Chicago—watching TV.

As I said, Cleo was a tremendous talent. In two hours on the floor in a hotel room in Dayton, O.—Cleo and I put together an entire program for Top Value Stamps. The name. The strategy. The symbols. And the advertising. The next day Kroger was in the stamp business.

In Houston—in the Exxon board room—we did the same thing in one evening when Exxon bought out the Signal Oil Company on the West Coast. Ditto in California—in a hotel room on a Saturday afternoon in L.A.—we created the entire program for Laura Scudder. New packaging. New theme. New advertising— even new products. It was great fun. We believed in extending a cogwheel idea through every communication device. Like a shish kebab.

We learned how a copy man and an artist should team together and not work in separate compartments like when I started in this business. We learned—the job is the boss. Not Ray Mithun. And firmly established that idea throughout the agency.

To answer your question about recruitment—again, we innovated. We hired an ex-agency man in New York to work with us full time. First he spent weeks in our office to learn about our people. Our spirit. Our needs. Then he worked full time as our headhunter —for top people. No ordinary employment agency approach. It really worked. Finally—we lost him because he was hired as a top executive in one of the largest agencies in New York.

Nowadays most of our people are home-grown. Minneapolis is fully recognized as an important advertising center. The talent pool here is tremendous. And almost everyone who aspires to get into advertising is knocking at our door. It's a marvelous situation —and a great contrast with the early days.

Over the years we have helped to spawn a number of other agencies and creative shops. When two of our hottest creative people decided they wanted to go in business for themselves—we encouraged them. Even provided them a loan to get started. They grew and prospered. Created outstanding TV for advertisers from coast to coast. One of the two is now back with us. The other is still doing great—on his own. It's all fun—to see men grow. And prosper.

When you finally decided to turn the management over to younger people, when was that?

Well, early on—I would guess that 10 or 15, maybe 20 years ago, I decided that it would be stupid to have all the know-how in management just in my noggin. I thought that other people ought to become involved. And so I formed an Executive Committee— there were five people on it—and I exposed that Executive Committee to everything that was going on, regardless—no secrets, everything out on top of the table—with the whole agency, for that matter, but particularly with the Executive Committee. So we've never had any problem with management. It's just an evolving situation.

And early on, Al Whitman became president of the agency, and I became chairman of the board and chief executive officer. But being CEO doesn't amount to a damn. So far as I'm concerned, we're all account executives. Later on—Stan Blunt, George Gruenwald and Dave Seibel—all grew up through our Executive Committee development.

How did you work your finances on a long-term basis? I thought that you had to give up your outdoor at one point because of 4A's ruling.

No, we never did. I was on the board of the 4As and Marion Harper was chairman, and I knew that there was some concern about whether an agency should own media, and so I went down to the 4As, in one of the board meetings, and told them that we were having a problem because of excess accumulation of funds, and I thought that we needed to diversify, and the intelligent thing would be to get into the media business. And I intended to get into the media business where it would not be a conflict of interest. We were going to buy an outdoor plant in an area where Campbell-Mithun was not using outdoor, and conceivably in the future was not going to be using outdoor.

Well, that caused some soul-searching, and almost everybody on the board thought it was okay, but Marion Harper put a halo over his head, and decided that it was wrong, and in the next board meeting, brought up a resolution that Campbell-Mithun should be expelled from the 4As. I pointed out to him that he was out of order; that there had been a system set up years ago by the board of directors and by the association on how to go about expelling anybody from the 4As, and he had better follow the system.

The board began to examine their own thoughts. They all agreed that it was inadvisable to try to throw us out of the 4As. So then we bought a second and a third outdoor plant, and these two radio stations, and those purchases turned out to be extremely valuable to us, in addition to buying the Dairy Queen business, and so forth. As a matter of fact, Campbell-Mithun, over the years, has made just as much money on the outside as we've made in the agency business. And whenever anybody has retired from the agency, we've given them their choice of shares in the outside activities, or shares out of our stock portfolio, or cash. And that went along fine.

And as I began to lose physical energy, lose the ability to run around the bases every day as fast as I think a man should in the agency business, I decided it would be time for me to not retire totally, but to lessen my grip on the agency, and to start selling my stock back to the employees.

All during those years, about ten years there, why, we were getting all kinds of offers from larger advertising agencies, people who wanted to buy us out. The first offer came from Howard Williams, who was the head of Erwin, Wasey at the time. Actually, he didn't want to buy us out, he wanted to merge with us. He said to me, "Ray, I don't want to run this business any more; I'd like to spend most of my time in Los Angeles and work on the Carnation business." He said, "We need leadership in New York and London and Chicago and Kansas City; and you've got an agency in Minneapolis. I'd like to have you go down to New York and take over the entire management of Erwin, Wasey, and we'll merge the two agencies." That was my first offer.

You didn't do that, because you didn't want to come to New York.

That's right. The second major offer that we had was from Y&R; but they kind of cooled on it when they found out, if we exchanged stock, that I'd be the largest stockholder in their company.

The third one was with Sullivan, Stauffer, when Brown Bolté was there, and he wanted to merge. But I didn't think that we were ready for it. The next one was from Kenyon & Eckhardt. They didn't have any food accounts. And then, of course, there was Ogilvy, who came out to Minneapolis, and made a presentation to our agency, and then asked me to come down to New York and become his partner, and to run the agency, and he would be the creative head and I would be the manager. And I told him I didn't want to move to New York, but I gave him a suggestion, and that was the idea that he become acquainted with Esty Stowell. So I think I was helpful there.

I'm sure you were. You and I both suggested that about the same time, apparently. Anyway, Esty ended up being the guy.

And after that, there were offers from Foote, Cone & Belding, and McCann-Erickson, about a dozen. Foote, Cone & Belding, for example—the last week, when I was deciding to turn over the business to our employees—Foote, Cone wanted to trade stock, which would have been tax-free to me, and their stock was then about $5 or $6 a share on the Big Board, and I guess it's $35 or $40 now, so it would have been quite a gain for me.

But we'd always worked on the basis of buying and selling stock at book value. In other words—they got the business FREE. They just paid for the cash in the business. I had one thought in mind, and that was to build an agency in Minneapolis that would continue in business. No single agency has ever extended its history in Minneapolis beyond the life of the founders. They've all folded and gone by the boards. I decided that that was unfair to clients, and that we should try to institutionalize the business. So I turned down all those offers for a hell of a big financial gain, and sold my stock back to the agency at book value—which means they got the business free—and gave the fellows five years to pay me. Of course, they made the whole thing back in less than five years.

I believe it took them just three years.

Wonderful.

As I remember, I lent some of them the money at 5% or 6% or 7% interest. And then they turned around and sold it at a hell of a financial gain, too.

Well now, were you involved in the sale to Bates?

Yes, I was on the Campbell-Mithun board, and it came up before the board, and everybody was in favor of the sale except me.

How do they feel about it now, or shouldn't I ask that question?

Well, the key executives who sold out to Bates made themselves independently wealthy, but the next generation will not have the same opportunity. So where I thought I had an unwritten covenant that they would continue to operate on the same basis forever, why, the signals have now changed.

Do I recall your telling me that there was some possibility of a McCann-Campbell-Mithun arrangement at one point?

Yes, many years ago, when Marion Harper was in charge of McCann-Erickson, they had some problems in that agency. Marion was a genius in certain areas, but from a management standpoint, he had screwed things up a little bit; and the board of directors there decided that they needed a change, and they came out to see me in Minneapolis, and we had a visit on the subject, and we finally decided not to become involved.

There were four members from the Board. They came out to see me, and it just didn't seem to make any sense with Marion still there. On that first visit, they were afraid to release him. At the time they were talking with me, Marion Harper was on his private airplane in Europe. When he came back, things got worse, so then these same folks came back to see me in Minneapolis a second time. And I said, "There's no point in this thing unless Marion Harper's out of the business, and then we might become involved." But fortunately, you know, McCann was a good agency.

And they had very good people, but their finances were all screwed up. Fortunately, several of their clients came to the rescue and provided the financial backing to get the organization straightened out, and Marion Harper was released, so everything worked out beautifully for their agency. They were overextended, and Marion had really abused his position. I could give you all the details but the story is best untold.

Tell me, Ray, I know that you're very close to the University of Minnesota, where you went to school. Do you recruit there? And if you do recruit there and at other places for Campbell-Mithun, if the agency recruits there, what are you looking for?

Well, we don't normally just recruit at Minnesota. We frequently have students from Minnesota working at the agency in the summertime, some of the better prospects. We usually have three or four every summer; and we have established scholarships at Minnesota, at the Journalism School, in advertising, and we've established a scholarship at the Art Institute School.

But we recruit all over the United States. As a matter of fact, we've recruited people from Japan and Europe, too. So there's no concentration on Minnesota.

What are you looking for in the young people?

I think the most important thing is *desire*. The average man can make a success if he has the desire to learn, and has the desire to do a job. The average man is going to fall apart and not be a success if he dogs it and doesn't have the desire to be a winner.

What about women?

Oh, yes, it applies to both. One of my many faults is that I think everybody should try to live up to his God-given talents. If a man's capable of running the 100-yard dash in ten seconds, I think it's a shame if he's doing it in 12 or 13 or 14 or 15 seconds. So for many years, I would push and urge and shove people to try to exceed their talent, to try to run the 100-yard dash in 9.8 instead of 10. And that irritated a lot of people who were more comfortable just coasting in life. So I finally learned, and it took me a long time, not to over-drive people, not to try to push people. Let them decide for themselves whether they really want to do a job. If they want to do a job, boy, then our doors are wide open, and we give them their head and let them run.

Do you look for any particular type of education when you

recruit? I mean, do you have to be an advertising major, or do you have to have an M.A. in Business?

No, we love it if somebody has worked at Procter & Gamble, or General Foods, or General Mills, or Pillsbury, or what have you. I mean, people who've really had their education in the business world.

Do you have a training program for these young people?

Well, we work them all the way through the agency, into every department.

Now, you came up as a copywriter. How do you attract creative people to your agency?

We usually try to hire people who have already evidenced their attitude to do a job. I started as a copywriter, and worked in creative, and actually never stopped working on creative all my business life. But when we were small most of us not only worked in the creative end of the business, but also contacted the clients and worked with the clients. So I became a creative account executive.

Your billing, having started out so modestly with $197,000 your first year? What will it be this year?

Oh, better than $250 million, close to $300 million.

Do you have offices outside of Minneapolis?

Yeah, we have a very fine Chicago office. As a matter of fact, the Chicago office, for many years, was larger than the Minneapolis office. And we have Colorado and Tokyo.

How about the Coast? Do you have any out there?

We did have agency operations both in San Francisco and in Los Angeles when we had the Hamm's Beer account, when we opened up on the West Coast. And we attracted quite a bit of business, and had a fairly good-sized agency in Los Angeles. But after we lost the Hamm business, why, it became rather unprofitable, and so we closed it up.

After you lost the Hamm business, the Hamm's beer business went to hell, too, didn't it?

Well, Hamm's was being served by an agency in Chicago, and they called us one day and asked us if we'd come over and have a visit, and we wound up getting the business. For about six months or nine months we floundered around and didn't know what to do—as a matter of fact, Mr. Hamm wanted to do nothing but just

247

imitate Budweiser. But we finally hit on a campaign, "From the Land of Sky Blue Waters," and sales started growing just like mushrooms. I mean, it was just a fantastic success. So Hamm's decided to open up on the West Coast; they bought a brewery in San Francisco and later in Los Angeles.

When we started with Hamm's, they were third in sales in Minnesota; they moved into first in Minnesota, first in Iowa, first in the whole western half of the United States. When we moved into California, we became first in that market within nine months. So Hamm's was the fastest-growing brewery in the United States.

Then Heublein came along and bought them out for $90 million. Most of that purchase price was in stock, which within a year and a half or two years, was worth $180 million to the Hamm family. We continued as the agency with Heublein for four years—maybe three years—and during that period of time, why, Heublein had five changes of presidents at Hamm's and each president wanted to put his stamp on the business and to change the campaign, until finally we didn't know which direction we were going, and we got fired. Incidentally, when we were fired, we had a 90-day clause, and we went down and got the Heileman account, so we were handling two beer accounts within 30 days.

So Heileman is now a much larger name than Hamm's ever was, and Heileman today is the fastest-growing brewery in the United States! Incidentally, Hamm's failed so badly that when Heileman sold Hamm's to the distributors, they sold out for what was really the equivalent of about $10 million, after you deduct some things.

Well, now, what are you doing, Ray? You pulled back, and you're still on the Board, but what are you up to?

This is sort of interesting for old folks in the advertising business, when they retire and need to do something else. If I took the cash that I was going to get out of the business, there would have been a tremendous capital gains tax. My stock probably would—after splits and so forth—have cost me 10¢ or 16¢ a share, and meanwhile I was selling out for, I don't remember now, $80, $90, $100 a share.

So I needed to get into some business where I could borrow a lot of money and get a deduction because of interest payments, which would offset my taxes. So I stepped out of the agency business and bought a bank. There's a lot of leverage in the banking business when you borrow money in order to buy a bank. So I had a tremendous cost in interest payments to the Northwestern Bank for the purchase of the suburban bank I bought, which offset the profit that I made on the Campbell-Mithun sale.

And that bank wasn't doing too well when I bought it. We made $9,000 the first year. This year it'll make about $1½ million, or $2 million. Then I bought a second bank and a third bank. And now we're in the process of buying a fourth bank.

So all told, I'm making a great deal more money in the banking business today than I ever did in the agency business.

Is your son involved with you in this business?

Yes, I thought I was going to die about three or four years ago— or five years ago—with cancer. And our son was then a vice-president of Y&R in New York; he'd been there for twenty years. I prevailed upon him to come back to Minneapolis and become acquainted with what I was doing, so that in case of my death, he'd be able to carry on. And he's very brilliant; he's a Phi Beta Kappa type of guy, and was valedictorian of his class, and went to Princeton and so forth. And he's doing a superb job.

Beyond the bank, beyond the agency, what else are you doing to keep youself busy?

Well, we have a real estate firm; we have a couple of insurance agencies; I'm still involved in International Dairy Queen. I'm involved in the agency less and less, but of course, I keep in contact with some of the principal clients.

There are some interesting things—to me, anyway—anecdotes that might be interesting.

I'll tell you one on Jeno Paulucci, who is sort of a well-known character. He came into my office many years ago, and set a can down on the desk and said, "Hey, I want you to advertise this." We opened it up, and it stunk to the high heavens. And what was it? It was a can of noodles and everything all mixed in one can, chow mein. I said, "Well, Jeno, if you advertise this, the more you advertise it, the faster you'll go out of business." And he was incensed. He said, "You S.O.B., to hell with you." And he picked up his extra cans and left the office.

A year later, he came back and set a can on the desk. He had invented the bi-pak, with a tape around two cans. He said, "Now, you S.O.B., will you handle our advertising?" We worked with them, and got fired, and then we worked with them again, and got fired, and finally I said I was willing to try it once more if he'd promise he wouldn't ever sell out, because there were rumors he was looking for a purchaser. He raised his hand and said, "I'll swear on a stack of Bibles I'll never sell to anybody." And the next time I came into his office, he had a plaque on the wall. It said, "Attention: Everyone who comes into my office—I will never sell this business." Two weeks later, he sold out to Reynolds.

Another interesting one: in the old days, when Green Giant was called Minnesota Valley Canning Company, Ward Patton was the sales manager. I was working in the office one Saturday, and in walked Ward Patton. He said, "Our advertising stinks. We need another agency. Will you come down and sell us? I want you to sell Ward Cosgrove." So we went down to see Ward Cosgrove, and made a presentation.

We had purchased the Daniel Starch Readership reports on Minnesota Valley Canning Company ads, and they were all like toothpaste ads. In one year's time, they never found a reader. And we showed this to Cosgrove.

Did he have an agency at that point?

He had Leo Burnett Company. He said, "I'll tell you what I'll do. I'll give you half of our business. You can take the pea account or the corn account." I said, "That doesn't make any sense," and he said, "Why?" I said, "You ought to have them both under one umbrella." In those days, they called their corn Del Maize Niblets.

And he said, "Well, what would you do?" And I said, "Give me a week, and I'll come back and I'll show you." And I went back home, and we designed a full-page ad for the *American Weekly*, which was then the No. 1 advertising medium in the country. And we drew a green giant the full size of the page, standing there with a case of peas and a case of corn on either shoulder, and signed it "The Green Giant Company." And we told them to put this green giant on both labels, the peas and the corn, and change the name of the company, and everything else.

Well, when we got down and showed him this, why, he just lit up like a Christmas tree. He said, "Okay, that's fine, but I'm not going to give you the business!" He said, "I can't do that because I guaranteed Leo Burnett I would work with them all of our mutual lives, because I furnished him the money to start in business." And he said, "I have a loyalty there, and I'm not going to change it. But you can have half the business." I said, "No thank you, it wouldn't work; you've got to advertise both." And he said, "Can I show this ad to Leo?" And I said, "Here, you take it."

And that's how it all started?

How Green Giant got started.

Oh, Pillsbury might be interesting. We first worked with Robin Hood Flour, which led to Occident Flour and Occident Cake Mix, which became the No. 1 selling cake mix in America, much to the irritation of Pillsbury, which was trying to get going in the cake mix business. And Pillsbury, at that time, bought out Ballard Flour. They bought out Ballard Flour to give them distribution and market leadership in the Southeastern part of the United States. Along with the purchase of the flour, they got the biscuit business.

Ballard Biscuits, which they really didn't understand, and didn't pay any attention to it when they were buying the flour business. Well, in the first week of our association with Ballard Flour, Bob Keith and I made a trip to the Southeast to observe the distribution in the grocery stores, and try to decide what to do. Every time we walked into a grocery store—this was before the days of open refrigerator cases—we'd go to the back end of the store and open up the refrigerator, and there would be the Ballard Biscuits, and they would blow up in the refrigerator, and they were causing the grocer a lot of trouble—the cans were blowing up. And the grocer would say, "You take those biscuits out of here, or I'm going to discontinue the flour business; to hell with you."

When we got home, Keith suggested to Paul Gerot that he'd probably better discontinue the biscuit business, because it was hurting the flour business. Well, at that time, we had a lot of experience in the refrigerator business, because we'd been working with Land O'Lakes for years. I'd learned immediately, of course, that the Ballard Biscuits were being distributed by Kraft's sales force, which was the greatest damned bonanza in the world, the greatest asset in the world!

I turned to Keith and Gerot, the two of them, and I said, "You don't know what a bonanza you've got there! You've got an oil well; you can pump it for years; all you have to do is fix that can so it doesn't blow up, and with the Kraft sales organization, this can become a No. 1 seller; you can be selling biscuits in carload lots!" Well, Gerot said, "You must be smoking marijuana!" I said, "No, just *please* fix the can!"

Well, Bob Keith went to work and got the can fixed, and it became the No. 1 selling item in the entire Pillsbury organization, and the biggest money-maker they ever had, until the hamburger business.

Then they gave us the biscuit business. We'd only gotten the flour business when we started. They gave us the biscuit business, and our first recommendation when we came in was a double-page spread in *Life* magazine advertising Pillsbury Buttermilk Biscuits— not Ballard—Pillsbury Buttermilk Biscuits—and use the Ballard brand as a hammer brand. Oh, gee. From then on, it was just like shooting fish in a barrel.

You still do business with Pillsbury?

No. Down the road, there was an erosion; we had about half the business and Burnett had half of it, and there was rivalry inside the Pillsbury organization between three guys, all trying to vie for Keith's job, and they were so jealous of one another and of our time, whether we were working with this fellow or that fellow, that it just became unbearable. One time, when Keith was in Europe on a vacation and Gerot was out of the country, we got in a real hassle with the guy in charge of the refrigerated business because he was jealous of our working on the other side of the business, and we just finally got to the point where life was unbearable. So we resigned from the business, and went over to General Mills and went to work for them.

Ah, and you're with them now.

Right. And what a wonderful organization!

Oh, did I ever tell you about Augie Busch?

One day I got a telephone call from Anheuser-Busch. They said, "Are you going to be there tomorrow?" I said, "Yes." They said, "We'd like to come up and see you."

And in walked a marvelous man—I'm getting awful, I don't remember names—he was the man in charge of sales for Anheuser-Busch. And he said, "You've done a pretty good job for Hamm's. You've caused us to investigate the Hamm advertising, and the Hamm marketing, and that's what led us to starting Busch Bavarian." But, he said, "Now we want to go into another business. We'd like to hire you to put us in the wine business. We'll pay you any fee that you stipulate. We want to start from scratch; it's in your hands. Name the products, package the products, help us find the sources of supply, and let's build the business."

So we worked for them for about a year, and designed an entire line of wines; helped develop the sources in Europe—it was all going to be imported wines, French, German, Italian wines, and Spanish. We worked for about a year, and had the whole thing all put together, and went down and made a presentation to Augie Busch, and the net of the recommendation was, "Don't go into the business."

Don't go into the import business, because it was too small a thing, and didn't fit the beer distributors, and so forth. So the whole thing was scratched. But it was a marvelous experience and Augie Busch and the Anheuser-Busch people were absolutely fabulous and thoughtful and gentlemanly to work with. It was a marvelous experience.

Got anything else there?

"Glass Wax"—do you remember that one?

I remember it was a great success of yours.

A fellow from North Dakota by the name of Harold Schafer walked into the office one day, and he asked us to help him establish a line of floor waxes. And we said, "What have you got that's better than Johnson's?" And we monkeyed around with the products, and he didn't have anything any better than Johnson's, and he didn't have any money. So we said, "Don't go in the business, forget it." He had distribution in North Dakota only, and only in hardware stores.

And as he was walking out, we noticed a bulge on his hip pocket, and we said, "What have you got in your hip pocket?" And he pulled out a pint bottle, not of liquor, but it was a liquor pint bottle, and in it he had a product, and he said, "I think this is a pretty good product." And we said, "What is it?" And it turned out to be a very good window-cleaning product.

We said, "Let's try it." It looked like it might work, so we put together a campaign for a product called "Glass Wax." And we designed the package, and everything we did in the campaign was a pioneer approach; pioneering in packaging, pricing, advertising, naming and everything. So it all was innovative in comparison to the then leader in the market, Windex. And in one year's time—

well, actually, he didn't have, as I mentioned, any money; so we decided that we would run a page ad in Chicago and Campbell-Mithun would pay for it, and if the ad didn't produce, we'd forget about it.

So we ran this page ad in the *Tribune,* which was, as I remember —in the area of $3,500.

You didn't have any distribution?

No, but we had a salesman down there.

Well, the ad just said that here was a revolutionary new thing. It was the so-called "Glass Wax" type of advertising; it became sort of famous for a while. It was an editorial-style page, made up just like the front page of a newspaper.

Well, we ran the ad; it cost about $3,500, as I remember, and the salesman had to work like crazy for the next week just filling orders. I mean, the orders came in from every warehouse in town. And in two weeks' time, we had distribution in every outlet in town; grocery stores, hardware stores, drug stores, and everything.

In six months' time, we went across the nation, city by city; opened up every market. He was making money like crazy. We came down to New York, and they laughed at him, and they said, "You boys from the country, you don't know what you're doing; any guy from North Dakota can't possibly do this." So nobody took it on, and we ran a double-page spread on Easter weekend in the *New York Daily News,* and we cracked this market instantaneously. Everybody took it on. So Harold Schafer just became a multi-millionaire overnight. He gave every one of us Cadillacs.

He didn't produce anything. He just sold. He had someone else produce the product.

He gave everyone Cadillacs. I'll never forget, he came and delivered a Cadillac car to our house on Easter Sunday. Our kids were so ashamed of having a Cadillac that when we went to church that day, our youngest boy yelled out the window and said, "Jay"—Jay Huebscher, our next-door neighbor—he said, "Jay, don't hold it against us. Somebody gave us this car."

That was back in the '50s.

What's happened to it?

He refused to improve the product. At the time he was not a sophisticated marketing man. Today he is. But at that time, he fell in love with his own product instead of trying to improve it. And others improved their products and passed us up, and "Glass Wax" became extinct. But meanwhile, we helped develop some other products for him. We developed a product called Mr. Bubble and created it from nothing, just created a package and a name and gave it to him. He went and found a maker, and it became the No. 1 bubble bath in the country. Then he became a leader in the dry bleach business with Snowy Bleach. So he's developed a very good business, and is today a very successful, sophisticated marketing man.

Is he still working out of North Dakota?

Oh, yeah, and he's become the No. 1 citizen of North Dakota, and has done some outstanding things in the state. He went out and bought a town, the old town where Teddy Roosevelt used to live, called Medora; it's in the Badlands. He bought the whole town, rebuilt it, and has made it the No. 1 tourist attraction in that part of the United States. He has an outdoor amphitheatre around the mountains, a natural amphitheatre, where he puts on Broadway-type shows every night that show to 2,000 or 3,000 people every night all summer. And he has built up the motels and the hotels and so forth, and he's got quite an attraction.

There's one thing you haven't asked me, which I think is more important than anything else. And that's the spirit of the place.

The *spirit* is all important. I think the spirit of a football team— you can take eleven men and line them up, and they can be perfect physical specimens, and you'll say they can win any game; but put them out on the field, and they're not going to win if they don't have the right total spirit. And I think this is true of a marriage. I think it's true of a family. I think it's true of a business. I think it's true of a church. God gives us a physical body, and gives us certain talents; each one of us has got a talent that can contribute some way or other to society. But I think that the spirit that's an unseen thing is more important than your brain power or your physical body or anything else. And that's what you either build or you tear down.

That makes a man. That makes a company. An attitude. And that's how I feel.

November 15, 1982

ALFRED J. SEAMAN

Upon graduation from Columbia in 1935, Al Seaman served his business apprenticeship as a grocery clerk, department store salesman, and mail order copywriter for Montgomery Ward before entering the agency business at Fuller & Smith & Ross, where he doubled as a copywriter and account executive. In 1941, he became a partner and General Manager of the Knight and Gilbert Agency, Boston and Providence.

He then joined Compton Advertising, where he worked his way up to Executive Vice-President and Creative Director.

In April, 1959, he joined Sullivan, Stauffer, Colwell and Bayles, Inc., as Vice-Chairman. He was elected President of SSC&B in 1961, and was made Chairman of the Board and Chief Executive Officer in 1979.

During his tenure, SSC&B billings grew from $38 million to over $250 million. In January, 1970, the agency bought 49% of the Lintas Worldwide advertising network, making it a major force in international advertising. After SSC&B was acquired by the Interpublic Group of Companies in 1979, he entered negotiations to consolidate the entire Lintas operation under the SSC&B/Lintas mantle, a deal that was concluded just as Mr. Seaman retired as Chairman in 1981.

He has served as a Director of the Advertising Council, a member of the Advisory Council of the American Association of Advertising Agencies, Director of the National Advertising Review Board, Director and member of the Executive Committee of the Outdoor Advertising Bureau, and as President of the 4A's Educational Foundation. In 1967, he served as Chairman of the 4A's.

He now is Chairman of the Advertising Educational Foundation after the merger of the 4A's and AAF Foundations.

Mr. Seaman entered the Advertising Hall of Fame in 1983.

ALFRED J. SEAMAN

Interview

I was born in Hempstead, Long Island, which in those days was almost a rural village. Hempstead High School in those days was really like a prep school. I think 85 to 90% of the graduating class went to college, lots of them on athletic scholarships. I spent my time running, which was good practice for the rest of my life. Aside from work, I was president of the class, and captain of the track team, and some things like that.

A leader from the very outset.

Yes, in a small way. I was president of my class in grammar school. I was president of the senior class in high school.

Then I registered at Columbia. My father got sick at that point; in fact, he almost died. He didn't die until very much later, but it sort of fouled up my plans for college. But I was determined that I was going to do it, and I did keep on at Columbia. They finally formed the School of General Studies, from which I was graduated with a bachelor's degree.

Did you have to work along with it, Al?

Yes, I worked, and I kept on doing this, even after we were married. And Mary was marvelous about it. I don't suppose I could have finished if she had been your average lady . . . I finished that with honors; in fact, the year I got my degree, I had the only straight A in English in the entire university. That was rewarding. It was a long, hard pull, but something I'm glad I did.

Did you major in English, Al?

Yes. And writing. In fact, that was the accent of the major. I majored in 16th- and 17th-century English literature and creative writing, the accent on creative writing. After college I'd started working fulltime in a department store for the merchandising manager, who was really running the store. I was, at the time, interest-

259

ed in psychology. I was reading a number of books on psychology, and I read one on the psychology of selling, which was written by a couple of professors at the University of Chicago.

And just about the time I'd finished that book and was all full of technical phrases, the merchandising manager said he wanted me to write a report on the store's advertising, which I proceeded to do. Three days later I was in charge of advertising and promotion for the whole store, which seemed like a great thing.

Well, the first thing I found out was that there was a big 12-page newspaper supplement which he didn't like, although it had all been set up and was in final proof form. My job was to get the whole damn thing changed around, and the sale was scheduled a week later. I worked days in the store and spent every night in the composing room of the old *Brooklyn Eagle.* That, I suppose, taught me about 90% of what I needed to know about print production for the rest of my life.

The advertising department had subscribed to a magazine called *Printers' Ink,* and one day I read an article about a thing called an advertising agency. It seemed to me like quite a fascinating place. A little later I read another article in *Printers' Ink* which said the way to get in to agencies was through mail order. I knew a guy who knew a guy who worked at Montgomery Ward, so I arranged to get an introduction. I took my proof book in and sold as hard as I could. This was when jobs were not growing on trees . . .

Depression time, wasn't it?

Yes, sir. They eventually gave me a job, and I learned a lot there. So, I had some possibility of having a mail-order career. However, I hadn't lost sight of the advertising agency. So I wrote some promotion pieces and then I clipped out little pieces and scraps to use and then I got my friends in the art department to put it together. So I had professional-looking mailing pieces which I sent out to the agencies. And, finally, one of my promotion pieces worked. I sent it to Fuller & Smith & Ross and they gave me a job.

I was an assistant account executive, but my main job was as a writer. However, you took your own writing out and presented it to clients. So I got involved in the whole thing, which, as it turns out, was the pattern of my career in advertising. And that was very solid experience. My first job was on American Can, which, incidentally, I worked on at three different times in three different agencies.

I was working for a man named John Wiley, who was the head of the New York office of Fuller & Smith and Ross. Wiley was regarded as the peppery boy in the agency, the can-do fellow. So it was kind of exciting, and, of course, a wholly new exposure to things. American Can Company featured Keglined beer cans, among other things. That was a big operation for its day, because they put a lot of pressure behind Keglined. You might say I was automatically in packaged goods, which was about the only opportunity at Fuller & Smith & Ross.

I remember I was given the job of writing a thing called "The Keglined Merchandiser." It was a newspaper for beer distributors. But it was very good. It was patterned on the *New York Daily News,* and Wiley had done it himself. I was given the job of doing it, and I remember, boy, I worked hard, nights and weekends, and thought my first edition was just great. He tore the whole thing to pieces, rewrote about everything. I was not only set back, but I figured there'd be a pretty good chance that I would lose my job.

Well, I didn't get fired, and within a couple of years John Wiley gave me some assignments that required the very best writing the agency could put forth. He came out to our house on Long Island on a Sunday afternoon from Westchester to look at the copy I'd written. After reading it a couple of times he said he wished he could write that way. That was kind of a triumph—from the guy who had torn all my stuff to pieces.

I was anxious to see Fuller & Smith & Ross get consumer business. It seemed to me that was exciting, and that was where the big action was, and where the prestigious agencies were.

One day I had lunch with a friend of mine whose father was general sales manager for the Axton-Fisher Tobacco Company in Louisville. He told me, "They're going to leave McCann-Erickson." So over the days and evenings I wrote a presentation, and I wrote some ads.

I've looked back at that presentation a couple of times over the years, and it was a damned good presentation. It was sound business, it was sound marketing, it was sound merchandising, and it was exciting advertising. It carried out what needed to be done. I showed the whole program to John Wiley, and he was very excited about it; he thought it was great. He said, "Allen Billingsley (who was our President) is coming down from Cleveland in a day or two. I'll show it to him."

I was sitting in my office, my little cubicle, when the great man himself came and sat down at my desk.

Wow!

He said he thought it was just great, and he appreciated the initiative, but also the quality of the work. It was something the agency would be proud to present. Then he said, "As a matter of fact, (somebody whose name I forget) will be going down through that territory in three or four months, and we'll have him stop in." I said, "But, Mr. Billingsley, they're going to make the decision in the next ten days. We have to go now." He said, "No. It's just not practical now but, believe me, we'll do it." About twelve days later, there was a big announcement in the paper that Axton-Fisher, which owned Twenty Grand Cigarets, and Spuds—one was menthol, and the other was the lowest-priced brand on the market—was leaving McCann-Erickson. It went to some agency that was not in our class at all, I thought.

Well, lo and behold, a little less than a year later, same friend, same source, said Axton-Fisher was going to move again. I thought, "Dammit, how am I going to do this? I'm *not* going to do it the way we did it last time." I got our art director and the owner of a studio we used together and made the presentation to them. I said, "Now, what I need is some comps, and I don't have any money." They were very excited about the presentation, and they did the most beautiful comps you every saw. I probably had, I would think, about 15 to 20 beautiful finished layouts. And I had booklets and all kinds of things, which they worked nights to develop.

I was told by my friend's father-in-law that by no means should I talk to anybody but the President. This was going to be settled at presidential level, and the advertising manager probably didn't even know about it. Now fortuitously, my vacation time had come, so what I did was pack the stuff in the car and drive to Louisville.

I got there at about 8:30 in the morning and asked to see the president. In effect, the receptionist said, who the hell was I, and what did I want to see him about? I told her who I was and what

I wanted to see him about. She said, "Well, you should see the advertising manager." I very resolutely said, "But I want to see the president." She said, "Sit down." In a few minutes the advertising manager came out.

Now, I had rather a tricky job, which was to get to the President without insulting the ad manager. I don't remember quite how I did it, but I did it. I went in with my black bag and my dog-and-pony show. The President said, "Now, this is a little bit uncomfortable, because we have one day a month when our agency comes down in force, and this is the day. They're all over the place, but anyway, go ahead." I started my presentation. The first thing he wanted to know was, "How was it that Fuller & Smith & Ross would speculate?" Of course, in those days, it was considered rather shabby to speculate.

I said, "Well, the agency doesn't speculate, but I do." I told him that I had initiated this on my own; that I knew, as far as the work and the thinking was concerned, it had the blessings of top management, but I was perhaps a little more agressive in seeking new business than this very fine organization would generally be. He accepted that. As we went through the first section, he kept nodding his head up and down. We went to the second section, and he nodded his head some more.

Then he said, "Mr. Seaman, why weren't you here a year ago? It's taken us a whole year to get approximately where you are now." I said it was just a matter of management's attitude, and that's why I'd come down on my own initiative.

"Well," he said, "I would like to show you the work we have, which is right in this direction." I said, "Do you want to show it to me so that I'll know you didn't copy my idea?" He said, "Yes," and I said, "I don't want to see it. I accept that. But," said I, "I have three more stages." We went through the three stages, and he couldn't have been kinder; escorted me to the door, and said, "I promise you that, if we ever change agencies, I will call you, and you and I will sit down together."

Well, just to round off that story: about a year later, there was an annoucement out of the clear blue that they had changed agencies again. So I picked up the telephone, called Axton-Fisher, and said I wanted to talk to the president. They said, "Oh, he's not with us any more. He left six months ago." So that was the end. But it did convince me, Bart, that there was no way that I was going to be able to stay at Fuller & Smith & Ross.

Well, coincidentally, I had a call from a friend named Jack Gilbert, at Livermore and Knight, a company in the printing business. First, he wanted me to go up with him, and I said, "Thanks very much, but I don't want to go to Boston." Then he called in another month or so, and said, "Hey, we've got a terrible problem up here. We need some new advertising, and would you come up over the weekend and do some ads for us? We'll pay all your expenses," and I think he said they'd pay me something like $50 or $75 a day. Fuller & Smith & Ross had no insurance business or anything near it, so there was no conflict. I took Skid Sidebotham, an art director at Fuller & Smith & Ross, with me. I guess Skid drove up; we went up together. Between Friday night, when I got the briefing (and it was late when I got it), and Sunday afternoon, I had written 13 campaigns with three ads in each campaign.

Howard Knight and his son Dick, who was a couple of years younger than I, came by, along with Jack Gilbert. I showed them the advertising; and they took Jack aside and said, "Offer him a partnership; we've got to have him." When Jack later reported this to me, I said, "No." Mary and I had just moved. We had lived in Forest Hills, in an apartment, at first; then with our daughter Marilyn, we moved to a garden apartment in Little Neck, Long Island; and then we got a small house in Hempstead. We had just moved in at about the time this happened. I didn't want to go to Boston, but they kept asking me and asking me, and sweetening the ante. They offered me $5,000 a year, which was pretty damn good then, and a partnership in the agency, and a great future, and blah-blah-blah. So anyway, I finally succumbed.

There was also the exciting prospect of building an agency, of course. We had John Hancock to start with, the prospect of building the company, and then spreading from Boston to New York. I guess everybody who's ever been in Boston has thought of that and almost nobody had ever done it. So I took off to take on my new duties, again driving. The day I left to take over these new responsibilities and live in Boston was December 7, 1941.

And so, of course, that turned the whole world topsy-turvy. Now, my first decision, you know, the first thing you think about, or at least some people think about, is should I go into the service. We had two children, and not a great deal of money, and I figured, I think rightly, that there were a lot of guys who should go first.

So we began the job of building the agency. Before I got there, by the way, I'd written an ad for the agency, which was published in the Boston papers, and as a direct result of that, we got Northeast Airlines—even before I got there. That seemed exciting at the time. As an account, if you'll pardon the pun, it never got off the ground—but it was exciting.

But we got Flash Chemical Company, I remember, and we got part of American Mutual Liability Insurance Company, and so forth. And the agency was really growing, except clearly I had inherited a problem with John Hancock. The advertising manager and his assistant wanted Knight & Gilbert out of there—that was the agency's name—because the relationship went back to Howard Knight and Howard Knight's influence with John Hancock's top management. They had spent $100,000, I think, on a research project, and my first duty was to do something with it.

The study was so wide that it was almost meaningless; trends in population, changes in social and economic status, life insurance holdings, savings, economics, etc., etc. My job was to take this and turn it into an advertising proposal, and a broad strategy for John Hancock.

It was then my job to present it to the executive committee, and it was a triumph. Here I was—I guess I was about 27 or 28—the world's expert on economics, population movements, and you name it.

Meanwhile, I'd become the head guy running the agency, and things looked good. However, Dick Knight had gone into the Navy about a year before, and I remember, I'd go home, and Mary and I would sit there by the fire and read the headlines about the ships going down. I got more and more uncomfortable. One night I said to Mary that if I could get a commission, I'd like to go into the Navy. We talked it over for a long while. Then Mary said quite simply and directly as she often did: "Do it."

Well, the end of it is, I got a commission as a JG, and in I went, and Mary went back to Long Island. This was in early '43.

I wound up as a Fighter Director Officer; I was in charge of the radar operation aboard the Kasaan Bay, CVE69. We were in the Pacific, the Atlantic, and the Mediterranean, where we covered the invasion of southern France. Then we came back and went to the Pacific. Then I had rotation of duty, and went back to St. Simon's for a refresher course, and from there back to another carrier. We were scheduled to cover the invasion of Japan, but there was a little guy named Harry Truman who dropped a bomb!

And then I came back. I didn't have a job; because after I left Knight & Gilbert in Boston, all the business went different places.

The agency dissolved, huh?

It was still there, but it did only a little sales promotion. Dick Knight came down to see me and said they were willing to lose $50,000 a year if I thought we could start it up again. Well, I had great regard for them, but I also knew how painful it was for them to part with $50,000. I said, "No, I don't think so, because it would take more than that." Well, of course, that let them off the hook, because they didn't have to hire a returning veteran.

There I was, by this time with three children, and no job. A friend of mine who was a photographer, Tom MacManus, said, "Why don't you call Dick Compton? That place is a revolving door." I said, "Mac, why do I want to go to a place that's a revolving door?" He said, "Because often that's where the opportunities are." A wise man, Mac, and a good friend.

So I got on the phone bravely, and said I wanted to talk to Mr. Compton. Well, Mr. Compton was away, and they transferred me to a man named Mr. Strubing. Of course, Jack Strubing was gung-ho for the military and anybody who had been in uniform was his buddy. So he saw me. Before the interview I had to decide what kind of job I wanted, because I'd been a writer and also done account work, and I'd actually run a small agency. I figured that since I'd been out of writing so long, you know, maybe the touch was gone, and maybe I'd be better as an account man. Jack listened sympathetically, and then he said, "You know, we can't do anything for you, because we have people coming back whom we have to take back, and we don't have enough jobs for *them.*"

On the way out the door, I said, "You know, I also write." Jack was glad to get off the hook, because he wanted to do something, so he said, "Let me call Joe Leopold." He called Joe Leopold, and Joe said, "Well, I can see him now."

I went down and talked to Joe, and Joe said, "Well, let me see some samples." I said, "I don't have my sample book here; it's at another agency." I said, "I have two or three proofs in my brief-case, but it wouldn't be fair to me or to you for me to show them to you. I'd rather wait until I have more representative samples." Well, finally, I thought, if I provoke him much further by refusing to show them, he may not see me again, so I sort of reluctantly got out the first ad and showed it to him. Joe was nodding and smiling as he read the ad. "You got any more?" he said. So I tried out a couple more. Well, by gad, he sent me to see Ed Dexter and Ham Mattoon on a Thursday afternoon.

And that got you the job?

Monday I was on the payroll as a copywriter, print copywriter, for Ivory Soap. And at $10,000 a year.

The first assignment I had, quite naturally, was to write some new campaigns for Ivory Soap. They thought it would be best, mind you this, they thought it would be best if nobody told me anything about Ivory Soap, and if nobody told me anything about the client. "Just write whatever you'd like to write." So I spent about a month generating ad after ad, and going down this road and going down that road and going down the other road.

Finally, I got to present them. Not one of those ads ever saw the light of day, of course. But it had established me, in the agency, as a capable person, if I may presume as much.

I think it was three months after the time I arrived that I was made print supervisor on all the P&G business. Then I had got involved in the New York Life Insurance business, because Ed Dexter was busy writing nasty notes to the Advertising Manager, who was writing nasty notes back to Ed. I was called in because of my experience with John Hancock. I did some ads which put out the fire. Al Thiemann, who was then the head of public relations at New York Life, felt he could do business with me. That ended up, as you know, with the ads I did one weekend, which made New York Life a national advertiser. It was a "short, short story" campaign, which I guess ran for four or five years.

You know the rest of the Compton story, so I won't go into that, except to say that I learned a great deal there that I've found not only useful, but extremely valuable, the rest of my career. I found the disciplines and even the frustrations, but especially the disciplines, of Procter & Gamble to be helpful to me, not only in my own thinking, but in building an organization. And I think it was just an invaluable experience.

But I suppose the big thing—the discipline, which I think in many cases is still missing among lots of advertising and lots of agencies—I learned there. Some of them were nice enough, as you know, to say I'd contributed to *their* thinking as well.

Anyway, when I went to SSC&B, I went with exactly the proposition that was described at the time, though I think most people thought I went over to be president. But that wasn't so. I bought the idea they had started with—Sullivan, Stauffer, Colwell and Bayles—four who called themselves "the partners". And in effect, although I didn't do the same things, I was meant to occupy the stall that had belonged to Don Stauffer. And in order to position me, I was made chairman of the executive committee and Vice-Chairman of the board.

I had known a lot of people there—Joe Leopold, Cliff Dillon, Beth Holmes. I knew Bob Colwell, who was then outside the agency. And, indeed, because he had asked me to go with them back in 1947, and I'd said no, I thought I had a career at Compton. I had got to know Heagan Bayles. But when I got to SSC&B, I found it was altogether different from what it had seemed to be on the outside.

To give you some feeling about what the problem was—and Heagan would agree with this—it turned out that the agency was losing money on almost every account it had except one or two. And if they lost one, the agency—I don't think would have been out of business—but for all practical purposes it would have been in very serious trouble. There was no substantial organization. Some of the account people were buying their own media. It was very unbelievable.

Who was the chief executive then?
Brown Bolté.

Ray Sullivan originally had been president, but he moved to Chairman of the board, and the by-laws of the corporation said the president was chief executive officer. That was true until we made the deal with Interpublic, at which time we changed it so the chairman would be CEO. Meanwhile, profit sharing had gone down to 5% and was sinking fast, and morale was very low.

When I got over there, as it turned out, nobody knew what I was supposed to do. Well, just by listening to what some of the problems were, I felt the best answer was to turn the executive committee into an *executive* committee. It would make the policy, and then the President's job was to carry out that policy. The Executive Committee was made up of Ray Sullivan, Heagan Bayles, Brown Bolté and myself. I remember I spent the first couple of weeks doing a kind of grand charter for the executive committee, and a program for the operation of the agency. Brown was somewhat surprised by this, as the others were when it was presented, but they all agreed it was a good idea, and they adopted it.

Did Brownie want you there?

No. He never said he didn't, but he obviously didn't. But they were in enough trouble, they were in a transition period, and I think Ray and Heagan were astute enough to know they needed help, and they were determined to have help. Inasmuch as they owned most of the stock, what they decided was the way it would be. The difficulty was that Brown agreed with the policy, and then went and did something different, sometimes just the opposite.

I thought it all through very carefully, and finally decided, Bart, that this kind of a system wasn't going to work. So I sat down with Heagan at cocktails one night, and I said, "This isn't my kind of operation. I think the simplest thing for me to do is find myself another job. It's no problem, you don't have to think a great deal about it, because I'm reasonably sure I can; and so, goodbye." Not quite that abruptly, but that was the message.

So they had a meeting and decided that Brown would become vice-chairman, and I would become president and chief executive officer.

When Heagan talked to me, I said, "There is one condition which I must have, and without it, I don't want the job. The condition is this: There's a great deal that needs to be done. I will do whatever I need to do, unilaterally make whatever decisions I have to make, because this is clearly not the kind of thing to be solved by committees. We've tried that. I'll tell you, sometimes, before I do something, but mostly I'll tell you after. And if you don't want that, let me go quietly on my way."

Yes, they did want that. Then—I think I was quite fair about this—I said, "Heagan, before we proceed any further, I think you should decide whether you really want to expand and become a big agency. You started off with the hope that you'd have a $10,000,-000 business. You have almost four times that now. You, personally, are very strong with American Tobacco, and you, personally, are very strong with Carter Products. And Ray Sullivan is strong, of course, with Noxzema. Here is a nucleus, Heagan, for you to have a strong small agency. You don't have all these miserable management problems. It's a little Jiffy Ad Shop, lined with gold. Why don't you do it?"

Well, he said he had thought that through, and rejected it—very wisely, as it turned out. So we proceeded. Bolté was shocked, but not shocked enough to leave. I suppose Ray Sullivan actually influenced me more in the area of reorganization than anybody else—not by what he said; Ray was always, totally, in support—but mostly by what I knew to be his feelings. Ray had a great softness about people; he would have been a great head of some eleemosynary society. In fact, as you know, he did a lot of that. He built a church in Korea—and supported missionaries.

He was a very nice man. I knew that Ray would be unhappy if we did what we *should* have done, which was to have a wholesale firing and cleaning out of underbrush. I elected not to do that. That set up a series of very big problems. One was that I soon found that if I wanted a weekly meeting with the senior executives in the company, I couldn't have a meeting with the department heads and the account people together, because we would have a Kilkenny fight. So I alternated: One Monday I'd meet with the departmental people, and the following Monday I would meet with the account people. Then I served as the liaison.

About this time we got a chance to solicit the Lipton Tea account. Gardie Barker, the (then) executive vice-president of Lipton, had known the SSC&B people when they were at Ruthrauff & Ryan. Heagan asked Gardie if we might solicit the account. Gardie was a man who wasn't going to give you anything, but he certainly would be interested in listening. My job was to resign the Salada Tea business before we solicited Lipton. The agency was in trouble with them and we were losing our shirts anyway. I went up to Boston to see the head marketing man of Salada. I told him why I was there, and took him through all the reasons, and said that the thing that made the most sense for us and for them was for us to resign the account. So the Salada executive said, "I understand. Let's go to lunch." That man is named Hugh Tibbetts, and he's currently the chairman of Lipton.

I led the charge on this. It was the damndest presentation you ever saw. I'd better not get into this, because it's too long, but it was a hell of a show. We just knocked everybody else out of the box and got the business. That gave a lot of publicity to the organization. It was worth three times its billings, because of that.

Well, from then on, the management of SSC&B was a kind of three-pronged job. The first thing was to get the organization right, which we did slowly. The second job was to build professionalism. The third one was to jack up the creative product. They did a lot of research and were trying desperately to build advertising which would sell the most product. But in the end, it had become pretty dull on average. In some cases, it was exciting—like Noxzema and Cover Girl—but the job was to lift the level of excitement without losing basic principles of selling goods.

All of our accounts were highly professional packaged goods people, all in highly competitive businesses, and they had to have selling power. The hope was that you could increase the effectiveness of that selling proposition by making the advertising more exciting—without having the excitement unrelated and false and from outside; that's the trap that so many of the so-called smart people fall into. And gradually, we did it. It was much slower than I had hoped it would be; and, of course, it's a thing that goes on forever anyway. But we began to pick up some power there.

What about the financial picture?

Profit sharing, which had been at a low of 5%, we built back up over the first five years to the point where the agency was even for the whole history of the company, despite all these bad years we'd had. As you know, you can make up for past short-falls, and one year we paid 27% in profit sharing. And when I left—well, when we stopped the profit sharing, that was the record: that we had paid the maximum allowance—15% across the board for the entire history of the company.

Anyhow, Bart, that's the story. I think what we did at SSC&B in the end was to build an organization that was highly professional, where I think politics was as close to a minimum as you can

271

get; where there was a feeling of esprit de corps; where there was a feeling of history, which, like all history, looks better after it's over than it did while it was happening. But I felt good—I think I left it with people feeling that they had been part of, and are part of, something very special.

I might say, parenthetically, that although I had established the right to do anything I wanted to do, in actual practice I never did anything to change policy, or anything that would lead to a change in policy, without sitting down and talking it over with Heagan to begin with. I am sure that was one of many reasons why he and I had such a fine and constructive relationship for more than 20 years. So he always knew in advance what was going to happen; and he respected my right to do what I felt was right, and he trusted that. It turned out to be very good.

He made out good. He should have. Heagan was a real entrepreneur. They all hocked their life insurance to start SSC&B, you know, and Heagan, I have been told, was the chief architect.

Now, Al, tell me whatever you can about the Lintas story—your merger of Lintas and SSC&B.

Well, I'll sketch the Lintas story for you. It happened, as far as we were concerned, accidentally, almost. I think it was about 1960 or 1961, we were invited by Lever Brothers to make a three-hour presentation to some of their colleagues from abroad.

Here, in this country?

Yes. They said we could talk about anything we wanted: our philosophy, examples of work we'd done, anything we wanted. And they also invited the other agencies who worked for Lever Brothers to do the same thing. The agencies, at that time, were: Thompson, BBDO, Ogilvy, ourselves, Foote, Cone & Belding, and a small agency—they handled a couple of products for Lever Brothers. We put on a show, and as you can imagine, it took up the whole three hours. Then we went back to work, glad to have *that* out of the way. Well, about two days later, two of the men came over to see us; one named Ivor Cooper, who was the retiring head of Lintas, and Tim Green, who was the emerging head of Lintas.

Maybe I'd better give you some background. This is very important in the whole concept of it. I think it was about 1902; Lever himself—later Lord Leverhume—decided that he'd better do something special about advertising. He was an instinctive believer in advertising. He felt that the Americans knew more about and had a better feeling for advertising than anybody else. So he came to America and got a man named Sidney Gross from Philadelphia—very likely with N W Ayer, but I'm not sure—to come over to be his advertising manager. Sidney Gross went over, spent about a year, and then went to Lever and said he could help more from the outside than from the inside.

At that time, Lever Brothers was beginning to expand geographically at a rapid pace. They grew in two ways: one, in marketing, and two, in supplies. They were buying plantations in Africa, they were building their own river boats to bring the oils up river, and they even had their own fleet of ocean-going vessels. And they were going into all kinds of out-of-the-way places. For example, about five years ago, we went to London to celebrate the fiftieth anniversary of Lintas in Nigeria!

But anyway, Unilever had some agencies they used in London. It wasn't a case of *picking* an agency for out-of-the-way places because if you went to Nigeria, there wasn't any such thing, so you had to be able to provide your own services. Sidney Gross's concept was that you would be better off having something called an advertising agency—outside the company—that could service the business. That took hold very well.

Which they owned.

They owned it, but they had no choice. What they wanted didn't exist. And this is a very important point, as we go into the present. Unilever never wanted to be in the agency business as a business. They never did, including the time we were associated with them, look upon it as a profit center because, you know, their turnover, as they call it, is probably about $28 billion now. So what can a Lintas do?

However, from the beginning, having a Lintas which provided a strong marketing service was absolutely essential to them. And over the years, they built up emotional attitudes toward it. Lintas began to grow. Then they came to the point: Did they want to put all their advertising in it? They decided "No." It was then, I think, probably in the '20s, when they were looking to the Thompsons and the Young & Rubicams and other agencies.

As a very young person, in 1925, Ivor Cooper became the head of the Lintas operation, but not the kind of head we would think of. He was basically a coordinator. Each one of the Lintases reported to the Unilever management of that country. For example, in Germany, Lintas reported to the German Unilever chairman.

That meant that some good things happened, and some bad things happened. The biggest bad thing was that money became of no importance, because it was a relatively small item, and if the chairman was getting the kind of service he wanted, who cared about a few extra dollars? So you had a marketing-oriented group, but not a profit-oriented group.

And Ivor's job was to run around the world and preach the good fight, preach new and emerging techniques of marketing and copy, etc., etc. But he had no power; he could simply say, "Here is the new thing, and this is what we ought to do, and I want you to come to London and spend two weeks with us, and we'll indoctrinate you in all this, and you'll come back a happier and better chap." Then when you go back home again, you would be the man in town with the latest information about what was going on in the big world. Of course, after the war, Lintas was big, flabby and sort of staggering along.

Well, by about 1959, Tim Green, who had been a Unilever marketing man, was made Chairman of Lintas London. George Cole, who was the chairman of Unilever, said to Tim that he wanted him to upgrade the whole Lintas system. But, interestingly enough, he gave him no power, except the power of persuasion. And this is where Tim, I think, is at his best. He's a great itinerant preacher. He learns a country very quickly, he absorbs information.

He went round and round the world, preaching the change in marketing, the change in advertising, the American dominance and influences etc., etc. He soon concluded, I gather, and sold to George Cole, the concept of "windows to the West."

Now you would think that Unilever and Lintas would have had access to the American market in any depth they wanted, except the American companies had always kept Unilever at arm's length.

Was this a matter of policy—this arms-length thing?

Yes. And a number of executives here, historically, had sold that idea to London, and it was generally accepted that this was hands-off, no invasion, no undue influence.

Getting back to the 1960s, the Lintas people could, on occasion, properly accompanied, come over and maybe visit a Lever or a Lipton, and then go home again. That was about it. So they had no windows to the West. Tim wanted that, and so did the others, and the idea was bought. They set out to find an agency with which to make an association. That was the background . . .

Of why the big presentations?

Yes.

Of course, you didn't know that.

No, we didn't know any of that. And frankly, I don't think most of us knew much about Lintas, because up until this time, Lintas was only for Unilever. If you were an outsider, the services weren't available.

So when Tim Green, who was the architect of this proposal, and Ivor Cooper, who represented the past and stability and all of that, came over to see us, they said they felt that we represented the kind of thinking that would be important to them—better than any of the other agencies. They emphasized there was no pressure from Lever Brothers or Lipton for us to do this, but they thought it would be great if we would train their top people in American marketing and advertising. They proposed we do that by a series of seminars over a period, and also by having some on-the-job trainees. For example, if they sent somebody over, it would be somebody, probably at the account group head level, people with considerable experience. And they would pay us for it.

Well, I don't think we looked very excited, because you can't make any money that way. But then they said the thing which made the little bird come out of the cage. The said, "If you people decide to go abroad, and we think you will eventually—and you're already a little late—we will roll out the red carpet, we'll open our books to you anywhere in the world, we'll help you get people, and Unilever may even give you some business in various places to help you get started."

That would perk you up a little bit.

Yeah, that got our attention right off. And we decided to do it, without too much deliberation. So—I guess it was in early '63, or maybe '62—we had our first seminar. And, of course, they sent their crack troops; they had the best from all over the world,

How many did they send?

Oh, I would think about 20. There was the chairman of France,

275

the chairman of England, the chairman of Germany, etc. A very bright lot, people who were very sophisticated. Many of them spoke quite a few languages.

How long would these things last, Al?

A week.

But back to New York; it was a big success. Our people made friends with them and vice versa. At the end of two or three years, they had absorbed a tremendous amount of new knowledge.

How often did you hold these seminars?

Well, at first, we would have a top executive seminar once a year. We would have a research seminar once a year. We did it by sections.

And none of the other agencies, at this point, were involved in this; it was strictly your own, right? Because they had felt that you had done the best job, and therefore could be the most helpful.

Yes. Well, the relationship began to grow and flourish. We made lots of trips back and forth, and we'd send people around to various Lintas offices. Heagan and I would make trips, and so on. By 1967, the relationship had developed sufficiently so that they sort of proposed that maybe we should have some kind of relationship that was more formal than what we had. It was the kind of thing that SSC&B had to approach very gingerly, because it would be all too easy for the word to get around that we had become a captive of Unilever, and we had become a house agency. So we were very careful. I remember talking to John Crichton [president of the American Assn. of Advertising Agencies] a number of times about it. But events kind of built up their own momentum, and the momentum was that, yes, this would be a good thing to do. It soon got to the point where we actually began negotiations.

Robert Siddons, who was the head of marketing for Unilever, was their chief negotiator. Marvelous man. Tall—if you sent to Central Casting for an English aristocrat—they might well have sent a Robert Siddons over. He spoke four or five languages very fluently. A very bright, perceptive, intelligent man of great integrity.

We worked out an arrangement—a "contractual agreement"—which averted any problems we might have about a house agency, and also avoided many of the problems you would have with a financial relationship because our profit responsibilities and needs were very much different from theirs.

So it seemed to me that a thing called a contractual relationship would be something that would let us experiment and would also protect us from whatever competitive attacks might be in the offing. The agreement was that we would service each other's clients anywhere in the world and that we would charge directly the time involved, but each group would be left to take care of its own overhead and profit. That eliminated overhead problems caused by London, for example. Lintas House in London was a fabulous office; they had their own building, they had 500 people at a time when they probably had $12,000,000, at the most, in billing. We didn't want any part of that overhead. So that was the basis on which we went in.

But underneath this, which was not known outside, we negotiated the possibility of our buying what they called the star agencies; those were the big ones—London, Paris, Hamburg, Milan and Sidney—at a time of our choosing. We agreed, as part of that, that we would train people for the remaining offices which Unilever owned. That was a very good deal.

I remember we did an ad. I was in London for a meeting of our Policy Committee. We had just finished our meeting when some proposed announcement ads arrived from New York. Unless you're really involved in it, and have the spirit of it, such ads are difficult to do, so most of the stuff was not usable. I told the others, sort of as a joke, "You gentlemen go in and have a drink. I'll be with you in about ten minutes. I want to write the ad." It turned out pretty well: *"With the stroke of a pen, a 300 million dollar agency is born."* That was fairly sizable on the world scene in those days. The copy was descriptive and competitive, everybody agreed, and we were off and running. I was only half a drink behind.

It went down very well with the advertising community. It did bring the relationship closer, and everybody felt better about it. We went along on that basis until about 1969; then a couple of things had happened. One on this side: we couldn't help noticing that when we talked to top executives about this great service, they would invariably say, "Well, now, tell us how it works." So we'd tell them how it worked, and their eyes would get a little hazy and they'd say, "Well, I'm still not sure I understand. Do you own part of it?" "No, we don't own any of it, but we have this contractual relationship."

We concluded that we should put some money in, so, for example, we could say, "Yes, we own 20%."

That was what happened in the marketplace. In Unilever, Robert Siddons had moved along to chairman of the overseas committee, which was responsible for all of the world outside the U.K., and a man named Ted Brough had become the new head of marketing. I hadn't met Ted Brough, but I'd heard a lot about him. I happened to be in London at the time there were hearings held in Parliament. You may remember this, because P&G and Unilever and Colgate all joined forces to fight against proposed regulations. Ted Brough was selected as the best man to do it. Ted Brough was so impressive in testimony that the whole scheme was dropped, and Ted was invited to become consultant to the *government* on matters of this kind. A marvelous man.

Well, we sat down with Ted, and said, "We've been thinking about this, and we would like to propose that we have an exchange of money." Ted said he was quite willing to do that; however, he had some misgivings about the limited nature of it, and from his point of view, Lintas had to remain a single entity. So we had to talk about all of it or nothing, inasmuch as we had just, at that time, won the Esso business in Africa. Because Lintas can cover Africa better than any two or three agencies put together, that was exciting, and it seemed to open up great possibilities.

Did you get deeply involved at that point?

We went through an arduous process, I must say. I was commuting to London about once a week. I'd go over by myself most times, knowing I was walking into this great morass of technicians, all behind the scenes, you know; but it provided a couple of advantages. One: it always gave me the chance to say, "Well, I have to go home and talk to my experts about it." And the other one was that a number of them, the technical people, got to the point where they'd say, "Tell me, just tell me in everyday language what it is that worries you about this point." So I'd tell them, and many times they'd fix it for me. So they became helpers rather than just "adversaries".

We finally worked out the proposal: we would buy 49% and

have an option to buy the remaining 51%. The intention was for us to buy the 51% as soon as possible. They had done some projections of profit, and we felt that with our impact—and incidentally, by 1970, Lintas had become a very different agency from what it had been before . . .

Because of all the training.

All the training and what you might call natural development. You could go into our office in Durban, South Africa, for instance, and think you were on Madison Avenue. The research people brought in geometric models, for which, incidentally, they'd send us the raw material; we would computerize it here and send it back. Then they'd put their little sticks together, and they were in business.

When did they start taking things other than Lever? During this training period?

Yes. In 1967 they started very slowly to take "outside accounts," and the pace picked up quite rapidly.

That Esso thing you mentioned—was that the first?

That was about 1968 or 1969—the first big one, the most dramatic.

And when we announced the deal, 49–51, we didn't say we had an option for the 51, but we did. Then a lot of things happened. Now let me pause to give you the structure. Unilever wanted 51%, not because they wanted to run it, but because Unilever was seen in any given country to be involved with Lintas, and whatever Lintas did that was not pleasing to the governments would be laid right at Unilever's doorstep. So they could not put themselves in the position of having another group of people do something that they couldn't live with. That turned out to be dramatized in Portugal.

There were a lot of good business reasons for getting out early, and saving ourselves a lot of heartache and a lot of money, as many agencies did. Unilever could not accept that position, and we talked it and talked it and talked it, but in the end decided to stay. And as a result of that, Unilever was very well regarded by the government; it helped in a lot of settlements, I think, and Lintas got a lot of business.

I'd say, if everybody left!

279

That's right. We were the only internationalists left. So they were certainly right about the 51% deal. The structure we set up was that there would be a Policy Committee which would have two Unilever representatives, Ted Brough to be the chairman and another man, who is now the chairman, called Hans Goudswaard, a very bright and very important director of Unilever. When Ted Brough retired, Ken Durham—a first-class scientist as well as executive—became a member. He is now chairman of Unilever. Heagan and I were members, as was Tim Green, who was the chairman of what we called SSC&B Lintas International.

This is the group we did not talk about publicly, because it was basically the capital investment, grand strategy group. We set up another group called the Operations Committee, which we all wanted to be seen as American-dominated. I was chairman; Heagan Bayles was on it; Tim Green was on it; and that was it, except we made Marty Hummel the secretary of it, after a while. That gave us another input without formally increasing the size of the committee. This was the committee responsible for the management coordination of the organization all over the world. And I think it worked surprisingly well. That was our structure, and we set about the job of building the agency into a bonafide entrepreneurial kind of enterprise.

Now, this is where SSC&B was really undone by our own success. What happened was this: we had the formula all worked out for purchasing the 51%, based, of course, on profit. The minute the word was out that an American agency had bought Lintas (although it was only 49%, the story apparently got around that 100% was in the cards), and that Lintas was now *seeking* outside business, lots of advertisers became interested.

We had an unusual and very appealing sales proposition, especially in Europe, where, as you know, card rates don't mean anything. The best deal is what you can get, and the average advertiser had no idea whether he was paying too little or too much for media. But inasmuch as Lintas did, and still does, buy all of Unilever's advertising, regardless of who the agency is, we were the biggest buying force in Europe. We knew where the bottom line was, because we made it.

In addition to all of that, we had begun to generate a very good creative product; we had become very sophisticated in research;

and we had an inheritance of being excellent marketing people. If you were a client or prospect, you could go into any office—Paris, Milan or wherever—and you would be talked to not only in English, but in American marketing language—the same thing you'd hear in Cincinnati or New York or Chicago. And that, again, was a very telling advantage.

So the business began to grow, which meant that the idea of just buying it out of profits went out the window. We decided—and Unilever was in agreement—that we would go public, which would give us a great deal more flexibility in the financial area.

We talked with one of the largest Wall Street firms. They were very favorably impressed. In fact, they were all ready to take us public at 14 times earnings. And we called it off. We felt that we had not yet got a full grip on the management of the worldwide operation, and that it wasn't cricket to go public and then have to tell stockholders that, yes, there was a problem, but we were not in a position to do anything about it, yet. It was kind of a chicken-and-the-egg thing; once you got the 100%, you would have full control, but until you had the 100%, control was limited. It had to be. So I had a nice talk with our friends from Wall Street and said we'd like to postpone it a year, and they said, "That's high quality thinking, and we appreciate it. We'll be back."

Two things happened. One: the business and profits continued to climb at a very good rate. We, the proposed buyers, had really, in many ways, given the stimulus that brought this about. And the other thing was, that there was a drop in the stock market, and for a long, long time, right up until about now, we did not have a climate in which it was very favorable to float agency stock.

At that particular time—1971 or 1972—the market was excited by esoteric stocks, including advertising agencies; and also "international" was the buzzword, and here we were with a fabulous, almost incomparable international setup. So 14 times earnings was fine, and everybody would have done well. And maybe we should have done it, Bart, I don't know.

Well, let me ask you this one, Al. That 51%—with this thing growing like crazy, wasn't that 51% getting more expensive all the time?

Well, that's exactly my point. The price kept going up—see, if it had had a very slow build, we could have paid for it pretty much out of profits. That was the plan, and that would have happened if we hadn't had this very rapid rise. But by the time you turned around, the price had gone up. So we were in a bind; there was no way we could do anything about it, except watch the price go up, but you couldn't do anything about that either, because you had to have a healthy organization.

So we proceeded, over this long period of time, with the agency growing and integration taking place. We had a couple of forces working, sort of, at cross purposes. We hadn't been able to go public, therefore making a whole new bit of financing available; and our major stockholders were retiring, or getting ready to retire, and that again was going to put some pressure on.

It was against this background that, one day, I got a call from Paul Foley (Chairman of Interpublic). I figured it was something special, because I'd known Paul a long time, but he hadn't been calling me every week for lunch. I said, "Well, I'd like to have lunch with you, but I just don't see any time open for the next month." And then I thought, and I said, "Are you going to the Four A's convention?" He said, "Yes, "and I said, "We can chat there." Well, he'd like me to meet Phil Geier.

So the two of them came down to our cottage one afternoon, and proceeded to say they'd like to buy SSC&B. "Well, it's very flattering," I said, "'but it's academic, because we have an agreement with Unilever that, if we merge with somebody, SSC&B must be the dominant partner. And unless you're willing to make certain financial sacrifices, I don't see how that's going to work." They said they wanted to buy the entire thing, including the 51%. So I said, "Well, I'll listen some more, then, because that does change things."

When we got down to further discussions later on, we had to work out a lot of things. For example, SSC&B had a profit-sharing plan; they had their pension plan. We never did argue about price; the details of the price, yes, but the price-earnings ratio was never debated. But that still leaves, as you know, a hell of a lot of stuff.

And we wanted to make sure that we had some kind of a workable proposition before we broached it to Unilever, because otherwise you're just upsetting a lot of people and possibly all for nothing. So we haggled out quite a few of the details, until we were sure that at least it was a sensible proposition. The situation was somewhat touchy, because McCann-Erickson had been, really, our biggest international rival. That made it sensitive! And I had no idea whether Unilever would just look at us in total disbelief, that we would even be talking about it, or whether they would think it was a good idea, Well, in the end, as you know, they thought it was a good idea, and the deal was consummated.

As you look back on it, Al, knowing what you know now, I suppose it probably would have been a good idea to try to buy the whole thing at once over a period of years.

No, I don't know, Bart. I think if I were in the same position again, I think I would have been influenced, by the same considerations, to do it about that way. First, we were dealing with something that was totally unlike any deal before. We not only were buying a property from a company, but we also had that company as our biggest client. And if that client said, "We don't like your agency," our business could dwindle away.

Where does that put you now.

Well, let me just finish the thinking there. Both parties recognized that there was a problem; it made our deal very different from the usual thing. Therefore, Unilever goodwill was always a very important consideration. Now, we were never, Bart, worried about an unfair deal. We were never worried that they would take our money and . . .

And fire you.

Right. They're just not that kind of company, and it would be totally foreign to their principles and to their way of thinking. But there was always a chance that, over a period of time, they might just have to say, "Hey, you fellows haven't done it and we want to do everything we can for you, but we can't sacrifice our margarine business in Germany," or whatever. Also, Unilever doesn't really, in a marketing sense, act as one big company. They operate country by country and industry by industry.

So if you look back, what we were saying was, "We don't have the money to buy 100%. But in a foreseeable, predictable period, we can proceed with a new input of capital, including earnings, to buy the rest of it." And it all made sense on paper, and in the normal situation would have worked out. But it was—not to lose the thread here—the experimental nature of it made it such that both we and Unilever thought it a good idea to go part way, get some experience with it, see how our people react to it when finally they're going to belong to somebody else. Both parties were safeguarded by a trial period.

Which worked out very well.

Yeah. So I don't think we would have done it differently.

Does Interpublic now own the whole thing?

No, Interpublic owns the 49% which we sold them, and they are about to acquire the 51%. You've had experience abroad, Bart. You know how many complicated things have to be worked out. And there are some of them that are still in the final process of being determined.

The lawyers have been very busy.

And financial people travelling all over the world.

Al, that's a fantastic story, and you deserve a lot of credit for building such a remarkable agency.

NOTE: Since this interview the deal has been completed: Interpublic now owns 100% of SSC&B/Lintas.

October 15 and November 18, 1981

NEAL W. O'CONNOR

Neal W. O'Connor, a native of Milwaukee, started his advertising career in the production department of N W Ayer & Son in Philadelphia in 1949, as a management trainee, following his graduation from Syracuse University with a B.S. degree in advertising.

Mr. O'Connor moved into the Plans & Marketing Department in 1951 to work on the agency's food and drug accounts. In February 1955 he was named an account executive on the Sealtest Foods account in Ayer's New York office. He was promoted to Account Supervisor in 1959 and elected a Vice-President in 1960.

He was appointed Manager of Account Service for Ayer's New York office in 1962, and held that position until elected President of the agency in 1965. As President and then Chairman, he was chief executive of America's oldest advertising agency for 10 years, until 1976, when he was named Chairman of the Executive Committee. He retired from Ayer in 1981.

Mr. O'Connor served as Chairman of the American Association of Advertising Agencies in 1975–76. He also served on the Board of Directors of The Advertising Council and is a charter member, President and Trustee of the Consumer Research Institute, Inc.

He also served as an advertising agency representative on the Board of the National Advertising Review Board and on its steering committee, and as a member of the Board of Directors of the National Outdoor Advertising Bureau.

NEAL W. O'CONNOR

Interview

I was born and raised in Milwaukee; German mother, Irish father, which accounts for my personality—stubborn on one side and very loose on the other side. I was the last of five children. A wonderful childhood, happy family, no problems; never rich, but never wanting. We were lucky, because this was the Depression.

My mother and father were Catholic, and I, being the youngest, in particular, was brought up in a pretty strict Catholic environment. Consequently, my high schooling was at a Jesuit school called Marquette University High School. I got out of there in June 1943, and was eighteen in August of '43 and went right into the service, like everybody was doing at that time, and found myself in infantry basic training. But four years of Jesuit high school really made basic training easy, because I knew discipline.

I wanted to get into the Air Force, but my eyes weren't good enough; my brother had been killed as a pilot on B-17s out of England, on July 4th of '43, actually, so it was just about the time I was thinking of what I would be doing.

Did you see a lot of action?

I went to Italy, and got wounded a couple of times, but very lightly. And as an 18 or 19-year-old kid, that's quite an experience. So, coming out of that, and with the G.I. Bill helping, of course, I immediately thought of college but I didn't want to necessarily stay in the Midwest. I really wanted to do something on my own. A couple of my brothers had gone to school in the East, and I'd been in the East. One went to Haverford, one went to Colgate. And I liked that kind of thing. Both my father and mother had gone to Syracuse, graduated about 1907.

It was near the end of 1945 when I got out of the Army, and frankly, I thought that I might just kind of sit back for a few months in the spring of '46, taking advantage of that wonderful "52-20 Club"—you got $20 a week unemployment for 52 weeks if you were a veteran. Then it was either New Year's day, or the day after, and my father said, "Well, here's a railroad ticket. I've enrolled you in Syracuse University, in the School of Journalism, because you like to write." And I did like to write, and draw. He said, "If you don't like it, you can always come back." And he kicked me out, the best thing that ever happened to me.

He knew you better than you knew yourself.

So I went to Syracuse. And I did go into the School of Journalism but shortly realized that that was a pretty narrow thing, and that there would be a much broader base of learning experience if I went into the College of Business Administration. So that's what I did, with a major in advertising. Then, as you approached your senior year, everyone was, of course, trying like hell just to get out and get a job. I accelerated; I went through the summer, so I would graduate earlier than I might normally.

I got out in '49. And I was taking all the inteviews from the P & G's, and Ford and General Motors were recruiting young veterans, college graduates, for their new training programs, at that time. I was hoping, certainly, that I'd be accepted in one or more of these programs.

One day, I was looking at the various people coming up, and there was this name, N W Ayer. And it turned out to be an advertising agency. I didn't know much about the agency business. I had thought that advertising would be something I'd be interested in, but I just felt that there was no direct entree into a field like that for someone without any background or experience, so I'd go into sales and marketing, and maybe then segue into advertising.

The placement director said, "Well, this is a large agency, headquartered in Philadelphia." That didn't have any significance for me then, but it should have. "And why don't you take the interview?" . . . I walked out of that interview thinking, "Well, hell, I've had it, they're not going to be interested in someone like me." But I wish I'd saved the letter I got several weeks later, from the personnel director, Theodore Whittlesey, Jr. It was a classic.

It was a classic; what it said was something like, "If you happen to be in the Philadelphia area on other business, we'd be delighted if you'd stop by to discuss opportunities further." What it really meant was they weren't going to pay my way down. And I did come down, and went through a pretty intensive grilling, because they had a training program, and they took four or five young men at the time, no women. And they offered me a job at $40 a week, and I took it.

So my resume is rather unimpressive, because it only has one company.

That's interesting, and unique.

They had a very detailed, very rigorous program. You started in Traffic—they called it Business Production. At that time, Ayer was very weak in broadcast, and what little broadcast activities there were were in the New York branch office, so your whole orientation was print. But you learned the print business; you learned engraving and printing and all of that sort of thing, and you learned how the agency work flowed, because you were at the centerpoint.

But it was far too long; they kept people there a year and a half, or two years. And then they moved people, traditionally, into what was called Plans or Plans Marketing or something like that. It was really one of the checks and balances that the management at Ayer had built into the business, because they were always afraid that the account management group would get too powerful. And so, the basic responsibility for strategic planning and laying out a marketing direction for an assignment was vested, not in the account management group, but in this separate department called Plans or Plans Marketing.

As a young guy, you'd be working under senior people there, and you'd be tallying up sales figures, and you'd be making store calls, and you'd be learning the business end of it. But it was a constant fight between this department, which had its prerogatives, and the account management department, who was responsive to the client. There was a tug of war—particularly if you were working on an account that was serviced out of one of the branch offices; because the management then had a deep conviction that everything should be centralized. Now, that's fine if you're in New York or Chicago. I mean, Ted Bates does it; Leo Burnett does it, largely—fine. But Philadelphia—no.

Philadelphia created a climate of comfort and ease, a lack of urgency, lack of responsiveness, which you would not have found in a major advertising center. And yet, clients as far as San Francisco were served, basically out of Philadelphia. Gradually, the only major exception to that came in Detroit, where the Plymouth account was being served. That client was sophisticated enough, and demanding enough, to insist that there be a major creative team out there on the spot. Still, a lot of the marketing and media work emanated from Philadelphia.

And that really led to a long slide of the company, because Ayer was simply not competitive. You cannot serve a package goods client in Chicago out of Philadelphia. It just doesn't work. Gradually, in the late '50s and early '60s, the base of business began to erode; accounts were lost. And yet, Ayer insisted on this style of working.

Did you people in Plans Marketing have any contact with the client at all?

Yes.

And so did the account people?

Yes. Actually, we were a crutch for the account management group, in that they did not have the basic responsibility for setting the marketing plan that was being recommended to the client.

What was their responsibility, basically?

A glorified traffic function.

Getting the creative in front of them, etc.?

Yes. And, of course, they were responsible for the client relationship and for a fair amount of the presentation. But, again, this check-and-balance thing that had been set up and the specialized departmentalization of the agency, over time, bred a very weak account management group. A strong account management guy would probably do things that would bring him into difficulty with the other department heads who, in turn, would complain to top management, saying "This guy's in trouble," and he would either get fired or disgusted and leave.

Again, I was fortunate. Very early on, after getting out of the traffic function and into this plans function in Philadelphia, I was moved into account management in New York. I was assigned, under one other guy—just the two of us—on what was then one of the largest, if not *the* largest package goods account that Ayer had at the time, the Sealtest account—milk, ice cream, and that sort of thing. Gradually, that business was diversifying into other products, albeit still in the dairy category. The client was a smart and demanding and sophisticated guy, who was a tyrant and a marvelous teacher.

I was fortunate in being around a man of that kind. He forced us, as an agency, to work the way we should be working. And the agency's management would come down on our necks, and the client would step in and take the yoke off. Because always, of course, the threat was that he could move the account. So, we were working in ways that were then quite unconventional to Ayer, but today are very conventional. I had great training experience in that.

How long were you in the New York office?

I joined Ayer in the fall of '49; went into the Plans Department about 1951; and moved to New York in 1954. And I stayed on Sealtest, gradually becoming the senior man on the account. As the guy ahead of me moved out, to head the Chicago office, I stepped into his shoes, and fortunately, the account was growing, and we were into television. Whereas earlier, Sealtest had been served by just two people, when I moved on from that assignment, we had an account group of six or seven. So I learned the business, and I also learned how to manage our own people.

Then, in 1959, I was made the assistant to the man who was head of the New York office, and was able to get into the other kinds of business; some proprietary business that Ayer had at the time, and of course, things like the telephone business which had been the anchor account at Ayer for years and years and years, and around which a lot of the agency policies and methods of working operated. In other words, what was good for the telephone company was good for Ayer, and vice versa. And other clients, if they didn't like the way the telephone company type business was being serviced, went elsewhere.

At this time, there was a series of pretty tough shocks for the agency. The Hills Bros. Coffee account, which had been the key account in San Francisco, was lost, and that meant the San Francisco office virtually ceased to exist. In the early '60s, the Chicago office began to lose important business, and that culminated in 1965 with the loss of United Airlines, which was probably, then, an $8–$10 million account.

That was a huge account for those days. Leo Burnett's had it ever since; and it was simply because we were not prepared to serve

United on the spot, with the kind of personnel and facilities that they required, that business was lost.

At about this time, I think the management was looking for a safe choice, and they elected me President.

You were still in New York then?

Yes. I was President without, really, any authority.

What was their purpose in electing you president and not giving you any authority?

I think they felt they had to show some changes were being made. The chairman, Harry Batten, was in his mid-sixties; Warner Shelly, the president, was about age 60. There was a lot of concern within the agency because of the gradual attrition of some of these larger accounts leaving. So I think they felt they had to do something; but they weren't about to give authority to a 39-year-old kid, which wasn't a bad idea. Looking back, I think what they did was rather risky.

There were a couple of other people, more senior than I, much more experienced than I, who felt they should have gotten the job. And in retrospect, they should have. But I think the management felt they might be too powerful, that they might rock the boat too much. They had revolutionary ideas, and I was just a young guy who had been going along and doing my job.

And so, it fell on me. How often have you heard that? You know, these funny circumstances that create the conditions. And at that time, this was right after the loss of United Airlines—in the summer of 1966, and I had been President for about a year—the Plymouth account was lost. At the time it was the largest account switch in history, some $30 million. I don't recall the exact numbers but it probably represented 35–40% of the agency's billings, and about 50–60% of its profits. It was a tremendously profitable account at the time. And that was a very, very serious blow.

Why did you lose it?

I think it wasn't because of the quality of work; it wasn't because of the lack of personnel—we had the best people in the agency servicing that account. And we had creative and media, out there; the whole thing. I think it was a political move, on the part of a man who wanted to shake things up, wanted to show his management that there was change afoot.

Ayer was old, conservative, the image tarnished, Philadelphia, in a long slide, all of those things. We were vulnerable at that time. Y&R, who got the account, was dynamic and strong, and moving, and they were attractive.

With that loss, things were very desperate, and so it was incumbent upon me to represent the rest of the people in the agency, mainly the younger people. And we had some long and very difficult sessions among just three people—myself and the two senior top management people—Harry Batten and Warner Shelly, men who had done great things for Ayer in an earlier day. There was no mutiny. There was no palace revolt or anything like that. We called everybody together; I was supposed to give a pep talk after the loss of Plymouth. We brought everybody into Philadelphia, and I was told to get the guys steamed up, it's not the end of the world, and all that sort of stuff.

But in the process, I said to our key people, "Now, I want each of you to give me, in longhand—*not typed and just one copy*—your recommendations as to what you think this agency ought to be doing in the next couple of years to turn the situation around. And I will promise you one thing; that you will never be directly quoted. And I'm going to pull together all these ideas and my own, and present a point of view to the management of this company, to the board of directors, which was a euphemism for these senior officers.

They heard you say that?

Yes, and frankly, they didn't like my statement. But it was said, and, in fact, that was the base on which I made my proposals to them. And I *didn't* quote those people, and I burned all the papers. I wish I hadn't. I'd love to have them now.

I kept everything anonymous. But there was such a unified point of view and concern. In fact, in the years that followed, this was the great thing to me. When you're under the gun and in trouble, there can be a tremendous gathering together of forces, and there's no petty fighting, and there's nothing to divert you from the main job at hand. So it acted as a unifying force.

These private sessions went on for something like a month. And at the conclusion, it was agreed that I would become chief executive officer. Again, I want to stress, there was no palace revolt; we weren't going to pull out and start our own agency, or any of that foolishness. It was tough to do, but it was, I hope, handled correctly.

How'd you persuade them?

The senior officers, who cared deeply about Ayer and its people, realized that there had to be change. We had to do what our competitors had been doing. We had to reorganize; we had to be much more competitive, much more responsive; we had to augment our facilities; we had to invest in people. We had to move out of Philadelphia.

What was your financial situation at this point?

Awful.

Were you in real trouble?

Well, no, it was okay at that time, but shortly afterwards—and I always have to go around with the concern that the strain of this whole thing helped cause it—Harry Batten died of a heart attack. I was named chief executive around early July, and he died of a heart attack, some time, as I recall, at the end of July. And immediately, his shares became due, and he owned about 60% of the agency.

And from that time until the early Seventies, Ayer didn't have much cash, because also, other older stockholders had been bailing out, or were bailed out, as it turned out, and we had tremendous cash obligations to them. And that re-buying yourself back, each generation of management, is just crazy, very expensive.

And it came at the worst possible time. Well, we got through that period, and we began. We reorganized; we decentralized. We created full-service facilities in Los Angeles, although there was virtually nothing there; we had closed down San Francisco. We closed down Boston, which was a drain. We kept Detroit for a while, but, not getting any automotive business to replace Plymouth, that then closed down. But we beefed up Chicago, and particularly New York, and went after new business.

In the middle of this, in the early part of 1967, a new Public Relations Vice-President had come into AT&T, which was the one big, solid account, and he put us on notice. He and his people were not satisfied with what had been going on. The old ties with some of the AT&T management had long since gone; people retired there and moved.

They had plenty of justification for looking around. Well, we scrambled and scrambled. It culminated in April of 1967, at a final presentation at Sterling Forest. And this man who was Public Relations Vice-President was out to do things with advertising that were probably far ahead of their time for AT&T, which was still a very structured and very conservative company, a regulated and protected monopoly. But he wanted to do things in advertising that, for that day and that time, would have revolutionized at least the image of the company. And he didn't think Ayer was prepared to make that kind of adjustment. And you know, looking back, he had perfect reason to think that and to start discussing things with other agencies.

Well, while we were trying to prove that we could meet this new requirement and prepare for this new day that he was trying to unfold, they got into very serious talks with another agency. And it was almost certain, as we went into this final presentation at Sterling Forest, that the other agency had the account. Now, had Ayer lost AT&T in 1967, after all the other things that had happened, I think what would have happened is that there would have been a choice, either to pull back and be a medium-sized Philadelphia agency—not even a medium-sized New York agency —or to really bite the bullet and try, with a much smaller tighter group, to begin again in New York. Both would have been extremely difficult. However, the first course, being a Philadelphia agency, would have doomed us forever to medium size. And starting in New York with, even then, very formidable competition here, would have been such an uphill battle that I don't think it could have succeeded. But we would have had to do one or the other if we'd lost AT&T.

Well, what happened was, we put on a hell of a presentation. The drill at Sterling Forest was, they came up after lunch one day, and the presentation lasted all afternoon, and then a smaller group was going to critique the presentation the next morning. We got through the presentation and, of course, we were all highly charged up, as you can imagine.

And we played poker well into the night, drank a lot, and yet no one said a thing.

Were you with them?

With them all night. And so we woke up the next morning,

everybody nervous, hung over and the rest of it. At breakfast I happened, by the greatest chance and fortune—boy, I'm not a Catholic any more, but if there are things like guardian angels, I sure had one that day—to sit down with this lovely woman who worked in the AT&T advertising department, and finally we were alone.

And since no one had said anything, and I knew I could talk to her, I said, "Well, how do you think it went?" She said—I'm not going to mention names but she said the top guy "thought that was the most smashing presentation he'd ever seen." And you know, I was just starting to rise up off the chair, literally, when she said, "*But*, he doesn't think you did it." And I said, "What do you mean, he doesn't think we did it?" "He thinks that you went out and bought freelance creative talent all over the town, and just did anything and everything to put on this presentation, but it doesn't represent the people at Ayer. It wasn't really done by the agency; it was done by a whole bunch of hired guns." I said, "But you know that's not true." And she said, "I know it's not true, but that's what he thinks."

At that point, we were interrupted and couldn't go on. We got into this smaller meeting and we had to go through the whole presentation again. We had a coffee break at one point, and I sat with our wonderful, then head creative man, Pat Gallagher, who later died of cancer—a most marvelous man. I told Pat this story. And he said, "My God, you know it's not true!" But then, we had to go on with the rest of the critique.

Meantime, as I recall, Pat is sitting in the back row, and he's writing on a little card like this. He's got his glasses on his nose and he's writing on this card; and I didn't know what he was doing. But eventually, the card got passed around to me, and I had a chance to look at it.

I still have the card. On one side, in his scrawl, it said, "There are 27 people at Ayer who worked on the AT&T presentation. These people have been at Ayer, assigned to AT&T, for more than a year, some of them for five and ten years. They all are at Ayer now, and they all will continue to work on the AT&T account, if Ayer keeps it."

And you turn the card over, and there are these 27 names, including his, and then all the way down the line. Many of the people, in fact, the majority of them were at the meeting, because they were the key people.

And so, we get finished with the presentation, and all along, the top client has been, again, praising the work, and saying "Now, when we do this, we should make that little change." And all the people on our side, who didn't know the story, other than Pat and myself, were really up, because they thought everything was fine. And so, the lights come up, and this man says, "Well, Neal, again I want to tell you that this is some of the most wonderful work that I've ever seen; but I want to share with you one concern.

"That is, I'm afraid is isn't really the work of the agency, that you just went out and got this done by free-lance people." I said, using his first name, because we were good friends, "I know that is your concern, and I want to read you something that Pat Gallagher, who knows that this was also a concern, has given me." And I read the card verbatim, and, honestly, Bart, without missing a beat, he got up, walked across the room, because we were seated some distance apart at that point, and he took out his hand and he said, "Neal, I hope we never go through anything like this again; you're going to be our agency forever." And we shook hands, and of course, the whole place exploded.

Wow!

From that point on, it wasn't easy, but that was a very major turning point in the affairs of the agency. It's one of those things where you're at a crossroads, or whatever, and one road leads down and the other road leads up. And after that, new business was coming in; the decentralization helped make us more competitive. But it was still a struggle.

Were you moving people from Philadelphia to New York then?

We didn't really make the move from Philadephia complete for a while. We were in process, always, of moving people and accounts up to New York, during this time, when we could. The truth of the matter is, we couldn't completely close down in Philadelphia and open up in New York, because we didn't have the money. It was a very expensive proposition. And there was an awful lot of attrition. In this process we lost a lot of good people who simply would not move out of Philadelphia. It would have been too disruptive to do this as we would have liked, to do it all at once. In fact, the move was finally complete in 1974.

It happens less and less today, but it's not surprising that we still, once in a while, get the tag of a "Philadelphia agency."

Do you have anything in Philadelphia now?

Nothing.

The good people that wanted to stay in Philadelphia? What did they do?

Three of them started their own agency, which has since sold out to Ketchum. A couple of them went into client situations, as ad or marketing directors; most of them went with other agencies.

Well, that was the real turning point. Since then, you fellows had a fantastic series of successes in new business.

Well, there was one summer where we got lucky.

Okay, but you must have been doing something right. Luck is only what you make of it, and there must have been something that you did to inspire your people to be able to get that much new business.

Well, sure. But it was—and this is not modesty—it was truly a total team effort. Out of adversity can come some awfully strong results. Because we'd all been through it, and you know, our careers, our lives and our fortunes, as the men of 1776 said, our fortunes were very much on the line and very doubtful. We couldn't even pay ourselves much money then. The stock wasn't going anywhere, obviously, because we weren't putting anything much into surplus. And so we had a lot to lose, sure, but we had more to gain. And that brought people together, with a unified spirit and feeling. The jealousies and the bickering and the politics, those were all gone. And while it was a difficult time, it was a very exciting time. Once you can see the turnaround, and things start to go uphill instead of downhill, once there is a trend going, it feeds on itself.

This is, as we say so often, a cyclical business, and it gradually, in the late '60s and early '70s, began to go up. And then, in '76, having been chief executive for ten years, I felt that was long enough. There were some things, however, that I still could do in the transition period. And Lou Hagopian took over, and actually, the real new business successes came after that, when he was chief executive—the big new business successes. But the base of the business had been growing steadily upwards. And sure, we all lose accounts, but I can't think of any shattering losses during that time. We were very fortunate. AT&T was solid again, and growing, growing very rapidly.

Was that same guy from the Sterling Forest presentation still there?

No, he left them and went briefly to another company, actually, a client that we got out of our Chicago office when he was still there, although he had nothing to do with the decision, the John Deere account.

Tell me, you probably had some guys that were working shoulder to shoulder with you during this terrible period. I gather Lou was one of them.

He became more and more the closest to me of all of those people. But from the standpoint of dealing with people, these were very, very tough times, because we had to make some hard decisions. But they were made, you know, for the benefit of the agency as a whole, and not for any one individual. And with that kind of a feeling and spirit, the place began to go ahead.

Lou was the No. 2 man in Detroit and he's the only guy that lost a $30 million account and got promoted. I took him out of Detroit, after the Plymouth loss, and made him head of the New York office, because he is a tremendously able guy, and that worked out very well. So that's a short history.

Now, I'd love to get your views on some other things. Let's talk about the creative side of the business, because I think we all feel it's such an important part of it. Creativity and new business are probably two of the most important things that we have going, and I'd like to ask you to talk about the creative philosophy of this agency, as you see it. You're the guy that probably had to help establish it through remaking of N W Ayer.

Every agency seems to want to grope for a reason for being, or a point of difference or distinction, and that question, "What is your creative philosophy?" is answered a million different ways.

I don't know how we were answering it over those years, except by trying to do the best possible work we could for each individual client, and use that as an example of our approach.

Ultimately, it evolved into a statement of this thing called human contact—the idea of talking to a customer, or a prospect as an individual; not above him, not below him, but right at him, and trying to have warm and involving advertising. A lot of the Ayer product then and today, I think, reflects that kind of attitude.

From an operating standpoint, what we really try to do is instill a spirit of joint accountability between the top creative guy and the top account management guy on a piece of business. These two people share every concern. The creative guy may not be as good at, but he should be just as concerned with the client relationship as he is with the product. And he ought to be concerned about the sales. Similarly, the account management guy has got to nurture and feed and create a climate for those creative people, to feel that they can be challenging and daring, and maybe go the extra inch.

You know, a client can always pull you back, but if you don't stimulate or don't provoke the client into thinking beyond a narrow point of view where he may be at the moment, you're never going to get brilliant advertising. And if we can take a very good top creative guy and a very good top account management guy, and make them work together with mutual respect and even affection—and it surely doesn't work all the time, don't misunderstand me—then that goes right through their respective groups of people, and you start to get that kind of spirit and cooperation at almost every level. But if you get a tough, arrogant creative person, or an overbearing or, worse, a timid account management guy, or whatever the characteristics of one or the other might be, that sours the whole thing.

And so there's that constant search to try to find people who can work in that spirit of respect and compatibility, and, to a very large degree, of liking each other.

But don't misunderstand me, Ayer has no exclusive on that. It doesn't work in many cases, because the people chemistry just isn't right, but that's what we're looking for. And in that kind of a climate, wonderful work can get done. It always amazes me, when you've got to save an account, or when you're going after a big new piece of business, the brilliant work that you can do, because there is that kind of attitude.

In many cases, you go much farther out than you seem to on normal, regular, day-to-day assignments, because you've got nothing to lose. But there's the spirit and enthusiasm, whether it's born out of fear of losing or the prospect of gaining something, that creates that climate. Now, if you can get that going on day-to-day assignments, then you've really got something.

What about the part that research plays in this process?

Well, if you drew agency functions on a piece of paper, there'd be these concentric circles, and each circle is a function. The two major circles that intersect are creative and account management; but certainly right under that, albeit not necessarily every day, and not to the same degree of intimacy and involvement that should characterize the team play between account management and creative, there are media and research.

Ayer tries to bring them in in the same way, but I must admit, not with the same intensity and not with the same deep involvement on a constant, continuing basis, because they come in and come out as the need requires. It is the account team concept, which certainly includes research and certainly includes media, that Ayer is trying to instill with all its people.

And the secret of a good account man is?

That he can lead all the other groups. As I say, when you're trying to rescue an account that's in trouble, or you're going after a piece of new business that's very challenging, the people come into that situation in that way.

So often on a day-to-day basis, things are going along, and people get within their little departmental walls, and memos are written instead of close relationships being developed. We tried deliberately to spread people around physically. You're not going to find creative people on one floor and account management people on another floor. They're all mixed up.

You lose a little control and you lose some supervision, because people are dispersed. But if you really believe in the team concept, this is what you should do.

Let's talk about how you get these people. I know you do some recruiting; I know you have an excellent personnel director in Ed Rogers.

He's a fine Personnel Director. But Ed will not hire a top account management guy. He won't hire top creative people. The management of those functions hire their people. Now, the personnel department can help on the administrative end, and does, in college recruiting; they are very important in that sort of thing. Bart, getting the best people is a tough one. You've got to be competitive in money and benefits, and those costs get higher and higher every year.

Ayer had a guy leave recently, a highly respected guy, and he was going to another agency, and I was staggered; his salary, with bonuses still on top of it, is $175,000 a year. He's a creative guy, but he's not, you know, at the top of the organization. He's a very good man, and Ayer was prepared to meet him part of the way, but not to that level.

That's incredible.

It is. It's tough. Assuming that you're reasonably competitive— and, of course, you have to be—on the money part of it, it's the kind of climate that the agency has, with the work environment, the people, that counts most. Is he going to be pushed around? Is she going to be yelled at? Is it going to be a pressure cooker, seven day a week forever?

What kind of an agency is it? If the agency is perceived to be a good place, a warm place, still professional, still demanding and all the rest of it, but not a slave ship, and not a torture chamber, and not one of these places where politics and cliques and groups exist to fight each other and vie with each other. I think you'll get a lot of good people who'll realize that that's really the priceless asset an agency can offer a prospective new person.

The money, you can quantify that; you can't quantify this other thing, but it's in the air. If it's a good place, with decent people, where you can have some fun and get a lot of satisfaction out of work, and you feel as though you're in the place that's going for- ward, that's thriving, dynamic, and that offers *you* opportunity. I think those are the important things, if anybody ever sits back and thinks about it, in considering whether to move to a new agency.

I know you do recruiting. What do you look for? I mean, are you looking for MBA's, or are you looking for undergraduates?

A balance, really. I think you can only take a certain number of these business school people, because they represent two things. They represent a high investment, because you've got to teach them, and it takes the time of senior people to do that; and a very high risk, because the turnover is nothing to be proud about.

After five years, you've probably lost three out of five, four out of five, of them. And why you lose them is because you've invested in and trained them, and they are now starting to become attractive, and you just haven't been able at this particular point in time to move them into the slot that they think they're ready for.

And there's responsibility and there's money involved, and some other agency, many of which don't do this sort of thing, comes around, and they offer a very attractive package *now*. And these young people are very much now-oriented, and they make the leap. It's understandable.

So, what we're looking for, what everybody else is looking for, is a person with intelligence, with curiosity, who definitely is going to achieve something in a career, whatever it may be. And again, it's a very frustrating thing, because I personally believe—and Ayer was guilty of it in the past, particularly when we didn't have the resources—that we close this business out to young people with no experience. And then we pay the price for it, because we haven't been developing our generations of management properly, and we do get this hired-gun syndrome going, and steal from you and steal from me and that sort of thing, when we have a personnel need.

I don't know what the balance is, but MBA's aren't the answer exclusively, although I think we should all respect an MBA, because it says that that guy or gal has achieved something. First of all, they must be interested in business; they're serious about it, they've invested time and money in it. And if they're coming out of a good school, and they're coming out with a good record, it says that they are able to accomplish something. But we never went after just MBA's alone. We took a lot of people right out of undergraduate schools.

Those that are advertising majors?

No. One of the most productive schools when I was involved, and I ended up being, among other things, in charge of personnel, was Princeton. And not boys, girls. The girls were so far ahead of the boys it became a problem. Our whole young account management group, particularly those recruited from off campus, was predominantly female.

What was their basic education at Princeton?

Liberal arts, of course. I'll tell you, they are bright, they are

303

attractive, articulate, very ambitious, and some of them around Ayer have done extremely well. And others who have been lost to other agencies have likewise done extremely well.

Do any of these women end up on your board?

Not yet. That's a disappointment to me, that in my time I was never able to offer that kind of an opportunity. I hope that very soon, there'll be a woman on the board of N W Ayer, and I think there will be. But the people that have been recruited in that last decade off campuses, no, they're not at the board level yet. That would be a pretty meteoric rise.

The Ayer Board is small—12 people—and largely functional. It's not, you know, one of those 25–30 person things which becomes the ultimate badge of honor. And that's a tough thing, to try to keep a board small enough to be useful.

And it probably has more creative representation on it than most agencies. There are four creative guys on the board of Ayer.

Let me jump back to the new business thing, because it's so important. You've had such tremendous success here. Is this because of one, or a few, people, or is this a big team operation?

Well, first of all, top management is involved in new business. But I don't think top management gets the business. If Ayer has been successful in getting business, it has been because in the presentation, the prospective client learns how Ayer would approach the assignment. And frequently, as you know, work is involved, speculative work, so they can see the execution of how that problem would be approached. But the people who have been responsible for the approach to the problem and execution of the solution are the major presenters to the prospective client, and they are the people who will be assigned to the account.

And so, if they like what they see, and they like the people, that's what they're buying. They're not buying just Lou Hagopian, as the Chief Executive. He's important to them for he represents the agency, its policies, and the ability to marshal its resources to serve the client. But the client, or prospective client, sees the actual people who will work with him. The presenters are fairly senior levels; I don't mean all the way down the line. But the promises are real. It's not one of these things where Lou says, "I promise to serve the account personally."

How often have we seen that? Now, the people who say they're going to work on the account *do* work on the account. And I think that's certainly one of the major factors. Also, you know, it's the work that you do for other clients. If a client sees a lot of good-looking, presumably effective, advertising, and feels he's going to get the same kind of thing, that, of course, is another important reason. Apart from this point of making sure that the people involved in the presentation are those who are going to be actually assigned to the account,

I think the best new business investment an agency can make is to look at its present list of clients, and say, "These four clients aren't getting as good a job as we're capable of giving them. Let's deliberately make an investment in those four situations, and try and do better advertising for them." Try and use—I say four—as almost a case history, and try to do better work for your current clients.

Don't worry so much about what you're going to do for a prospective client. Because if he can see a high level of good work throughout the agency for its entire client list, I think that's his best assurance that he's going to get something good if he goes to the agency.

You work on a team basis?

Absolutely.

I'd like to go back to one thing. This thing that ten years of being chief executive is long enough. A lot of guys in this business have stayed there longer than that. I'm just curious; what made you decide that, Neal?

Well, it wasn't anything as arbitrary as ten years, Bart, but I had seen the problems that accrued to the company because of the former management holding on, and holding on, and holding on. And I'm sure that conditioned me. I'm sure I could have stayed another five years, because I almost did, in terms of staying with the agency, albeit not as chief executive.

But the time seemed right to me, the successor was there; maybe five years later he wouldn't have been there. And I had this awful feeling that I was going to con myself into saying, "Well, the time isn't right," or "This guy isn't just absolutely perfect," and maybe I would start to worry about my stock and my bonus and all that sort of thing, and forget that this is a small, personal-service business that has to have a very high energy level from its top people.

I certainly wasn't tired. I'm not tired now; quite the contrary. But whether it was ten years or twelve or fifteen, the time, I felt, had to come, and it was about right. You know, ten years in a life-time of most agencies—that's a very long time. A lot of things change. So I'm very comfortable with my decision. I had enough interest in other things that I wanted to do, so that was not difficult.

I'm not the kind of a person who only knows how to play golf as a second life or a second career. I'm lucky in that regard, again. I have had a lifelong interest, even as a little kid, in World War I aviation, which sounds strange. Over the years, I've collected an awful lot of material; I have files and research and photographs and materials connected with this thing, and it's gotten to be quite an extensive set of documents and other artifacts. I have established a foundation for this, for the research and preservation of this kind of thing, and am building a small museum to house it at this very moment.

In Princeton?

Just outside. Of course, I am the president of the foundation, but to be legitimate, I have a board of trustees that should hold me accountable and I'm working quite hard at it. I have at least two books that I want to write in connection with this, that some day may sell at least fifty or sixty copies. It's almost a passion, and it's very time-consuming and a lot of fun.

I still have ties with Ayer, and they have first call. And I might be working, in a given year, up to 20% of my time on various project-type assignments given to me by Lou, as chief executive, or by the board.

I participate in some of the management conferences, and act as a general outside consultant and a sounding board to Lou and to the board on matters of policy and long-range direction. I am certainly no longer in the day-to-day at Ayer, and I don't want to be and that's as it should be. I'm not looking over anyone's shoulder.

April 21, 1982

BROWN BOLTÉ

Brown Bolté is past President of SSC&B and past Executive Vice-President and Chairman of the Plans Board of Benton & Bowles, two of America's greatest advertising agencies.

He founded Bolté Advertising Companies in the New York/Connecticut area, an outdoor advertising concern, in 1961; a consulting firm, Bolté-Lukin & Associates of Palm Beach; Realty Enterprises Corporation and Bolté Investment Group, both active in industrial and residential real estate in Florida. He is a residential architectural designer, an industrial designer, an inventor, a published poet, author and composer and has been elected to the American Society of Composers, Authors and Publishers. His inventions are in the fields of glassware, baking equipment, medical instruments, packaging, drug and food products.

He had served on the boards of medical institutions including The Norwalk Community Hospital in Connecticut, The Palm Beach-Martin County Medical Center, and the Community Mental Health Center, both in Florida.

During World War II he served as a Field Service Officer and Deputy Chief of the Athletic Branch of U.S. Army. He composed and wrote for the Army some of its best known WW II music, including "The Soldier's Prayer," "The Allies Victory March", "The Army Fighting Song", "Bring Peace, O Lord", and others.

He has received honors from the University of Missouri School of Journalism, the National Defense Transportation Association, the Institute of Outdoor Advertising, the Child Welfare League of America, the American Red Cross, the American Cancer Society, Boys Club of America, Boy Scouts of America, and others.

BROWN BOLTÉ

Interview

I was born in Winnetka, IL., Dec. 23, 1908. My father was a graduate of Michigan State University, as was my mother. My family, to my great good fortune, were very, very literate and very intellectual.

I started in public school in Winnetka. My father, at that time, was Assistant Advertising Manager of Sears Roebuck, in charge of the Special Catalog Division. We moved to Indianapolis when I was in the fourth grade, and my father became Advertising Manager of the Reilly Creosote Company there. At the same time, he became an Associate Professor, not of Agriculture, in which he had graduated, but Professor of Marketing, at Indiana University.

I went through Arsenal Technical High School, then the largest high school in the world, with just short of 8,000 students and 72 acres of campus and 14 buildings. And at that time, I thought I wanted to be a doctor. I was ready to graduate at the end of about three years, and I was only fifteen, but my parents made me stretch the last year out, so at the age of sixteen, I entered Butler University.

But I had started to work long before this; I went to high school half-days, I went to Butler half-days. And I used the other, the remainder of each day, working. I worked for L. S. Ayres, the largest department store in the state; for Kroger Co.; for an Indianapolis jeweler; and numerous others. Until, at 19, I talked a little print shop into getting the Flexlume sign franchise, and I became head of that division.

Then I found, during the Depression, that a lot of people had signs and weren't replacing their signs because they felt they couldn't afford it. Flexlume made an arrangement whereby I could offer five-year leases on new signs, and I got the amount of electricity consumed by neon signs, and I'd find that I'd be illuminating a new sign for about one-tenth of the electrical consumption the sign on the building lit with normal bulbs was using at that time.

Well, it was an irresistible approach to the sign business, and resulted again in my making so much money that my father was having fits. I was making over twice what he was!

And you were still in your teens.

Yes.

When I was 21 years old, I decided that I wanted to be an advertising man—I wanted to be with an advertising agency. I didn't know a damn thing about advertising, though my father was in the business, but I had found that I had certain talents that could be employed from an advertising agency base. I refer, for example, to the fact that I had fooled around with inventing things, and had found that I had a talent for developing new products, or improving old products; but I had no place to take them, and I had no way to present them. I found that I was playing the piano by ear, and was composing music, but I had no place to take it; there were no composers in Indianapolis. I found that I could write rhyme as rapidly as I could write prose. So I felt that the one place in the world where I could pool all of these talents together and make them work in unity was within an advertising agency, because of the diversity of activity and the diversity of product an advertising agency produces.

So I went to Howard Caldwell Sr., a fraternity brother, who was—I think it's Sidener, Van Riper & Caldwell now.

In Indianapolis?

In Indianapolis. And I was making somewhere around—oh, at this time, shall we say, $150 a week, which was a lot of money for a kid 20 years old!

I'll say it was!

And I said, Howard, I want to go into the agency business, and if you're interested, I'll go to work for $15 a week." And the following Monday he called me in, and said, "Brownie, I'm sorry, but things are so tight and so tough, I just simply can't hire you. I can't afford to pay you $15."

So I went back to what I was doing, and about four or five months later, I went back to him, and I said, "Howard, I am not a very good man with money, but I do happen to have enough to carry me for a few months. I'll go to work for nothing!" And he said, "Brownie, I can't afford to do that." So I gave up.

So Merve Hammel, a friend of my father, started a stationery business and hired me as a salesman. I had a drawing account of $75, plus a bonus and commission on sales made to new accounts I brought in. I was 21 at the time. I went to Kansas City, with my wife and baby daughter.

Aha, you'd gotten yourself married.

Yep, I fell in love with Bunny when she was 14 and married her when she was 19.

I married her the last year of the sign business. I didn't tell you why I got out of the sign business, and I think I should.

I found that I was making wonderful friends of my customers, my clients. And I found that there was no way I could cash in on that, because they only needed one sign each. So there were no resales. And I decided that I just was wasting my time making money on one-time sales, and I simply had to get into a business where whatever contribution I made was a continuing one, and I received a continuing income as a result. So I left the sign business, and went into the stationery business.

Either I was a hell of a salesman, or I was very, very lucky, because I averaged about seven new accounts a week. And out of that, I paid my expenses; and it's hard for you to believe this, but I traveled 22 states—that was my territory. Everything east of Colorado, and everything south of the Mason-Dixon Line, from the Mississippi River to the Atlantic Ocean. I did it all by car, and traveled 52,000 miles a year, on the average. And I was making about $175 a week.

So anyway, I continued that for 3½ years, with one break. Two breaks, as a matter of fact. I got fired because I did not turn in written reports, and within six months was rehired because the company missed the volume that I'd been flipping in.

So after 3½ years of that, I had gotten to the point where I was about 24, maybe 25; headquartered in Kansas City—

You and Bunny, and—

And my daughter Celia.

So anyway, I found that selling, while it is a fascinating occupation, is stultifying. It was boring, though rewarding financially.

My mind kept turning back and turning back and turning back to advertising. My Uncle Guy, who was in the advertising business in New York at that time, as a rep, was with *This Week* magazine. And I loved him even more than my father; I absolutely idolized him. So I wrote to him, and I said, "How do I get in this business?" Well, it happened that that letter coincided with his resignation from the Hearst organization, and his acceptance of the Advertising Managership of Barron G. Collier—the car card organization. And the first thing I know, I got a letter from Barron Collier, and it said: "I am not prepared to pay you what you are making at the present time" (which, I would say, was $650 a month, after I had paid my expenses), "but I will start you at $225 a month, and will pay costs of moving to whatever area we decide." And I wrote back and said, "Sold. I'm your man. Where do I go?" Back came a letter saying, "Report to C. C. Chase in Cincinnati." And then I was ordered to Newark, N. J.

Well, when I arrived there, I received half of the expenses of moving, and then suddenly my salary checks began to be deferred, so my $225 a month was practically nothing. And at the end of seven months, Mr. Collier owed me four months' back salary. And he was over in New York, and I had no money to buy food for my daughter or my wife, and I was fit to be tied. I borrowed from neighbors and borrowed from friends. So, it turned out that my daughter had saved 80¢, and I got on the subway and headed for Mr. Collier's office in New York.

Mr. Collier had a male secretary, but he had a very mad young man to deal with. I shoved him out of the way, and I walked into Mr. Collier's office, and he was asleep at his desk—an enormous office. And I said, "Mr. Collier, I've come for my money." I said, "You owe me roughly $900, including some expenses." And he said, "I'll send it to you." I said, "No, you won't send it to me. Either I get it or I will have the sheriff in here tomorrow morning and close you down. I don't give a damn how many millions you owe other people. You owe me $900."

Finally he got his man, and said, "Will you settle for half of it now and the rest tomorrow morning?" And I said, "Yes, providing you put me up at the Astor Hotel, because I am not going back to Newark and back here again, and I want that money no later than 10:00 tomorrow morning." So at 10:00 I walked in, and I got the remainder of the money. And he offered me the manager's job in Dayton, O. And I said, "The hell with you! It's almost impossible to get to you from Newark! If you did the same thing to me in Dayton, what do you think I would do?" I said, "For your information, I quit!"

And with the $900, I started a new company, called Candy Cod Laboratories; it was cod liver oil and chocolate. I was President; my uncle put in $10,000; Howard E. Spaulding put in $30,000—I raised $50,000, which was an unbelievable sum in those days. And I owned 20% of the company.

We ran three tests; we ran a test in Rochester, and one in Buffalo, and then one in Syracuse; and then no tests whatsoever, but just put the product on sale, in Cleveland. And we used radio in Rochester, radio and newspapers in Buffalo, newspapers only in Syracuse, and we just eliminated the media in Cleveland.

At the end of the first year, we got back $3.99 for every dollar sold in the market with the radio and newspaper combination; and we had a winner! So I took my first vacation in 22 months, and when I came back, the business was closed down. My friend, Mr. Howard E. Spaulding, had been brought up on a bigamy charge. He had to turn all of his assets over to his wife, to avoid a divorce; and she, while I was on vacation, had sold Candy Cod Laboratories . . .

Well, anyway, that company lasted about two years, and the whole thing just went off the market.

During that time, I had developed patents in the medical field, and I had two that were particularly promising which I sold to Scott & Bowne, and I went over there under contract to complete the work in their laboratory, because it had to be completed.

At the end of that time, the President of the company, Bill Mathe, asked me to take the job of Advertising Manager (their agency was Young & Rubicam, but they did not have an Advertising Manager), and I finally wound up as Assistant to the President in charge of advertising and marketing for the entire hemisphere.

And once again, I found, after almost four years with them—during which I developed some other products; I developed the first tablet shaped like a capsule. I did that because my wife gagged and couldn't swallow round tablets, and I named it Caplet. This was about 1935–36, something like that. And Scott & Bowne just thought, you know, "It'll go nowhere, what the hell, what do we want to put that out for?" Well, the funny part about it is, today, over 50% of all the tablets in the United States are sold in capsule-shaped form, and surprisingly, in the trade, they're called Caplets.

Generic, huh?

And also, during my stationery days, I told you that there were two episodes when I was out. I was down in Florida, selling writing paper, and I saw dropped fruit in every grove, the ground covered with grapefruit and oranges.

Cocoa Beach?

We were staying in that hotel at Cocoa Beach. And I said to the manager, "Why the hell all the dropped fruit?" And he said, "Because when we ship it North, people can't afford to buy it, just cannot afford to buy it; so we're letting it drop." I said, "Well, what would happen if we squeezed it, and froze the juice, and shipped the juice North, and had the juice delivered house-to-house by the dairy companies with the milk, and also had it available at stores?" "Hell," he said, "that sounds like a hell of an idea!" I said, "You'd cut your shipping costs down to practically nothing, compared to shipping the whole fruit." So we did; we froze the stuff. We used the ice cream freezer to freeze orange juice, and we served it to all the guests, and no one knew it had been frozen. Then I named it "Tree-Ripened Orange Juice, right from the groves to you." I went to every damned potential source in Florida; I went all over Florida, and *no one* would buy that idea, and I gave it up and went back to selling writing paper.

Well, would you believe that I had it in—it had to be 1933? That's thirteen years before its time came. Same with the capsule.

And then I developed another thing. I said, "You know, one way to get rich is to develop a product that will sell for 10¢ or less, in high volume, and repeat." [Bolté conceived the idea of an alkalizing chewing gum, and registered the name, "Alka-Gum."] "Stomach bum? Chew Alka-Gum!" And I took it to Scott & Bowne but they didn't want to do it, so I took it to White Laboratories, which is now part of Warner-Lambert. And I got them to make it for me, and people loved it. The war came on, and I volunteered for the Army, went over and tried to get White to put it out and give me a commission, and they said that they never introduced products that they did not develop themselves. And when I came back from the Army, they had a product on the market called Chooz!

I remember.

And Chooz happens to be Alka-Gum. I could have sued them. My attorney said, "You can. But if you want to be an agency man, and you start out returning from the Army and suing a manufacturer, your name is going to be mud in the agency business." So I just let it go.

Well, I am confused. Because you were at Benton & Bowles before the war.

Yes. But I owned Alka-Gum at that time.

I see. You developed it while you were at Benton & Bowles?

No, I developed it while I was at Scott & Bowne.

Before you were at Benton & Bowles?

I left Scott & Bowne. I'll have to pull you back because—after four years with Scott & Bowne—and by that time I was one of the four top executives of the company—I did a very careful analysis of the advertising business and of my own capabilities, and I came to the conclusion that the most secure and the least productive job in the advertising business, in those days, was Advertising Manager. You created nothing; you were a critic of other people's work; and you were solely responsible as a staff executive. You had no line responsibilities, even in your own company, except running the department if you had one, and many in those days had none— just Advertising Managers. It was the lowest-paid, but most secure.

Then you moved to Media Sales. There, once again, you get back into selling, the same thing, over and over and over again, by rote; and you get paid more, and it is less secure. You go to the advertising agency business, and you get paid the most—or you did in those days; it's not true now, but then it was true—you had a much broader spectrum of activities, and you could see your own productivity contributing. And therefore, I felt, again, that the agency business was the one for me. I'd gotten up to about $12,000 a year; I'd gone to Benton & Bowles earlier, and had been offered about $28 a week as a trainee, because I was older than most trainees, and had had sales experience; and I had to turn it down, of course. I asked for $65.

But anyhow, I got a call, and it was from Benton & Bowles. I went over and saw them; and they were having problems on Richard Hudnut at the time, and surprisingly Chet Dudley was the Account Executive. They offered me $7,500 a year. I went back and talked with Bunny, and said, "Here we go again. Every time I seem to make some money, I go somewhere where I'm not going to make the money." So I resigned, and took the job. And I was there—this was about 1939, I believe, because it was only about a year or so later that I resigned to go into the Army. I volunteered for the Army. My daughter was eleven by this time, ten or eleven.

I had some very interesting experiences. I was ordered to Washington University for orientation and training. I remember that I had charley horses, and I couldn't march for three days after the first march. Boy, I was in great physical shape! And then, they ran us through a series, a battery of physical tests; and one of them was chinning yourself. Well, I managed to do it 1½ times. So, they made me Deputy Chief of the Athletic Branch of the whole damned Army. Would you believe it?

And you could chin yourself 1½ times.

First I was at the Port of Embarkation in New York, and then I wound up on the staff in Washington. And that's the title they gave me. But I discovered why; they didn't give it to me because I was the world's greatest athlete. But they had discovered that I could write, and was able to speak, and could represent the General at affairs where he was supposed to speak, but preferred not to. And primarily, I served more or less as an overseas liaison officer. I had the title and the rank; I became a major, and I'd started out as a second lieutenant. But my job was going over to ETO, or Peninsular Base Command in Italy, finding out from the commanding general what changes he needed in his ETO and his Table of Organization, and his basic Table of Equipment; making the studies, writing the reports, coming back, and submitting them to the special staff, and to the general staff. So, really, my job was almost that of an Account Executive in an advertising agency. I was in sixteen countries, and on seven ships. And I don't know how many times I flew that Atlantic. But that, primarily, was my job. I always managed, somehow, to stay at least seventy miles behind the front lines.

That's smart.

Just a matter of, you know, precaution.

Okay, did you go back to B&B?

Yes, but when I was in the Army, I found new talents, shall I say. Number one: I did an awful lot of speeches. I was scared to death, before I went in the Army, to get on my feet and talk. And the other thing that I found is that I could really make my ability to play the piano by ear an important asset. And I began to seriously compose. I wrote the *Soldier's Prayer*, the *Allies Victory March*, *Bring Peace, O Lord*, the *Army Fighting Song*, and God knows what else, while I was in the Army, and all of them were published; all of them were played over national network on major shows, and when I came back, I had a reputation as a composer and lyricist.

So I was offered the Advertising Managership of Gillette because of my gorgeous title, Deputy Chief of the Athletic Branch, and they were completely tied up in athletics as an advertising medium. Craig Smith, who was the Advertising Manager of Gillette was promoted to Vice-President, with the responsibility for areas other than advertising, and he wanted me to take his place as Advertising Manager in Boston, and he offered me considerably more than I was making at Benton & Bowles. But I returned to Benton & Bowles, at a salary of $12,000 a year, and discovered that they'd been paying my wartime replacement $30,000 a year and letting him work two days a week in a defense plant, so that he wouldn't be drafted—which didn't make me happy at the moment, I might say, nor did I feel very secure.

And I had a most difficult time the first two years I went back to Benton & Bowles; I found it very hard to get out of the service. The regimentation and the fact that when you once learn it, you are free to do anything you want to do, providing it does not violate regulations, had given me a sense of security that money, salary, position in the business world had never provided. And it took me a long time to break out of that mold and become competitive again, and start to become really productive. Benton & Bowles had the patience of Job, and they put up with me for two years when, if I had been in charge of Brown Bolté, I'd have thrown him out so damn fast that he never would have hit the revolving door on the way.

But they did; they stuck with me. And then I started to move; things began to go. Procter & Gamble, in large part, played a role that was just so supportive that it's hard to describe. Here I was, a country boy from the Midwest, didn't go to the right colleges, was creative in a way that their other advertising men were not, and they accepted me completely.

Then my management at Benton & Bowles began to take the same attitude. Like all people, you have your pluses and your minuses; I think my greatest personal negative is the fact that I, by most standards if not all, talk a great deal.

I did a lot of writing, though I was not in the Creative Department. I wrote most of the copy for accounts like Procter & Gamble's Prell. I did not write the copy for Crest; I wrote the copy for many of the Norwich products; I was successful, I brought the account to the agency. And then, Bob Lusk made a decision that ran counter to Procter & Gamble's policy; and that is that a Procter & Gamble man cannot work on two accounts. "If he's going to work on Procter & Gamble, that's his job, and we don't want our agency executives on other accounts." And Bob went to them and said, "Look, Brown is handling Prell and Crest and experimental products for you in the Drug Division." (I was considered two things; a drug expert and a new products expert, development and introduction.)

So, he said, "We want Brown to have the Norwich account." And Howard Morgens and Neil McElroy agreed, and I wound up with two accounts rather than one. That meant that I had another Account Executive reporting to me, and I got into the Group Head situation. From there, it expanded and expanded and expanded, until I had over 50% of the total billing of Benton & Bowles under my supervision. I had Procter & Gamble, and later, 50% of General Foods; all of National Distillers; all of Norwich Pharmacal; all of Grove Laboratories in St. Louis; and Schick Shavers, in Lancaster, and *This Week* Magazine.

    Quite a responsibility.

It was too big. And I said to Bob, "Bob, I'm spread so thin that I literally am not giving the time to"—what I referred to as—"the independent accounts." Procter & Gamble and General Foods were the "bellwether accounts." And I said, "I can't get in bed and sleep with all of these accounts at the same time, and we're going to have trouble." And sure enough, I was asked by Joe Cullman, who is a very dear friend, as well as a wonderful client—he took his Benson & Hedges over to Philip Morris, and became the top man there—and he said, "We'd rather have good, constant, personal attention than occasional genius," and he said, "Can you replace Brown and have someone who can give us more time?" That was the first one. And the second one was National Distillers, I was called in by the VP in charge of advertising (Alan Schilling) and he said, "Brownie," I want you to know you're fired." I said, "That's very interesting. Would you mind telling me why?" And he said, "Because you don't seem to be part of us. You are on the periphery. You are there with your recommendations and your advertising and all of the basics, but the warmth and the cameraderie and the intimacy, and so on, that we require is nonexistent; and we would rather have an agency executive with fewer responsibilities, fewer accounts, and more time for us." And I said, "Well, Alan," I said, "you've made only one mistake." And he said, "What's that?" I said, "If I had been in your shoes, I would have fired Brown Bolté two years ago."

As time went on at Benton & Bowles, my career progressed. They understood me; they put up with my idiosyncracies to get what I could contribute. And if Bunny was ill, which she was most of the time—as a matter of fact, of the 48 years we were married, we were separated some eight years, with mental hospitals and divorces and remarriages and all of the things that happened, and I've often wondered how the hell I became as successful as I did under the circumstances. . . [Bunny Bolté committed suicide after treatment in several mental hospitals.]

But Benton & Bowles put up with that. Many employers would not. Benton & Bowles is like Compton; once you're in, you're family, and they accept your minuses because they want your pluses. It's the greatest organization I ever worked for, and gave me the eighteen happiest years I ever had in my life. And they still treat their people the same way.

Yes, they do.

But to get back to the career: I wound up as Vice-President and a Group Account Head in charge of account management. But I was noodling all the time in other fields; I was noodling around in music, and I was designing packages, and inventing new products —Gravy Train in itself is a story, quite a legend. And as these things continued, I think primarily with Hobe's backing (Atherton

Hobler, agency Chairman)—I was more or less Hobe's protege, whereas Alan Sidnam, a very, very talented and wonderful fellow, was closer to Bob Lusk, and Bob was President. And over a period of time, I was given more and more responsibility, and more and more recognition. So, here I was—a man who writes advertising, makes layouts, understands art, understands the media, then I am a true advertising man. But I never thought of myself as such, because I had all these other things I was doing within the agency. I founded the School for Returning Veterans at B&B, and we had some seventy returnees; and for two years they worked half-days and went to lectures half-days by those of us who were teaching them the agency business.

Even though you were a returning veteran.

That's right. And I think that's one of the greatest contributions I've made, not only to Benton & Bowles, but to the industry as a whole, because so many of those men, over 50% of them, stayed with the agency, and some are still there. Others have gone to other agencies, and have risen to the top positions. Bruce Crawford (now CEO of BBDO) is an example. He was my trainee.

But generally speaking, getting back to where I finally arrived; I was offered the Presidency of Ruthrauff & Ryan. I was offered the Presidency, three times, of Campbell-Mithun. [Having turned down that offer, Mr. Bolté told Bill Baker, then B&B President, that he would consider staying with the agency.]

I said, "I might consider staying if you make me an Executive Vice-President, and I will refuse it if you don't make Esty Stowell an Executive Vice-President at the same time." And I said, "I consider myself Mr. Outside. Esty is an introvert; one of the world's most magnificent jazz pianists, but he's a Harvard, Brooks Brothers introvert; and I love him, but he is, and I am a Middle Western ambivert. I will be Mr. Outside, and Mr. Stowell will be Mr. Inside and run the shop, run everything." So Esty and I were made Executive Vice-Presidents. Same amount of stock, same benefit programs; same everything. This was in 1954.

By that time, roughly half of the agency was General Foods/ Procter & Gamble, and the other half was the other accounts. We didn't have many; we started with nine, and then we started to expand, and I believe at the time I resigned, we had fifteen. Esty began to have some difficulties with General Foods, but it was not Esty that was causing the trouble; it was a man that was working for him, called Bill Lewis—(so ultimately I was asked to take over the cereals and dog foods at General Foods).

So I talked to Bob Lusk the next day, and he said, "The company would be better off without Esty." And I said, "Look, this is utterly ridiculous. Esty came in here as a trainee, directly out of college; and he's come all the way up to Executive Vice-President, and he and I are the two largest stockholders of this company, aside from you. You have 15.6% of the stock, and I think mine is 11.2%, and Esty's is 11.2%." He was adamant. And Esty is an extremely sensitive man (and ultimately resigned).

So I went home, and I had a long talk with Bunny—oh boy, was I upset. And I told her, "I'm going to give it exactly 12 months." I became more and more unhappy. Esty had gone. And he really had retired; I mean, he went home, he was so hurt that he didn't do a damn thing for a year. And then, for reasons that you know, he became President of Ogilvy & Mather.

Yeah, he came to see me, and I called David Ogilvy and sent him over there, because I knew David needed a good administrator and marketing man. And wanted one, what's more. Anyway, it was a great thing; he went over there, and in short order, became President. He did a lot for Ogilvy.

That's right. I know he did. So, suddenly a fellow named Sid Schwinn, who had been at Ruthrauff & Ryan, and then became a consultant to SSC&B, suggested they talk to me. And SSC&B had been on a plateau of $39 million for years, and needed new blood. So they called and I had luncheon with Ray Sullivan.

They offered me the Presidency of SSC&B, and a stock position that was comparable in percentage to Benton & Bowles; but, on the other hand, Benton & Bowles was billing $150 million or so, and they were billing $39 million.

I said, "Fellows, I'm making almost a quarter of a million dollars a year where I am! I think my salary is either $65,000 or $70,000 a year, and I get a hell of a bonus; and with 11% of the stock," I said, "My God, my stock dividends average $2 a share, and it puts me well over $200,000 a year! I'll go to work for you for $65,000." Which I did.

I went in to resign; Bob said, "Why do you want to resign?" And I said, "Bob, I've lost confidence in you, and I don't want to work for you. You're the four-star general, and I'm the three-star general; and I've asked you repeatedly over the last year to stop making unilateral decisions, to come back to the old way we had before Esty left; and that is to come in and discuss the problems before you make the decisions. And I am not saying 'do what I say,' but 'listen to what I think.'" And Bob's reply was, "Brown, you'll be President of this agency, and running it your own way, within the next eight years; and by gosh, as long as I'm President, I'll run it my way." And out the door he went. So, a week later, I went into his office, and resigned, and out the door I went.

When I moved over to SSC&B, I think most of my friends were totally horrified, because they knew that the character of SSC&B was utterly different than the character and personality and modus operandi of Benton & Bowles, and that I just simply was not the right person for the job. Also, many of my friends, like Hobe and others, felt that I was destroying my creativity by accepting the administrative responsibilities at SSC&B. And Hobe said, "Listen, you gave up being one of the greatest creative men in the field to become just an average administrator." Which was true, and I found it out very fast. I never should have been President of anything. I should have been put in a corner, and made Chairman of the Board or whatever, and just allowed to think and talk with creative people. At SSC&B I scared the hell out of them. I had Heagan Bayles in a state of shock! I had him in a state of shock because my thinking was so unorthodox as compared to theirs. That agency, at that time, was more inclined to say "Yes" to clients. Whereas I would go out with a recommendation and those recommendations could be turned down. But if they ordered us to do something that I felt was not proper and good for business, I would tell them so.

But at SSC&B, things weren't the same, right?

No, they weren't. If Barney Walker (President of American Tobacco) said, "Jump," you jumped. I was out on a hunting trip in Wolsey, S. D., with Gordie Fawcett and on Sunday, my secretary called and said Mr. Walker wanted me in his office at 9 on Monday morning.

So, I chartered. We had Pall Mall, billing $33 million. You know, the billing those days just doesn't compare to the billing today. I just have to sit in a state of shock. You know, Toyota, $65 million!

That's right, things have changed. Inflation has done it.

So, it was tough as hell. But I got there, and I sat until 10, and there was no Barney Walker. And I went to the receptionist, and she got on the phone, and she said, "I'm very sorry, Mr. Walker is too busy, and cannot see you. Bob Heinmann, the Executive Vice-President, is coming out." So Bob came out, and said, "Hi, Brown! You want to come into my office?" And I said, "For what purpose?" And he said, "Barney's too busy to see you, so I will talk to you." I said, If I can come 2,000 miles and make this 9 a.m. appointment, and he's now too busy to see me, I'm too damn busy to see you; and I suggest that Mr. Walker call me when he's free, and I will come over and talk to him at any time." And I walked out.

Well, the place blew up. So you see, I was an independent cuss, compared to some agency men. The result was that I told Heagan Bayles that I really was incompatible. There was personality conflict, and I felt that he should put someone on the account in my place; which he did, until they brought out Montclair, and they got in trouble with Montclair, and Barney Walker then asked that I come back and make a study and re-orient the whole damn thing.

So, I switched the campaign over, took it away from men, got women with their hands on a cigaret and so on, and Montclair started to grow.

But I learned one hell of a lot in my last several years. I became very unhappy with the move; not because it was the Presidency, but when Al Seaman became President, I moved up and replaced him as Vice-Chairman, but I became Vice-Chairman without responsibilities. I had two accounts that I had brought in; I brought in the tea account, and turned it over to him to run. I was never back in that job. And I had had a tremendous experience with Lever Brothers; we turned Lifebuoy completely around, and as a result, that wound up in the Lintas association, and Al took that account over. So I kept being cut back. Mr. Seaman may give you

323

other reasons for it. I find a personal incompatibility—it's still there, was there; it started with the day he came in; he ignored me completely, and went over my head.

He came in in '59, was it?

Yeah, somewhere around there.

It was then that he left Compton, you see.

Well, you see, I moved over in January '58.

So anyway, I had a broken leg, and couldn't get into the office for quite a long period of time—I was in the hospital for damn near three months—and what took place, I really am not qualified to say, except that there was a marked change when I came back. I had Bulova, and I had Seagram's, and that was $15 million in billing that I brought in, and that was it, and they were solid.

But—I had made a decision. First of all, I described my position. I said, "As Vice-Chairman of SSC&B, I am like the spare tire on a bus. All of the action is going on inside, and I'm going along for the ride; and only in case of emergency am I called upon to help move the bus down the road. Otherwise, 'you're not part of us.'" And I said, it made me very unhappy.

And I decided at that time that I was going to make a change into a business where I would be my own boss, would have time to do outside things as opportunity arose, and that I never again would report to either an individual or a Board of Directors.

That decision was challenged twice. Both times, if I had reneged on it, it would have made me, probably, a wealthier man than I am today. So after I left, I did not try to become wealthy, personally; I tried to become family-wealthy. My money, and the money I've made, has made my children multi-millionaires, as well as me; but it has made me a hell of a lot smaller millionaire than I would have been if I had stayed and kept it all for myself.

The first was by Elmer Bobst and Bill Lasdon, president of Warner-Lambert. They said, "We want you to come over, and we want you to work for a year as assistant to Elmer Bobst, and then succeed," said the President, "me as President of the company." And I declined. I said, "I'll think it over," and I never called them back.

The second was Armour & Co. The President of Armour & Co. was a delightful man named Wilson, and he'd gone past the retirement age of 67, and they were looking for a new President.

So he came to me, and he said, "We have 4,000 profiles of 4,000 executives, and we want you to come out to Chicago to be interviewed by Prince and Wilson." So I went out, and damned if they didn't make me a similar offer; an apartment in New York, a country club, a car and limousine, a salary that was 80% of what Wilson was getting, because Wilson was supposed to retire. And I turned that down. And they came back and offered it to me a second time; and by this time I'd been studying the outdoor advertising business for two years, and found that Minneapolis is the absolute headquarters for outdoor advertising—or was then. Foster & Kleiser, of course, has come along since, as part of Metromedia.

But I said, "I've decided I'm going into the outdoor advertising business, and I think there'd be a conflict of interest. I don't see how I could be President of your operation and own two or three outdoor advertising plants at the same time." Though I could; the Four A's had waived the old rule that if you were in the agency business, you couldn't own *any* media.

I know. I'm the guy that got rid of that rule when I was 4A's Chairman.

I'm not sure I would have made a good Chief Executive Officer of a manufacturing company. I might have.

So those were the only two major offers, outside of the agency business; but I tried—no, another: Lever Brothers offered me a consulting operation, going to London three months each year. I turned that down because of Bunny's health, and also, I think Lever Brothers were a little embarrassed after having made the offer, because they were making the offer to a retiring SSC&B man who was tied up with Lintas. So, it worked to their advantage for me to say no. And I'm sure, though, I would have loved to do it.

That would have been a lot of fun, sure.

I turned it down. So, I had decided to leave SSC&B, and I made one unforgivable move. In order to buy the Hartford Outdoor Advertising plant, I needed to raise a quarter of a million dollars down payment. And I wanted no more partners, as well as Board Chairmen, or Boards, or anything else. So I sold back enough of my SSC&B stock to make the down payment. Well, that was like putting one foot out the door. The only question was, how much longer would the other foot stay in the door? Was

I going to move it out, or were they? Well, two years went by. I bought Hartford the weekend of the Kennedy funeral—that would be in 1963.

And I stayed, and left SSC&B on June 30. SSC&B had agreed to pay me for my stock over a period of four years, and I said, "One of the requirements of this agreement is that you will pay me in cash." Which they did. Now the question is, did I move that second foot out myself, or did they remove it? So I can't tell you whether I voluntarily left SSC&B; I might have stayed another six months. I had found out that I could make enough money in the outdoor advertising business; I didn't *need* to be in the agency business.

On the other hand, they had found out that I had interests other than at SSC&B, and they felt that they didn't need me. So, one of us fired the other.

I'm sure Al Seaman was happy to have you leave.

He's the one who conducted the negotiations.

So I managed to scrape together about a million bucks under these circumstances, and decided that outdoor advertising had a future that was simply unbelievable. And now we get into an area that most people don't know anything about, or very little. The agency business was absolutely elated to have a top agency man leave the agency business and come into the outdoor business. That's sick—the no good, dirty, beautification, problem business, hated by the President and his wife, and all this and that; and here I come, and throw a million bucks into it.

And I made a speech at the Waldorf, and it made four-column headlines—where I attacked David Ogilvy, who had said that if he had his way, every American would have a hatchet and would go down the road and would chop down every sign in the country. And in this speech, I said, "I would like to read from Mr. Ogilvy's book. Mr. Ogilvy has said, or asked, in this book, 'Have you ever heard a sales clerk in a retail store sing a selling message to you? I think singing commercials are utterly non-productive and ridiculous.'" And I said, "I will now read from his media purchases during the last twelve months." And I said, "Some 30% of his radio and television commercials are musical."

I said, "Mr. Ogilvy has stated that he would have you all go across the United States with hatchets and chop down every sign.

Last year, David Ogilvy spent X % of the total expenditures in outdoor advertising. So what Mr. Ogilvy says and what Mr. Ogilvy does happen to be two different things."

I had to get insurance to make the speech. They were all scared to death that he'd sue me. For slander, libel, or what. Lloyd's of London wouldn't issue a policy! But it made headliness, and I think David loved it, because he likes anything, as long as David's in it. Great. So, anyway—

Well, they always say, just be sure you spell the name right.

Yeah. He's a friend of mine; I wouldn't say a warm friend, but he is a friend; and we've worked together on committees, Four A's, and so forth.

Very talented guy.

Oh, I'm sure he is. Of course, creativity, to me, means more than just the ability to write.

Let's have the Gravy Train story, Brownie.

Well, I'm sure, Bart, by this time, there must be a dozen people who have done Gravy Train, so it's going to be fun to tell you exactly how it came about. I was responsible for the dog food products of General Foods, and the most successful, by far, was the dry dog food, Gaines' dog food. We had some 31% of the market, I think, at that time, by Nielsen count, 31–32% of the market; and we had a concentrated pellet, about the size of rabbit droppings. And we sold it in 5- and 10-lb. sacks. And Ralston Purina, brilliant, able competitors, proceeded to take the same nutrients, and they made a biscuit of them; in other words, they puffed it. Well, it turned out that our 10-lb. sacks were about 50% the size of their 10-lb. sacks. And then, in addition to that, they had taken a vegetable oil and given it a meat aroma, and had it sprayed; and then had lined the bags so that the oil didn't seep through; and the dog, of course, could smell the meat smell. And then they ran some commercials.

They would say, "Now here is America's most famous dry dog food, and here is new Purina Chow. And here are the two dog dishes. Now I'm going to pour water in both of these, and let it stand for just about five seconds, and now we're going to see what happens." And a door in the wall would open, and out would come a medley of dogs, ranging from St. Bernards to Pekingese, and they'd go sniff Gaines, and they'd sniff Purina Chow, and they'd all go around the Purina Chow dish, and here's our product sitting there all alone, and the dogs are really digging into our competitor. Well, our volume dropped from about 31 or 32% down to 10%.

And Herb Cleaves was the Executive Vice-President in Charge, and Charlie Mortimer—not only a client, but a very good friend of mine—was President of the company, and he called me. He and Cleaves got hold of me and said, "Brown, we're being driven out of the dry dog food business, and by God, you have to do something about it." And I said, "I do? Look, we're handling the advertising, and the advertising got you up to 32%! It's a product problem; you've been outsmarted by Purina Chow. Those commercials, it's impossible that Purina wouldn't win!" And they said, "We don't give a damn. You're either going to correct it, or we're going to turn it over to Young & Rubicam, or Foote, Cone, or somebody else."

So I went home, and I took all the research with me, and I noticed that Mom treats a dog just exactly the way she does a baby. She has to take it out to piddle it; she has to take it to the doctor; she has to bring in food for it; she has to have it baby-sat if they're going places or taken to a kennel; and her love for it is the same maternal love that you have for a small baby. And I was lying in bed, stewing this thing over, and suddenly it dawned on me, "By Gosh, Mama buys this. So what we have to do is change the product so that we have a plus that Mama will believe is better for her dog than Chow."

I'd eaten every dog food that was made; I'd eaten it to see what it tasted like. I had the Gaines pellets downstairs, and I had a big mixing bowl; and in that, I put a quarter of a cup of Kitchen Bouquet, and a quarter of a cup of water, and then I put in about two quarts or so—maybe not that much—of Gaines.

And I began to mix it by hand, until all of it and the liquid had been absorbed. Then I left it in the oven at 200 degrees, and went back to bed. I woke up again, the product was dry, and I took it out and put it on the counter.

So the next morning at breakfast, I said to Bunny, "Now let's see what happens." And I put the product that I had just created, if you want to call it that, in our dog-food dish. We had two

328

collies. And I poured water on it, and it turned brown. And I said, "See Honey, we make our own gravy."

That morning, I stopped at White Plains, and at Herb's and then Charlie's office; I had them bring out two dishes, and I poured it. And I said, "Now, our product makes its own gravy, and Mama is going to think it is better for her dog because it has gravy, than Purina Chow, which has no gravy." And I said, "Don't let Kankakee louse it up! If you send it out there to your New Products Group, they didn't think of it, there's going to be the usual professional jealousy." I said, "Just send it out there and tell 'em this is what you're going to do, and that they are to perfect the production of it and the packaging of it, and they're to spray it with a meat fragrance."

And what happened next?

Within 12 months we were back on top; and then they screwed up the product. And what the hell, now it's back, and doing very well.

I did *not* create the name Gravy Train. We had a brilliant copywriter who, having seen this function, called it Gravy Train.

April 4, 1982